IN DEFENCE OF
REALISM

Raymond Tallis

Edward Arnold
A division of Hodder & Stoughton
LONDON   BALTIMORE   MELBOURNE   AUCKLAND

This book is dedicated with my love to Edward and Mary Tallis without whom I should have had no access to reality.

British Library Cataloguing Publication Data

Tallis, Raymond
  The defence of realism.
  1. English literature, 1800- Realism.
  Critical studies
  I. Title
  820.9'12

  ISBN 0-7131-6593-6
  ISBN 0-7131-6577-4 Pbk

Typeset in 11/12 pt Plantin Compugraphic
by Colset Private Limited, Singapore
Printed and bound in Great Britain for Edward Arnold,
the educational, academic and medical publishing division of
Hodder and Stoughton Limited,
41 Bedford Square, London WC1B 3DQ by
Biddles Ltd, Guildford and King's Lynn

Contents

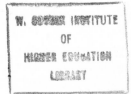

Note

I have referred to the reader throughout this book as 'he'. This is not because I believe that only men read books or that males are the only readers worth considering. I did experiment with 'he or she', 's/he' and 'he/she' but found the results at best clumsy and at worst distracting. And for a male writer to refer to the reader consistently as 'she' would be hypocritical pretence. And so I have conformed to normal usage, fully aware that behind linguistic use there is much extra-linguistic abuse. The fact that 'he' is the unmarked and 'she' is the marked form of the third person pronoun is directly connected with the marginalization of women and the implication that the male is the normal or canonical form of the human species – or of the common reader. Even so, I should prefer that my feminist credentials were judged by my ideas rather than by a nervous linguistic tic. If those who defend realistic fiction have natural allies, they are to be found amongst the ranks of the feminists.

Acknowledgements

I am very grateful to the two anonymous readers of this manuscript who made numerous helpful suggestions. One of the readers, Professor Jeremy Hawthorn, subsequently revealed his identity and made further very useful comments. I found his observations on Part IV especially valuable. I should also like to thank Dr Simon Dentith who read the manuscript at an early stage and whose criticisms of Part I in particular strengthened the arguments while his encouragement strengthened the author.

An earlier version of Chapter 1 was previously broadcast as a talk on Radio 3 and published in the *Listener*. The material in Chapter 2 was previously published by the *Cambridge Quarterly* and the material in Chapter 3 previously appeared in *Critical Quarterly*.

Aperture: The Realistic Novel under Attack

That realism is outmoded and the realistic novel a form that has had its day is a critical commonplace sufficiently widespread to be familiar to anyone who glances through the book reviews in quality papers – irrespective of whether he reads a novel from one year's end to the next. Not long ago, the popular idea was that the novel was on its death bed; but now we learn from certain quarters that only realism has died, while the non- or anti-realistic novel is flourishing. Such posthumous life as realism enjoys (so one current orthodoxy runs) is exemplified by the novels of middlebrow and best-selling authors – mere entertainers, some superior, others inferior. Outside of the novel, the true nature of contemporary realism is betrayed in the vulgar naturalism of television serials such as *The Archers*, *East Enders* and *Coronation Street*.

On the basis of such evidence, it is concluded that the realistic novel now serves only to sedate (that is to say, kill) the higher reaches of the mind, or (in the case of those readers whose minds lack such reaches) to kill time when the television has broken down or has become, as on a train journey, temporarily unavailable. Realism is cultivated either by an, admittedly talented, *arrière garde* or, more conspicuously, by talentless millionaire hacks who sell their worthless products in millions. It has been evicted from the Literature shelves and squats ingloriously (but lucratively) in paper-back bookstands on railway stations and at airports. It has, with a few striking exceptions, lost its literary function; and if it has any political function, it is to support the status quo, to collude with one version of reality and pass it off as if it were reality itself. The serious reader must look elsewhere, outside of realism, for instruments to sharpen his perception of the world and to heighten his awareness of the significance of things; even, paradoxically, for fictions with which to explore reality itself.

This is of course a parody of one – very influential – vision of the current state of fiction. It is not based upon observed fact. For the truth is that realistic fiction is very much alive and kicking, though realism seems to have conceded much of the experimental high ground. Realistic novels of a very high standard, as well as the rubbish, continue to be written and read. And realism continues to be appreciated – if the awarding of major literary prizes can be counted as a criterion. The great majority of novels short-listed for the Booker Prize are realistic.

So the facts are not entirely in favour of those who, like Michael Boyd, claim that the modern novel defines itself in terms of its rejection of the conventions of formal realism[1]. Nevertheless, there are many critics who wish that the modern novel would behave in this way, believing that those who continue to write in the realist or naturalist traditions are 'like headless chickens unaware of the decapitating axe'.[2] Moreover, many of the acknowledged giants of contemporary fiction – Beckett, Pynchon, Barthelme, Borges and Marquez, to name a few – are committed to the creation of non-worlds, dream-worlds, word-worlds or anti-worlds. The works of the campus heroes of recent years are stepped in myth and fantasy. So-called science fiction is more often given serious attention as a literary form and its reputedly better practitioners, such as Moorcock and Le Guin, are considered appropriate for postgraduate research. At least one novelist, Doris Lessing, who began her career as a serious, if for some tastes rather dull and moralistic, practitioner of realism, took to writing 'space' fiction which, she has implied, is the only suitable mode for the contemporary novel. Even those writers who locate their fictions on earth and still have a use for characters drawn from daily life are apparently unashamed by implausibility. Nor are they criticized for this. Iris Murdoch, to cite an author who enjoys a very high critical standing, often relies heavily on improbable coincidences to keep her plots going. This particular failing reached its highest expression in her absurd *The Sea, the Sea* which won her the Booker Prize. Indeed, a modest degree of implausibility, along with other kinds of timid rebellion against 'realism', seems to metal the royal road to critical favour. This may be why many 'serious' novelists, in whose work formal experimentation is not especially evident, now include goblins, or unfortunates who are twice-born or undergo one or more reincarnations, lucky creatures with magic powers, and other implausibles in their casts of characters. The booming genre of 'black comedy' provides a favourite place of refuge for writers whose fictional fancy outstrips their imagination. Perhaps the most telling sign of the favourable climate enjoyed by piecemeal anti-realism is the way critics accept the most absurd of plots, which they retail with poker faces.

When the house of fiction is overrun by fabulists, by writers with their hands deep in what Philip Larkin called 'the myth kitty'; when even the least visionary of practitioners seem to trouble themselves less and less with precision and plausibility; when many intelligent critics see plausibility as a literary vice, a kind of confidence trick, ought we not concur with the growing body of opinion that realism is increasingly outmoded?'

No we should not, if only for the reason that realism has not yet begun to

---

[1] Michael Boyd, *The Reflexive Novel: Fiction as Critique* (Toronto: Lewisburg Bucknell University Press, 1983) p. 9.
[2] Robert Scholes, *The Fabulators* (New York, 1967) p. 6.

exhaust its possibilities. If it seems to have done so, this is only because of a persistent tendency to confuse the *aims* of realism with certain techniques used to achieve those aims – techniques developed largely by the great nineteenth-century novelists. Understood as an attempt to do justice to, to express or to preserve, a piece of reality, realism is not the dead hand of the past but the challenge of the present and of the future. A defence of realism does not imply an opposition to experimentation. Quite the reverse; for it is precisely those most concerned to express reality with maximum fidelity who are required to be most daring in their experiments.

The increasing consensus, uniting literary journalists and radical academic critics, that realism is outplayed, is difficult to oppose because of the inextricable mixture of half-truths and whole falsehoods on which it is based. The present book is a continuation of an argument developed in an earlier work and I think a few words on the relationship of the two books may be helpful to the reader.

In *Not Saussure*, I examined the claims made by post-Saussurean thinkers about the relationship between language, the self and reality. In particular, I investigated the claim that words could not refer to a genuinely extra-linguistic reality. I was able to establish that most of the celebrated post-Saussurean assertions – 'there is nothing outside of the text'; 'all texts are about other texts'; 'the world of words creates the world of things', etc. – are based on serious misreadings of Saussure. These misreadings, and the often elementary philosophical confusions underlying them, have gone undetected because lost in opaque texts where key terms are strategically mishandled. Post-structuralists, in particular, find it useful to confuse or conflate the signifier with the sign, the signified with the referent, reference with meaning, verbal token with verbal type. The radical nominalism of the post-Saussureans is, in short, founded not upon Saussure but upon bad linguistics and even worse philosophy of language.

There are two reasons why it is important for the reader of *In Defence of Realism* to know what was established in *Not Saussure*. Firstly, he might otherwise think that, in the first two parts of the present book, where I deal with the case against realistic fiction, I have failed to take account of the quasi-philosophical arguments associated with structuralist and post-structuralist thinkers. Secondly, when, in the third part of the present book I ask the question, What if the ideas advanced by certain radical critics were true?, the ideas referred to are not only those discussed in the earlier parts of *In Defence of Realism*, but also those examined in *Not Saussure*. For the convenience of the reader, I shall briefly summarize these at the beginning of Part 3.

There are many reasons why critics may subscribe to the ideas that seem to provide a theoretical basis for hostility to realistic fiction. I discuss some of these in Part III, notably in Chapter 8, where I connect the attractiveness of these ideas with the critics' loss of confidence in their traditional tasks of exposition, interpretation and evaluation. In particular, with the lack of control of the PhD supply, many critics are depressed by the pandemic of interpretosis that has broken out in the republic of letters. Much criticism is surplus to requirement and the role of the critic seems in need of re-definition. The displacement of literary criticism by literary theory and of the latter by 'theory' has provided the longed-for solution, reviving a lost sense of purpose.

The contents of this book are organized as follows. In Parts I and II, I deal with some of the reasons that have been given for the widespread critical position that fiction should abandon its attempt to represent reality and that realism should give way to fantasy or to self-referential meta-fictions. Chapter 1 examines the historical and sociological reasons for asserting that, as 'reality is no longer realistic', realism is inappropriate. Chapter 2 investigates whether, since stories and experience, telling and living, are different, there can possibly be such things as true (or true-to-life) stories. Chapter 3 looks at the reasons for believing that the rise of the cinema has 'dealt a *coup de grâce* to a dying realism'. Chapters 4, 5 and 6 uncover the contradictions in the 'ideological' arguments against realism originating from Althusserian and other brands of Marxism. Chapters 7, 8 and 9 look at the relationship between critical theory and novelistic practice. In Chapter 7, we discover that no fictions as yet answer to the specifications that radical critical ideas would, if they were true, demand. Chapter 8 looks at the absurd and often self-defeating pronouncements of radical critics. Chapter 9 documents the necessary retreat from theory. In the fourth, and final, part of this book I discuss the nature of realism, its problems and possibilities, and try to indicate how much is lost when novelists abandon the attempt to 'represent reality'. A conciliatory postscript (Closure) suggests that the relations between realism and anti-realism may not be entirely adversarial and that anti-realism, although secondary, may serve to waken realistic fiction out of unquestioned assumptions and routinization of what were once revolutionary techniques.

This book, like *Not Saussure*, has been written in the belief that current trends in literary criticism represent a real threat to the development of fiction. Critics have often been wrongheaded but they have never before been so well-funded, so numerous and so naked in their ambition to expropriate the prestige of the creative writer. With the professionalization, indeed the industrialization, of literary criticism and the replacement of the Man of Letters by the Man of Signifiers, the risk that critics may actually pervert the course of literature is greater than ever before. It is unlikely that they will succeed in preventing great artists from doing what they do best; but they will make life more difficult for them. The republic of letters cannot be a more healthy place for being wrapped in a fog of bad philosophy and worse linguistics and such a fog can only slow the appreciation of true worth.

If there is such a thing as a literary morality – and I believe that there is – it consists at least in part of devoting the higher attention of one's more inspired moments to coming to grips with the reality that has oneself and others in its grip. It is in the name of this morality that I have tried to defend the novel – potentially the supreme adventure of human consciousness –

and to clear away some of the critical errors that have threatened to smother it. It is less for the sake of the artists that I write – they are well able to look after themselves – than for the sake of their readers; those who, like myself, felt their critical senses being bewitched by ideas whose strength lay not in their truth but in the confusing manner of their presentation.

Realism, Representation and Reality

1

Is Reality no Longer Realistic?

> Marvin asks Sam if he has given up his novel, and Sam says 'Tempo-
> rarily'. He cannot find a form, he explains. He does not want to write a
> realistic novel because reality is no longer realistic.[1]

The case against the realistic novel is usually developed in regions of discourse where the intellectual air is so thin that the mind, presented with ideas
that are easy to recite or quote but impossible to think or imagine, can
scarcely breathe. On the lower slopes of literary theory, however, homelier
arguments are sometimes advanced in support of the claim that realism has
had its day. Some of these stem from a consideration of the changing nature of
reality itself. For there is now a widespread belief that twentieth-century
reality is 'unreal' and that it is therefore unsuitable for realistic treatment.
The conclusion does not, of course, follow – there is no reason why a novelist
should not attempt to deal realistically with the sense of unreality – but it has
been drawn often enough for the premise upon which it is based to warrant
critical examination.

Philip Rahv[2] informs us that 'it is no longer possible to use realistic
methods' without taking reality for granted – 'and this is precisely what
artists cannot do *now*' (italics mine). Bernard Bergonzi[3] believes that we are
unable to write now as Tolstoy did

> because we have no common sense of reality. We are saddled with all
> kinds of relativistic structures of consciousness. We do not believe in
> there being 'one reality' out there as undoubtedly Tolstoy did.

Even Gerald Graff, a hostile and sometimes penetrating critic of postmodern
or ultra-modish critical postures, appears to accept, quite uncritically, that
'contemporary capitalistic reality' is qualitatively different from all that has
preceded it, and that its essence is 'unreality'[4]. And he speaks elsewhere of

---

[1] Norman Mailer, The Man Who Studied Yoga in *Advertisements for Myself* (New York, 1959, London: Panther, 1970).

[2] Philip Rahv quoted in Damien Grant, *Realism* (London: Methuen, 1970) p. 4.

[3] Bernard Bergonzi quoted in Grant, *op. cit.*

[4] Gerald Graff, *Literature Against Itself: Literary Ideas and Modern Society* (Chicago: University of Chicago Press, 1979) p. 10.

'the kind of unreal reality that modern reality has become'[5]. He cites, without apparent protest a passage from the American novelist and critic William Gass in which it is suggested that

> the world [has] become, for many novelists, a place not only vacant of Gods, but also empty of a generously regular and peacefully abiding nature on which the novelist might, in large, rely. . . .'[6]

Literary journalists, *avant-garde* novelists and advanced critics, then, are united in the belief that contemporary reality is totally different from that of preceding centuries.

Different writers would give different answers as to what it is about twentieth-century reality that makes it no longer amenable to realistic treatment and why realism, which flourished in the nineteenth-century and was apparently able to respond adequately to to its realities, should be quite unable to deal with the world that emerged a few decades later[7]. Certain themes, however, are sounded again and again: modern reality, we are told, is more horrible than anything that has gone before; it is more vast and complex; it is pre-digested, in a manner that has no historical precedent, by the organs of the mass media; human artefacts now intervene between man and nature to an extent not previously seen, so that the individual's environment is a rapidly changing man-made rather than a stable natural one. Not to be appalled by the complexity of the age, by the scale of its achievement and its cruelty, not to feel bemused by the unremitting assault upon the mind of the products of the mass media, is therefore to betray an insensitivity unworthy of a serious writer. Authors who feel defeated by a world that sprawls beyond their comprehension will be sure of the applause of critics if they exhibit this feeling of defeat. After Auschwitz and the more recent events in Kampuchea, the argument runs, can any man of feeling put pen to paper and hope to express what lies around him? When (to cast the argument in the usual journalistic terms) the world has a population of over 3,000 million, when science progresses at such a rate that ten years is a geological era, when the human race lives daily on the brink of destruction, can any individual, least of all a writer, believe that he is able to make sense of the world or that his sense of reality can withstand critical scrutiny? And when, every moment of the day, television and newspapers and the radio mediate between him and the reality, can any thinking artist trust his own perceptions? Is it not an infallible sign of stupidity to write as if one were at home in the world?

It is a peculiar but not uncommon kind of snobbery to believe that one lives in the worst of all historical eras – the most abominable, the least compre-

---

[5] Graff, *op. cit.* p. 80.
[6] Graff, *op. cit.* p. 10.
[7] There is a good deal of uncertainty as to when it was that reality became unsuitable for realistic treatment. Erich Auerbach, for example, seems to believe that even Flaubert (whom he agrees is a 'realistic writer') 'suffered from a lack of valid foundation for his work': *Mimesis*, translated by Willard Trask (Princeton, NJ: Princeton University Press, 1953) p. 551. See also the observations on Eliot later in this chapter.

hensible, the most rootless. Such a belief is a sure sign of an underdeveloped historical sense. Anyone with the scantiest knowledge of the past will know that the history of the world is largely the history of pain, injustice and chaos. As Nietzsche wrote, 'the whole of history is a refutation by experimentation of the principle of the so-called "moral world order" '[8]. Men have always lived in dark times, though some have been more conscious of it than others; and certain individuals in every era have derived a perverse comfort from believing that they lived in the darkest times of all. Revolting cruelty is not a twentieth-century invention; nor is the application of technical advances to bestial ends. Moreover, the whole of 'reality' has never been within the grasp of an individual mind. Why should anyone imagine that it could or should be? How could one mind comprehend a world containing many millions of other minds? Human life has always been torn with extremes and extremes have always outreached the consciousness of a man with a pen in his hand. The Black Death was proportionately more destructive than the events at Hiroshima; or – to compare human acts with human acts – the Thirty Years War and the American Civil War were on a scale of horribleness comparable to that of more recent catastrophes. There is nothing intrinsically more revolting in the slaughter of a thousand Americans in a semi-religious cere-mony at Jonesville in 1979 than the massacre of 80,000 victims in an Aztec religious ritual at Tenochtitlan many centuries previously. It is, therefore, no more a sign of moral or intellectual insensitivity to try to write a realistic novel in the 1980s than it was in 1922 or 1857.

If recent horrors seem more horrible than those of earlier centuries, it is only because they are apparently less excusable. They seem less excusable because we like to believe that the world is – or should be – more civilized than it was. This belief in turn derives from the idea that the material benefits brought by technology should make men less rapacious and cruel. Instead, all that has happened is that, in certain quarters, the appetite for power has replaced the drive for the necessities of life as a mainspring of behaviour; or, rather, that technological advance has allowed the latter of these appetites to dominate over the former. Cruelty as a by-product of the struggle for survival has been replaced by manifestly senseless savagery.

Contemporary reality shocks us more because we assess it against improved expectations of our fellow men. And, perhaps, also because its excesses and atrocities are more widely known. A massacre of children in Central Africa would have gone unreported in the western press in the nineteenth-century; and the appalling conditions endured by the labourers working on the Great Wall of China would have passed unremarked in some contemporary *Washington Post*. So the complacent, even self-admiring des-pair and cynicism of the well-heeled owes more to an all-too-easy apathy than to a profound appreciation of the history of the world.

[8] Friedrich Nietzsche, *Ecce Homo* in Walter Kaufmann, *The Portable Nietzsche* (New York: The Viking Press, 1954) p. 660.

Some writers have concentrated less upon the mass evil of modern society than upon its complexity, multiplicity and discontinuity. Everyone is familiar with the claim that the present age is more fragmented than past ages. According to Graff, not only war but also

> Modern technology . . . politics, commerce, social engineering, and journalism, which, by promoting continuous discontinuity and upheaval, have assaulted our assurance of reality[9].

Moral, technological and organizational differences have combined to produce a contemporary reality that is metaphysically different from past realities. We, unlike our predecessors are 'saddled with all kinds of relativistic structures'. Unlike Tolstoy and his contemporaries we 'do not believe in there being "one reality" out there'.

These claims do not stand up to the briefest reflection on the phenomenology of human experience. Human consciousness has always been riven by discontinuities. To dwell merely on the physiological facts, the outside world has always been refracted through bodies that have had fluctuating and different neurophysiological and neuropsychological properties. Throughout history, human life has been marked by intermissions of consciousness itself: sleep, dreams, delirium, coma and epilepsy are scarcely creations of the twentieth-century. Individuals experience the world totally differently as neonates, as young adults or in advanced old age. The invention of the motor car or the micro-computer has not cut deeper into the continuity and the uniformity of an agreed-upon reality than do sleep or coma.

In fact, physiological and educational considerations suggest that inter-subjective reality is now likely to be *more* uniform in advanced countries. To focus upon just one small, but vitally important, aspect of history (at the risk perhaps of seeming to be absurdly specific in a realm of argument where facts are usually viewed with disdain or treated as irrelevant), there has always been a certain proportion of the population who are brain-injured and consequently profoundly alienated from an agreed-upon reality. This proportion is now lower, not higher, than it was in the nineteenth-century when realism was supposed to be at its appropriate zenith. For there is now a lower incidence of cerebral damage due to starvation *in utero*, to birth injury, malnutrition during critical growth periods or to accidents. The subjectivity of the brain-injured hardly belongs seamlessly with that of the non-injured in an unfragmented, collective reality. (It scarcely matters, from the point of view of the victim, whether the injury was the product of an organic fist being smashed into an organic face in an organic community, or whether it was the result of a more 'clinical' accident in a factory.)

To take a less extreme example, the destitute and starving do not participate in the same reality as the well-fed and well-heeled and the former, in those (affluent) countries where 'the unreality of reality' is most likely to be

[9]Graff, *op. cit.* p. 8.

complained of, have become somewhat less numerous. At present, as many as 25 per cent of USA citizens may live below the official poverty line. This, in the wealthiest country in the world, is an abomination and cries to heaven for rectification. Even so, it is an improvement on the situation one hundred years ago where the vast majority of the population lived in what, by modern standards, would count as extreme poverty.

Furthermore, the higher prevalence of illiteracy in the past meant that much greater sections of the population were cut off from the discourses of power and from making those *formulations* of reality that have come down to us as the images of the past. Indeed, the spread of a certain sort of literacy, enabling more individuals to participate in centralized discourses disseminated by the mass media, discourses that are increasingly tailored to mass consumption, has suggested to some commentators that reality is becoming *more* uniform and *more* unified than it was before. Herbert Marcuse, for example, has worried about the 'closing down of the range of consciousness' and the emergence of one-dimensional man in a one-dimensional society. As Alasdair MacIntyre has written

> Marcuse's vision is of a single systematic web of interconnections by means of which each part of society is dominated in the interest of the total system. He . . . sees such societies as among the most highly integrated in human history[10].

So there are equally strong (or, more precisely, equally weak) grounds for believing that contemporary reality is *less* various, *less* fragmented and *more* unified than earlier versions of reality and that 'conflicting subjectivities' are increasingly swallowed up in a monolithic, repressive, totalitarian consciousness.

The same sort of false conclusions have been drawn from considering the changing relationships between man and nature – in particular the progressive distancing of man from nature as a result of the proliferation of technological artefacts. William Gass, in the passage quoted earlier, referred to the loss of 'a generously regular and peacefully abiding nature' that earlier novelists could presumably refer to to underpin their idea of a unified reality. One would be curious to know where on earth this nature was to be found. It is certainly not a notable feature of the recorded past. An interview with the parent of a sick child in the eighteenth-century, with a sailor in the twelfth-century or with a farmer in the fourth-century looking across his flooded fields to his future ruin and probable death by starvation, would be unlikely to add much weight to the idea of 'a peacefully abiding nature'. If nature has ever been 'peacefully abiding', then it is in those corners of the twentieth-century where it has been subjugated by technological man. And this view has been taken by Marcuse who speaks, somewhat prematurely, of the 'pacification of nature' as a modern phenomenon. It cannot be denied that in advanced industrial societies there is

[10] Alasdair MacIntyre, *Marcuse* (London: Fontana, 1979) p. 70.

an increasing distance between man and nature. But this has resulted in a further socialization of reality which could scarcely be expected to make it more fragmented. It will certainly not make it less collectively real.

We can see, then, that there is little foundation for the idea that contemporary realities are metaphysically different from earlier realities or that the latter were more unified. Certainly the past was different from the present but not in such a way as to justify the belief that the reality which was continuous and 'realistic' before is now no longer so.

The belief in a metaphysical difference between past and present is founded less upon a mistaken conception of the present than upon a misreading of the past and it is interesting to speculate where this misreading comes from. Where did critics derive the idea that reality was previously a seamless continuum? Or that earlier realistic novelists believed in such a reality or needed to do so in order to write realistic novels? Not from the facts of history; nor from the novelists in question.

When seeking the source of implausible ideas entertained by literary theorists, we often need look no further than the implausible ideas held by earlier literary theorists, often of an opposite persuasion. For a long time, critics earned their living by discovering organic unities in works of literature. In certain crucial cases the unity of the work was thought to reflect the unified consciousness or unified world-picture of the author[11]. It was further implied or suggested that behind this again was an experience of unified, unfragmented external reality. Highly dubious, of course, and literary criticism of this sort is now rightly execrated. Unfortunately one absurd fashion tends to be replaced by an opposite and equally absurd fashion. Works of literature are now explored with the aim of demonstrating their inconsistencies[12] as if this were what they were 'really' about. Sentimental rhetoric about

[11] See, for example, Jonathan Culler, *The Pursuit of Signs: Semiotics, Deconstruction, Literature* (London: Routledge Kegan Paul, 1981) – especially Chapter 3, Semiotics as a Theory of Reading. Authors, of course, have world pictures only to the extent that other people have them. It was, however, better for critical business to think of an author as someone who had 'a vision of the (or a) world'. Now the opposite view is regarded as a revelation and this, again, is good for critical business.

[12] The career of Hillis Miller illustrates this very clearly. Imre Salusinsky (*Criticism in Society*, London: Methuen, 1987 pp. 210-11) has discussed how Miller directly contradicts himself.

In 1965, Miller informed his readers that 'all of the passages [in a novel] reveal a profound harmony. Taken together [they] form the imaginative universe of the writer'. Through them, the 'critic can hope to glimpse the original unity of a creative mind. For all the works of a single writer form a unity, a unity in which a thousand paths radiate from the same centre. At the heart of a writer's successive works, revealed in glimpses through each event and image, is an impalpable organizing form, constantly presiding over the choice of words.' (*Charles Dickens: The World of His Novels*, Cambridge, Mass: Harvard University Press, 1965, p. ix). In 1970, he writes with equal authority that 'we must put in question certain habitual metaphors' of criticism, including those which 'propose to explain the text by something extra-linguistic which precedes it – the life or psychology of the author, historical conditions at a certain time, some event'. There are certain theorists whose tone of confident, dogmatic authority persists unchanged through any number of changes of opinion.

'organic unity' and 'coherent visions' has been replaced by an opposite rhetoric that would persuade us that works of literature are distinguished by their total incoherence[13]. All of this would be fairly harmless if the shifts of fashion in critical rhetoric were not thought to represent a transformation of the nature of reality itself; if changes in some interpretations of certain parts of reality were not confused with changes in the nature of reality itself. Unfortunately, minor events in the university library and seminar room are taken to be representative of what is happening in the world at large – in the lives of Kalahari bushmen tending their flocks as much as to lecturers in English tending their post-graduate students.

The idea that past reality – such as is supposedly reflected in nineteenth-century realism – is somehow organically whole in the way that contemporary reality is not, is a powerful prejudice. For it springs almost directly from the most intractable occupational hazard of scholars contemplating the past. This is the habit of confusing the unwritten history of experience with the written history of ideas. That the *experience* of reality is not the same as *ideas* that have been put forward about that reality is often overlooked by non-historians. It is equally invalid to equate ideas as they are recorded in print with their life in the minds even of those individuals who seemingly subscribe to them. One presumes that Tolstoy seemed to Bernard Bergonzi to have 'undoubtedly'[14] believed 'in there being "one reality" ' because Tolstoy had expressed ideas adumbrating this at certain times. Bergonzi may have been thinking of the famous Epilogue to *War and Peace*. But it is naive to confuse Tolstoy's ideas with his experiences. The novels bear eloquent witness to his vision of a fragmented, discontinuous reality, of conflicting subjectivities, at odds with the unifying vision he strained after. And the novels are a much more powerful testament to the nature of the novelist than any number of formal pronouncements tacked on to them. It is probable that if Tolstoy *had* believed in *a unified* reality, he would have been a philosopher rather than a novelist. A man as deeply possessed by the metaphysical impulse as he was became a novelist rather than a philosopher *because* the world refused to submit to the unifying intuitions he had, *because* it resisted being encompassed by the definitive thought he so enormously ached for[15].

Erich Auerbach asserts that

> as recently as the nineteenth-century, and even at the beginning of the
> twentieth, so much clearly formulable and recognized community of

---

[13] Jonathan Culler's admirably lucid but insufficiently critical *On Deconstruction* (London: Routledge Kegan Paul, 1983) summarizes this trend well. See also Michael Boyd, *The Reflexive Novel. Fiction as Critique*, (Toronto: Lewisburg Bucknell University Press, 1983) and William E. Cain (Ed.), *Philosophical Approaches to Literature*, (London: Associated University Presses), 1985 where even mainstream nineteenth-century realists are claimed to be concerned to undermine the premises of their own fictions and to be aware of the inevitable contradictions within discourse.

[14] We shall deal with the symptomatic 'undoubtedly' shortly.

[15] See, for example, Isaiah Berlin's *The Hedgehog and the Fox* (New York: Mentor Books, 1960).

> thought and feeling remain [in Europe] that a writer engaged in repre-
> senting reality had reliable criteria at hand by which to organize it[16].

How is Auerbach led to believe that he knows this? Possibly he is influenced by the fact that religious belief was more in evidence then than now. But it is naive, even irresponsible and certainly fallacious to accept uncritically the idea that a society which has prominent religious beliefs, an official state metaphysics, is more unified in the higher levels of its collective consciousness than one that doesn't. This is akin to the kind of historical simplification that Sellars and Yeatman parodied so brilliantly in *1066 and All That*.

Even a society apparently unified by religious belief may be deeply fragmented – as indeed Victorial England was. Karl Marx recounts the story of an interview between a factory inspector and some children working under-ground in a coal-mine. In order to assess their level of religious knowledge – a matter supposedly of great concern to their masters – he asked the children who the Virgin Mary was. Their spokesman stated that she was a kind of sweet stuff, 'like chocolate'.

The unified reality of past societies was at least in part a creation of munici-pal rhetoric and has been re-created by uncritical critics with their own kind of rhetoric. Even 'secure' ideas in 'secure' societies – and I am thinking in par-ticular of theological ideas in predominantly religious societies – are elusive to those who try to live them. There is a world of difference between the public acquiescence of interested parties in the religious rhetoric of the parish and their intersubjective coherence in a sustained, collective vision of God. As the testaments of the great believers show, religious belief has always been only an asymptote towards which the believer's imagination and faith struggle.

Many of those who pronounce on the uniquely disordered nature of contem-porary reality have been influenced, albeit indirectly and unconsciously in some cases, by T.S. Eliot's magisterial but often confused critical essays. In his, alas seminal, piece on James Joyce[17], he tells us that the narrative method must be replaced by the mythical method because the realistic novel was simply 'the expression of an age which had not sufficiently lost all form to feel the needs of something stricter'. Myth is

> simply a way of controlling, of ordering, of giving a shape and a signifi-
> cance to the immense panorama of futility and anarchy which is contem-
> porary history

What a curious statement! Once history is viewed as a 'panorama' it is difficult to imagine it seeming anything other than futile and anarchic. But there is nothing special about contemporary history in this regard. The history of all ages is the history of men who are born for no clear reason, live lives over which they have relatively little control and die for no better reason than that they

---

[16] Auerbach *op. cit.* p. 551.
[17] Ulysses, Order and Myth in *Selected Prose of T.S. Eliot*, ed. Frank Kermode (London: Faber, 1975).

were born. We have already quoted Nietzsche to this effect. It might be argued that Eliot felt that in previous eras the spectacle of human life would at least be encompassed within a framework of religious belief that conferred meaning upon it. In his essay on Tennyson[18], however, he refers to Victorian England as

> a time busy in keeping up to date. It had, for the most part, no hold on permanent things, on permanent truths about man and God and life and death.

But this was also the time when the realistic novel, and the narrative as opposed to the mythological method, were in the ascendant. Sooner or later, *terribles simplificateurs* run into self-contradiction.

It is probably unnecessary to appeal to historical and empirical evidence when debating whether or not contemporary reality is amenable to realistic treatment. It is sufficient to attend to the way in which writers who deny the reality of modern reality present their cases. Take Bernard Bergonzi's pronouncements. He assures us that

> *we* have no common sense of reality. *We* are saddled with all kinds of relativistic structures. *We* do not believe in there being 'one reality' out there as Tolstoy *undoubtedly* did [italics mine].

We should note how the scope and confidence of Bergonzi's assertions is at odds with what they say about the 'we' who have no common sense of reality. The total lack of confidence that should follow from the collapse of such a reality is signally absent. Who, moreover, is this 'we'? Does it include me? Does Bergonzi mean to include the whole world? Or only the students who attend his seminars?[19]. If his 'we' encompasses more than the few people he knows, does this not imply that the common sense of reality that he deems to have come to an end is in fact very much alive? And consider his 'undoubtedly'. If we no longer share with Tolstoy a belief in 'one reality out there' how can Mr Bergonzi be so confident about the difference between 'our' beliefs and those of Tolstoy? For if there is *really* no continuous 'out there', then the nineteenth-century becomes a very doubtful entity; so too does Leo Tolstoy and, *a fortiori*, that writer's vision of reality. If, furthermore, there is no unified reality how can we speak of 'now' as in: 'we are unable to write *now* as Tolstoy did'. What is the scope of his 'now'?

Bergonzi's merely typical claims about contemporary reality and the modern novel illustrate the way in which many critics' assertions presuppose a

---

[18] Essay on In Memoriam in Kermode, *op. cit.*
[19] Bergonzi's 'we' is reminiscent of Lionel Trilling's 'we', of which an anonymous reviewer in the *Times Literary Supplement* wrote that it sometimes meant 'just the people of our times as a whole; more often Americans in general; most often of all a very narrow class, consisting of New York intellectuals as judged by his own brighter students in Columbia'. To his credit, Trilling quotes this in the preface to *Beyond Culture* (London: Peregrine Books, 1967); but he does not attempt to answer this, very penetrating, criticism that throws into question his (or anyone's) credentials for carrying out the kind of inquiry he claims to be conducting.

much more understandable and unified reality than common sense would normally allow while at the same time they postulate a lesser degree of either of those things than anyone in his senses would accept. Gerald Graff has put this point succinctly:

> The rhetoric carries an authority and an assurance that quite belies the self-doubting tenor of what is said in this rhetoric[20]

It is not only academic critics who are prone to pragmatic self-refutation of this kind. The more journalistically inclined practitioners of the novel seem equally fond of practising self-refutation. One of the clearest, and hence most clearly absurd, statements of the view that modern reality is peculiarly resistant to treatment in realistic fiction is to be found in Philip Roth's essay 'Writing American Fiction':

> The American writer in the middle of the twentieth-century has his hands full in trying to understand, describe and then make *credible* much of American reality. It stupefies, it sickens, it infuriates, and finally it is even a kind of embarrassment to one's own meagre imagination. The actuality is continually outdoing our talents[21].

The passage contains two quite distinct grumbles. The second is easily dealt with. The complaint that truth is stranger (or more extravagant, or more improbable) than fiction should not cause the serious novelist anxiety. Truth has *always* been stranger than the serious fictional presentation of it. Only the writer of *Ripping Yarns* should be worried when actuality outdoes his talents; it is such a writer's job, after all, to *produce* strangeness – and stale, familiar strangeness it usually is. The serious novelist on the other hand has to *mediate* between the strange and the ordinary. To see him as being in competition with reality, trying to make fiction stranger than truth is wholly to misconceive the purpose of serious fiction. (This is not to deny the importance of realistic fiction in defamiliarizing the familiar – see note 23.)

The other complaint that 'much of American reality'[22] is especially difficult to 'understand, describe and make credible' is interesting only because the route by which this conclusion is reached makes helpfully explicit the pragmatic self-refutation implicit in the all-too-typical assertion originating from Bernard Bergonzi cited at the beginning of this chapter.

For the quoted passage is offered as the 'moral' of a story which takes up the

[20] Graff, *op. cit.*, p. 4.

[21] Philip Roth, Writing American Fiction. This essay is available in *The Novel Today* ed. Malcolm Bradbury (London: Fontana, 1977).

[22] *How* much, one is tempted to ask. How much of 'American Reality' does Mr Roth (one American out of over 200,000,000) imagine that he knows? Unless he believed that American reality was sufficiently unified, uniform and simple to be containable within one mind out of the 200,000,000 or so that contribute to it, he would recognize that he is not in a position to pronounce upon contemporary reality, even less to say in what ways it differs from earlier American reality. The only people qualified to do this kind of thing are the headline purveyors, the masters of Newspeak and the one-sentence paragraph – in a word, journalists.

first half of Roth's essay. This story, based upon newspaper reports, which Roth retells very racily, in a realistic way, is a particularly unpleasant one about a double murder turned by the newspapers into an occasion for a readers' competition and for various other 'media' events: horror made more horrid by flippant treatment that reduces it to farce. The story, which it must be re-emphasized, Roth *tells quite well and makes convincing*, is intended to illustrate the very reality that he argues is indescribable, incomprehensible and incredible. But unless we comprehend the story and accept it as a description of events that we believe in then this point is not made. Roth, in other words, is in the position of describing a piece of American reality in order to demonstrate that that reality is indescribable; of telling us a story about reality, expecting that we will understand it and believe it, in order to exemplify the mid-twentieth-century American reality that, he claims, is almost impossible to understand or make credible. Need one say any more?

There *is* perhaps one more point to be made. Roth's story is based upon newspaper material. Nature herself did not write the news reports and the feature articles he drew upon to make his story. Does Roth really believe that the *Chicago Sun Times* has the last word on the events in question? Surely for the novelist the newspaper story is merely a beginning. His very disgust and anger at the inadequacy, the superficiality and the distortions of media coverage imply this. Stendhal *began* from newspaper reports he did not, however, feel that his job was to 'out do' the 'actuality' (*newspaper* actuality) that he read about, but to penetrate more deeply into it. Had he merely dismissed the story of the woman cradling her lover's decapitated head as she drove away from the guillotine as 'stupefying, sickening, etc', we should not have had *Le Rouge et le Noir*. And did Tolstoy find the newspaper story of a woman who committed suicide, because of the collapse of an illicit love affair, immediately understandable? (What, after all, is love? What is death?),[23] Are we to accept that modern reality is so fashioned that it can be presented to us through the newspapers but not in the novels of a serious fictional artist? Why should we believe that contemporary reality is such that it can be televised and newspapered but is not amenable to reflective, analytical, compassionate and indignant treatment in a serious realistic novel?

The self-contradictions of Roth's essay should suffice to make us suspicious and certainly unimpressed when someone informs us that reality is 'incredible' or, worse, 'unrealistic'. The 'unrealistic nature of reality' is less apparent when one is running for a bus or suffering from toothache or hungry than when one is

---

[23] cf. Milan Kundera in an interview (*Granta* 11, London: Penguin, 1984 p. 35): 'Take jealousy, for example. It is so commonplace as to make any explanation seem unnecessary. But if you begin to pause and think about it, it is different. . . . Suddenly the commonplace becomes difficult, troubling, enigmatic.' For Kundera, one of the purposes of the novel is to question the commonplace, make it seem surprising, enigmatic: 'It doesn't just represent situations – jealousy, say, or tenderness or the taste for power – it arrests them, comes to a halt by them, looks closely at them, ponders them; interrogates them, asks questions of them, understands them as enigmas'. It does, in short, all those things that the *Chicago Sun Times* has no inkling of.

contemplating reality through the windows of a sheltering text in a well-appointed library.[24].

The fallacy of pragmatic self-refutation was brilliantly encapsulated by F.P. Ramsay in an imaginary dialogue[25]

A Say 'breakfast'.
B Can't.
A Can't say what?
B Can't say 'breakfast'.

We could adapt this dialogue to apply to some recent critical theory as follows:

A Express reality!
B Can't.
A Can't express what?
B Can't express reality.
A Why not?
B Because reality is . . . [Description of reality then follows].

As Passmore (to whom I owe my use of the concept) defines it, in pragmatic self-refutation 'the speaker's action is the best possible counter-example to what he asserts to be the case'[26].

Reality has always been a huge panorama of reali*ties* and that panorama has always been stupendous, complex, magnificent, vast and cruel. Contemporary reality is, in these respects, no different. One does not have to be insensitive or politically naive or indifferent to its iniquities and horrors to believe that this age is no worse, no more complex, no more resistant to complete understanding than any other. Reality is as 'realistic' as it ever was; or, rather, reality remains neither real nor unreal: it simply, inexorably, is.

> Our destiny . . . is not frightful because it is unreal; it is frightful because it is irreversible and ironbound. The world, unfortunately, is real; I, unfortunately, am Borges[27].

And so the novelist remains in at least one respect what he always has been: a real man or woman addressing other real men and women in a world – partly their own, partly held in common – that is, fortunately or unfortunately, real. There seems to be no compelling reason why he or she should ignore that world or talk about as if it were unreal.

---

[24] Behind many assertions about the unreality of reality may be an over-reaction to the fact that reality does not quite correspond to the expectations fostered in childhood. Experience, or (more usually) other people's experience as reported in newspapers, does not match the world-picture presented to the privileged few in their formative years. The world proves to be more complicated, less moral and perhaps more governed by accident than one's parents and teachers had led one to believe. A theatrical over-reaction to this discovery seduces some writers into self-refuting pronouncements about reality itself.

[25] F.P. Ramsay. *The Foundations of Mathematics* (London: Routledge & Kegan Paul, 1931) pp. 77–8.

[26] John Passmore. *Philosophical Reasoning* (London: Duckworth, 1961), ch. 4.

[27] Jorge Luis Borges, A New Refutation of Time in *A Personal Anthology*, ed. Anthony Kerrigan (London: Picador, 1972) p. 49.

2

'As if there Could Possibly be Such Things as True Stories'

Telling stories is telling lies

B.S. Johnson, *Albert Angelo*

'The novel' Michel Butor tells us[1] 'is a particular form of narrative'. Until recently, this assertion would have seemed unexceptional to the point of banality: *of course* a novel tells a story. Increasingly, however, 'serious' novelists and those regarded as serious have been unhappy about the narrative function of the novel. There is an influential body of critical opinion that would discredit the whole business of relating realistic, or even coherent or intelligible, stories. Serious fiction, it has been suggested, should be devoted less to recounting stories than to meditating on the nature of narration. It should certainly not be concerned with telling stories that are like 'real life'.

Many different arguments have been advanced in support of the view that apparently realistic narratives are a kind of confidence trick. Some of them have been directed against the explicitly or implicitly omniscient narrator; others against the supposedly related belief that reality can be rendered intelligible from a single, coherent point of view; and yet others against the notion of a world populated by recognizable characters with distinctive voices, styles of behaviour, etc. We shall discuss these in later chapters. A particularly interesting group of arguments derives from an unease with the fact that reality has to be ordered or structured before it can be narrated. This order or structure is alien to reality itself. A narrative is therefore an artefact whose shape and structure, whose internal connectedness, is quite different from that of reality as it is actually experienced. Narration, in short, inevitably distorts reality, and so-called realistic fiction, which conceals the extent to which a story is a construct upon, rather than a representation of, reality is, therefore, a confidence trick. Verisimilitude, fidelity to a world outside of the text, is an illusion; to use Barthes's phrase, a mere *effet de réel*.[2]

One classic statement of the novelist's anxiety about realistic narrative is to

---

[1] Michel Butor, The Novel as Research. This essay is available in Malcolm Bradbury, *The Novel Today*, (London: Fontana, 1977 pp. 48–53).

[2] The analogous but more radical argument that language itself is a closed system is examined in Chapter 3 of my *Not Saussure* (London: Macmillan, 1988).

be found in Sartre's early (and compellingly realistic) novel *Nausea*. The hero Roquentin reflects how

> for the most commonplace event to become an adventure you must – and this is all that is necessary – start *recounting* it. . . . When you are living nothing happens . . . There are never any beginnings . . . There isn't any end either . . . But when you tell about life, everything changes; only it's a change nobody notices; the proof of that is that people talk about true stories. As if there could possibly be such things as true stories; events take place one way and we recount them the opposite way. You appear to begin at the beginning: 'It was a fine Autumn evening in 1922. I was a solicitor's clerk in Marcommes'. And in fact you have begun at the end. It is there, invisible and present, and it is the end which gives those few words the pomp and value of a beginning. . . . And the story goes on in reverse: the moments have stopped piling up on one another in a happy-go-lucky manner, they are caught by the end of the story which attracts each of them and each of them in turn attracts the preceding moment. . . .[3]

The very process of recounting experience transforms it; or rather past reality becomes stories only at the cost of being changed into something that wasn't, or couldn't be, lived. Narration dramatizes, and hence distorts. We don't live inside the referent of stories; and since there is no livable reality corresponding to them, all stories must, in an important sense, be untrue:

> I wanted the moments of my life to follow one another in an orderly fashion . . . You might as well try to catch time by the tail.[4]

Comparable worries have been expressed by certain narratologists and it has been suggested by some that temporal processes are recognized as such only to the extent that they can be recounted. Others have suggested, more radically, that an action has a *beginning* only in a story that it inaugurates.

At the very least, a story relates a number of events placed, explicitly or implicitly, in some kind of temporal order. The latter exists only insofar as the experiences that the story purports to recount are articulated into a narrative. Individual experiences, isolated events do not (by definition) stand in a temporal relation to one another; nor are they related to a 'beginning' or an 'end'. One could go further and assert (quite plausibly) that there is no sequence of events existing in itself independently of the discourse that orders and presents them. Events form sequences only when they are ordered

---

[3] Jean-Paul Sartre, *Nausea*, Trans. Robert Baldick, London: Penguin, 1965, pp. 61–2. Contrary to Roquentin's claim, recounting is *not* sufficient to transform experience into an adventure or even into a story. Recounting will generate an accumulation of facts but something more is necessary for these to add up to a story. What that 'something more' is, no one can say; just as no one can say what it is that determines that a sequence of notes will count as a melody rather than a mere succession of sounds. It is one of the great mysteries of psychology.

[4] Sartre, *op. cit.* p. 63.

and presented or conceived of as ordered and presented.

Culler's implied criticism that many narratologists do not go far enough seems just:

> I am claiming that the narratological analysis of a text requires one to treat a discourse as a representation of events which are conceived of independently of any particular narrative perspective or presentation, which are thought of as having the properties of real events.[5]

The assumption that such events have a demarcated existence independently of the discourses about them is as vulnerable as the less fundamental assumption that they (intrinsically) 'have a temporal relationship with one another', each one being 'anterior to, simultaneous with, or posterior to every other event'.[6]

If, as is often stated, structure and event are interdependent, the structure of the narrative will not only determine that events are related to one another but also dissect out the events that are to be related. Happening becomes events – discrete patches of space-time, occurrences obtruding out of the continuum of experiences – only in relation to descriptions that narrate it. Only when it is articulated does it acquire edges: articulation confers boundaries upon portions of reality and joins those portions together in sequences. It is the significance of an event to a whole narrative that confers its shape as a 'setting' that may be differentiated into background and foreground. Experience granulates into 'events', into 'experiences' only in the context of actual or possible narration. This is what lies behind Roquentin's eloquent denunciation of 'true' stories.

Now one can concede all these points without being forced to the conclusion that there is an especially pernicious distortion at work in the construction of realistic narratives. If the arguments presented so far were to count as adequate grounds for discounting the implicit claim of the realistic novel to cast light on the nature of the – or a – real world then much more would have to be rejected besides.

In the essay quoted earlier, Butor points out that

> . . . narrative is a phenomenon which extends considerably beyond the scope of literature; it is one of the essential constituents of our understanding of reality.[7]

And not merely of our *understanding* of reality; but also our knowledge of it. The world that we think of ourselves as being surrounded by is presented to us largely in the form of stories. Our knowledge is mainly – to borrow Russell's[8]

---

[5] See the discussion in Jonathan Culler, *The Pursuit of Signs: Semiotics, Deconstruction, Literature*, (London: Routledge & Kegan Paul, 1981) Chapter 9: 'Story and Discourse in the Analysis of Narrative'. The passage is cited on p. 170.

[6] Culler, *ibid*, p. 170. [7] Butor, *op. cit.* p. 48.

[8] Bertrand Russell, 'Knowledge by Acquaintance and Knowledge by Description', in *Mysticism and Logic and Other Essays*, (London: Penguin, 1953).

terms – 'knowledge by description' rather than 'knowledge by (direct) acquaintance'. Most of the reality that we know or know of has not been experienced by us but has been presented to us as narratives or narrative fragments. Even within the realm of knowledge by acquaintance, narrative is a major presence; for the very process of remembering our experience or, indeed, of laying down retrievable memories may depend at least in some degree upon their being located within verbal structures. Amnesia for early childhood (up to the age of two or three) is almost total; and this is not solely because the child's way of perceiving the world is so different that the two worlds are almost mutually incomprehensible[9] but because a very young child does not *talk* about his experiences and memories. Experiences that are not linguistically coded cannot be stored in such a way that they can be retrieved. They are not, to use computer terminology, 'addressed':

> You can get back to an adult memory by reconstructing it from a verbal description or 'tag'; such verbal tags are not available for very early experiences.[10]

Ordinary recollection, therefore, depends upon language-mediated structuring of experience. Life remembered is not the same as life as it is being experienced. We are not, however, justified in concluding from this that all memory is false; that re-lived experience is a falsification of lived experience. Such a view would run into immediate and insuperable difficulties. By what criterion could we judge that a particular moment (of experience) was more 'truthful' than the recollection of it? What would one be comparing the recollection with? Raw, unprocessed reality? A *forgotten* primal chaos of sensation? Even if it were possible to compare the two, how could one adjudicate between them? Experience cannot of itself be true or false since truth values can be assigned to experience only when it is reflected upon and articulated into propositional form and made the basis of an assertion – as when, that is, it is recalled at a later date. As for sensation itself, this cannot be accounted 'truer' than memory since unrecollected, that is to say uninterpreted, sensations no more carry truth values than pebbles do. (This point, fundamental to the understanding of the relationship between language and reality, is one to which we shall return shortly.) The attack on realistic narratives – that they are necessarily false because they are structured in a way that the reality or experiences they apparently refer to are not – has therefore as little validity as an attack on realistic memories.

---

[9] Dan I. Slobin, *Psycholinguistics* (Glenview, Ill. and London, Scot Foresman & Co.), p. 105. Even Freudians, who invoke repressive mechanisms to explain amnesia for early childhood experiences, accept the crucial role of language in making memories accessible. For Lacan, language is central to the acquisition of a world picture shared with others, and to very process of becoming 'worlded'. That which is accessible and that which is intelligible coincide with that which is publicly acknowledged and mediated by language (See *Not Saussure*, Chapter 5).

[10] Slobin, *op. cit.* p. 106.

Or – to change the direction of the argument slightly – as an attack on realistic facts.

Everyone is familiar with Nietzsche's slogan, directed against naive positivism, that 'there are no such things as facts, only interpretations'. It is a reminder that 'the' facts of the case are selected in accordance with the observer's point of view – his changing personal interest, his unconscious ideology, his narrative purpose, and so on. The facts are not only selected by the observer; they are also in a sense constructed by him. For facts, like stories are, of course, artefacts. They are not secreted by nature, do not partake of the status of material objects. They are constructed out of the interaction between language, experience and memory.

But the constructed or artefactual nature of facts – their being *'facta'*, 'mades' – does not impugn their truth. A statement such as 'there is a dog in this room' is highly constructed and it is certainly not isomorphous with the state of affairs that it refers to: it is neither dog-shaped nor room-shaped; nor is it dog-in-room-shaped. Nor was it secreted by that state of affairs. Nevertheless, it may be true and its truth will depend upon whether or not the state of affairs that it is used to assert is actually the case. Its truth conditions are independent of the statement; and they will not be fulfilled by the process of its formulation. Facts are selected and constructed but they are not invented; they are made but they are not made up. Between the reality that determines the truth value of the statement and the statement itself there intervenes an enormously complex process of selection, abstraction, generalization, analysis, synthesis, etc. But this will not preclude the latter from being true or false. Just because physical reality – material objects, sensory experiences, perceptions of presence – is not a nexus of 'natural' facts, we are not entitled to conclude that there are no true or realistic facts or that factual truth is an illusion.

A fact, then, is as much a product of the ordering of experience as a story is; indeed, a fact is a kind of mini-story. There is a sense in which a fact is a story given all at once and a story is a special or privileged fact disclosed by slow degrees. More precisely, a story is a fact or set of facts released in a setting (itself constructed out of other facts) that make it significant and make knowing it desirable; an aspect of expressed reality that becomes, in virtue of the gradualness of its disclosure and the expectations raised in relation to it, the deferred goal of a listener's or reader's aroused attention.[11] The difference between a fact and a story is not absolute or even intrinsic but a matter of degree and of context. So anyone who denies the validity of true stories must also deny the possiblity of true facts. More particularly, anyone who asserts that stories are false on the grounds that their construction involves the ordering of experience in a way that does not reflect any inherent order it may

---

[11] We could define a story as 'a fact or group of facts, together with the means of generating an appetite for them'. Such a definition might identify more precisely, but it would not of course solve, the mystery alluded to in Note 3.

have must hold the more general belief that *any* ordering of experience necessarily falsifies it.

In practice, few of those critics who adopt an extreme, sceptical position *vis-à-vis* stories would be willing to hold the more radical position that all facts are lies or in some other way false. While Roquentin, Sartre's fictional *alter ego*, finds it easy to dismiss the possibility of true stories, Sartre himself does not seriously question whether there can be true facts. His eloquent, well-documented, denunciations of political evils, those generous angers for which he was so famous, bear witness to a man who in practice believed passionately in factual truth.[12] There are, however, some bold critics who are willing to defend the more radical position. Two frequently encountered confusions help writers to the conclusion that there is no such thing as objective factual truth: one arises out of an uncritical acceptance of the Nietzschean position alluded to earlier; and the other is the result of a mistaken belief that an assertion needs to be either part of, or isomorphous with, the reality it is apparently about in order to be true of it.

The first confusion is presented with exceptional clarity in the opening chapter of Terry Eagleton's *Literary Theory*.[13] In an attempt to demonstrate how the difference between fact and interpretation is illusory, he invites us to compare two statements, one apparently a straightforward neutral assertion of fact and the other an explicit value judgement:

(a) This cathedral is a magnificent specimen of baroque architecture.
(b) This cathedral was built in 1612.

At first sight it would appear that (b) is an 'objective' statement of fact while (a) is a 'subjective' value judgement. This difference, Eagleton believes, disappears on closer consideration; for even the apparently factual statement is or implies a value judgement.

> Statements of fact are after all *statements*, which presumes a number of questionable judgements: that those statements are worth making, perhaps more worth making than certain others, that I am the sort of person entitled to make them and perhaps able to guarantee their truth, that you are the kind of person worth making them to, that something useful is accomplished by making them, and so on.[14]

Facts, he implies, are riddled with implicit value judgements inasmuch as the assertion of a fact implies the making of a choice – dictated, like all choices,

---

[12] See, for example, the essays collected in *Between Existentialism and Marxism*, Trans. John Mathews (London: New Left Books, 1974). The distinctive tragedy of Sartre's intellectual journey was his inability to reconcile the radical vision of the philosopher with the noble (and sometimes less than noble) anger of a man with an acute sense of the appalling suffering caused by global injustice. The absolute metaphysical freedom of the existentialist prophet could never (without a good deal of dialectical clap-trap) be intelligibly united with the relative, contingent, limited freedom that the politically committed social observer saw around him.

[13] Terry Eagleton, *Literary Theory* (Oxford: Basil Blackwell, 1983).

[14] Eagleton, *op. cit.* p. 13.

by values. And of course there is also implicit evaluation in what we, however indirectly, choose *not* to say: to select one remark is to discriminate against other possible remarks. As Brecht says, 'To talk of trees is to pass over so many crimes in silence'.

The initial plausibility of Eagleton's argument does not survive examination. Consider the following statements:

(a).1 This cathedral is not a magnificent specimen of baroque architecture.

(a).2 This cathedral is a magnificent specimen of modern architecture.

(a).3 This cathedral is monstrously ugly.

(b).1 This cathedral was not built in 1612.

(b).2 This cathedral was built in 1988.

A dispute between someone maintaining (a) and someone maintaining either (a).1 or (a).3 would be manifestly an argument over value judgements. Even the difference between (a) and (a).2 could be regarded as a matter of terminology in an area where terms notoriously have rather fluffy boundaries. It would be very odd, however, to suggest that (b) versus (b).1 or (b) versus (b).2 was simply a question of different values. It is not merely a matter of your, my, or the community's opinion that this cathedral was built in 1612 rather than 1988.

We are able, therefore, to distinguish without difficulty, matters of fact from matters of interpretation or judgement, in the very example that Eagleton has provided. The statements belonging to the (a) series are riddled with evaluation, while those belonging to the (b) series incorporate values only in their having been chosen, not in their content. So the truth of the latter cannot be entirely assimilated to value judgements. Just as my values or interests may be implicit in my assertion that Terry Eagleton's book *Literary Theory* was published by Basil Blackwell in 1983 though they do not determine the truth value of that assertion. Whether or not I assert it is independent of whether or not it is true.

The underlying muddle is between the role of the subject as one who articulates reality into facts on the one hand and the truth-conditions of factual statements on the other; between what motivates the formulation of reality into statements and the reality that determines whether or not they are true. My current interests (influenced, perhaps, by preceding conversation) will determine whether I explicitly notice that there is a dog in the room, as well as whether I consider it worthy of comment, but not whether there *is* a dog in the room. Failure to observe this distinction will lead to a kind of idealism that holds that reality itself is created out of values – in short, to magic thinking.[15]

15 Marx, at whose shrine Eagleton worships, is careful to avoid magic thinking. He recognized that even where reality is apparently constructed, where it is historically derived, it is external to the value systems of individuals and their momentary interests: 'Men make their own history but they do not make it just as they please; they do not make it under circumstances chosen by themselves but under circumstances directly encountered, given and transmitted from the past. The tradition of all the dead generations weighs like a nightmare on the brain of the living.' *The Eighteenth Brumaire of Louis Bonaparte*, Progress Publishers, p. 10.

The other confusion that may lead to a denial of the possibility of realistic or objective factual statements derives from the assumption that discourse can be genuinely 'about' something only if it is structured like it. This, which may be called the Isomorphic Fallacy, leads inevitably to the conclusion that language, since it is composed of arbitrary signs that have their own rules of combination, is essentially a closed system.[16] The belief that an utterance has to be ordered like reality in order to be about it is rooted in the more general premise that a sign can signify truthfully or without distortion only if sign and significate share an identical form. This is, of course, untrue even of non-arbitrary, natural signs: clouds do not signify rain in virtue of looking like rain. Moreover, the cloud that signifies and the rain that is signified also differ in being respectively particular and general. Furthermore, an identity of form guarantees nothing: Object A does not count as a description of Object B just because it looks like it. Isomorphism is thus neither a necessary nor a sufficient condition either for expression or for truthful reference. On the contrary, a lack of such identity is essential in order that sign systems can create those distances from which expression is possible and which reference can then cross. Far from being a barrier to truthful narration, to successful reference, non-isomorphism between discourse and reality is an essential precondition of it. Only where there is a distance between what is said and the reality that is spoken of can a narrative, or any description, be 'about' anything.

Behind the belief that factual reality is distorted reality – because statements are structured differently from the reality they are about – is a yet more interesting misconception which we touched on earlier. It is that reality is *in itself* true – so that spoken or written reality, which is ordered differently from it, is false.

Physical reality, understood as the object of pre-linguistic, or even asemic, sensory experience, is not itself true or false. It is only in judgements on experience, formulated in statements which can then be asserted as facts or told as stories, that reality acquires the status of being in some sense true. Even then, the truth of reality is borrowed from the truth of the statements that are true of or to it; for truth and falsehood as fully explicit categories are posterior, not anterior, to language. They are categories to which one can assign statements (stories, descriptions) not objects or events. Anyone who maintains that reality is in itself true is committed to assimilating the category of truth to that of existence: whatever is, is true. Or: truth is whatever exists. Truth would become a redundant category, entirely superseded by that of existence. Statements would then all be true in virtue of their existence: they would have the truth enjoyed by objects or events. But they would be false in virtue of their reference. Or they would be true insofar as they were mere

[16] Similar arguments have been developed by Structuralist critics to suggest that language, having rules of its own, must be cut off from reality and that reference to reality must therefore be illusory.

sounds but false insofar they had meaning. The ordinary distinction between true statements and false ones would have to replaced by the distinction between true reality on the one hand and truefalse statements on the other: statements that were all inevitably true in their being and all inevitably false in their reference. This is manifestly absurd – aside from the fact that it would force us to jettison the inescapable everyday distinction between true and false assertions. (If there is a dog in the room in question, then the statement 'There is a dog in the room' is true and certain other statements, such as 'There is no dog in that room' or 'All the dogs are in the street' are false.)[17]

So we must reject the notion that reality is in itself true and that that truth can be approached, but not reached, by statements about it. Truth and falsehood emerge as fully explicit categories only in relation to statements that formulate reality in order to present it as facts. This must not, however, be taken to imply that truth and falsehood remain intralinguistic. Although there can be no fully developed truth or falsehood without explicit formulation of reality – without assertion – the *truth conditions* of a particular assertion are to be found in reality outside of language. A pebble existing in a certain place is neither true or false: it merely is. The assertion that 'There is a pebble in such and such a place' does, however, carry a truth value and this will depend upon whether or not in reality there is a pebble at such and such a place. It is in virtue of language that a piece of reality becomes a set of truth conditions – the truth conditions of the assertion that that piece of reality exists (is the case). The linguistic operation that produces 'R is the case' out of reality R makes R the truth condition of the proposition P which asserts 'R is the case'. R becomes that which would have to be the case for P to be true. It does not, however, thereby become true in itself.

This position is a complex one and therefore liable to be misunderstood and confused with adjacent positions between which it takes a middle course in order to avoid the error of regarding factual truth as independent of language[18] and the opposite and currently more fashionable error of seeing it as entirely internal to language.[19] Without language there could be no

---

[17] Truth presupposes explicitness, disclosure, assertion. In language explicitness is made explicit and truth (and falsehood) emerge as fully developed categories. 'Explicitness' is close to *aletheia*, 'uncoveredness' that Heidegger used in his later essays. (See, for example, *On Time and Being*, Trans. Joan Stambaugh, New York, Harper & Row, 1972) I prefer it to 'uncoveredness' because the latter may be taken to suggest that truth is purely a revelation of the inherent properties of prelinguistic reality.

[18] It should not be confused with a naive Correspondence Theory of Truth or (worse) a Mirror Theory. I do not see reality as already ordered into facts, waiting to be reflected in the mirror of language. On the contrary, it is language that orders reality into factual reality; it transforms reality into truth conditions of factual assertions.

[19] This position is, of course, especially associated with the name of Derrida for whom both truth and meaning are effects of language. Such radical nominalism is absurd: there must be differentiation of meaning prior to language, otherwise language would be entirely redundant. The difference between nutritious food and deadly poisons may be brought to full explicitness and formalized in language (language may make possible secondary symbolic developments constructed upon that opposition) but the final home of that difference is not the opposition between those two terms.

facts – for facts do not inhere in uncommunicated physical reality: the latter is not a network of facts. Even the most laboriously *chosiste* description is not a direct translation from Thingish into English. The fact that my pen is approximately 3,000 miles from New York could hardly have come into being without the mediation of language – nor indeed could the relations that they express have acquired independent existence without being made explicit linguistically. Facts, then, are in a sense the child of language though their status as facts – as opposed to errors or falsehood or lies – is determined extra-linguistically.

By way of conclusion, let us return to Roquentin's worry that stories are different from life and that telling is different from living. A given moment in a story, but not in life, is ordered with respect to a future towards which the story is unfolding and related to a past from which it has explicitly sprung. The moment of lived consciousness that the story may be about does not yet know which story it belongs to. Unlike the corresponding moment in the story, it points to no exclusive destination, no clear ending that will in turn pick it out as the beginning. So narration transforms experience: it turns temporal reality into something that is layered, a series of corners to be turned, a progressive disclosure; and makes time itself more explicit as the vector connecting an explicit future with an explicit past, the no longer with the not yet, Page 10 and Page 100, rather than a scalar non-sequence or dis-sequence of nows.

So telling transforms reality. But is this grounds for complaint? Surely not; for if telling were *not* different from living, it would be redundant. One can reasonably resent the fact that stories do not simply replicate reality only if one subscribes to, or is in the grip of, an extreme version of the Mimetic Fallacy; if, like T.E. Hulme for example, one believes that the purpose of literature (in his case poetry) is to persuade language to perform some act equivalent to the 'bodily handing over of sensation'. For language, of course, cannot replicate the realities of which it speaks.

But even if this were possible, it would be an empty feat; who wants a week with two identical Tuesdays – one lived and one recounted – in it? Do we really want language or the realistic novel to be committed to the mere duplication of experience? Or demand of fiction that it should be devoted to the equivalent of the futile literary task Pierre Menard proposed for himself:[20] to re-write *Don Quixote*, using only Cervantes's words. If the condition of fictional truth were an absolute identity between the text and the reality referred to in it, then the only true fictions would be pieces of reality itself. All descriptions would have to be full-scale reproductions of the settings described: the *reductio ad absurdum* of the *chosiste* enterprise. As Dr Johnson observed,

[20] Jorge Luis Borges, Pierre Menard, The Invisible Author of Don Quixote in *A Personal Anthology*, (London: Picador, 1972).

If the world be promiscuously described, I cannot see of what use if can
be to read the account; or why it may not be as safe to turn the eyes
immediately upon mankind as upon a mirror which shows all that
presents itself without discrimination.[21]

It is the difference between telling and living that gives the former its purpose. To criticize a story because it is differently constructed from experiences it reports would be like criticizing a summary because it left out certain
details. The inevitable difference between telling and living does not, however, eradicate the difference between truly realistic and unrealistic stories
any more than it abolishes the distinction between true (accurate, etc.) and
false (inaccurate, etc.) accounts of real events. A patient does not reproduce
his illness or his experience of it in giving an account of it to his doctor; but the
difference between a true and false medical history remains a very real and
important one. His life may depend upon the doctor eliciting an accurate
history of the illness.

The differences between telling and living do not, therefore, provide compelling grounds for denying the possiblity of true stories that have more than
the mere appearance of verisimilitude. Anyone who would reject realistic
fiction as a fraud because reality is structured differently from stories must
also be committed to rejecting realistic non-fictional stories, realistic
memories and those realistic mini-stories we call facts. The more radical position that facts, being contructs, have no objective truth depends, as we have
seen, upon the convergence of two muddles: one concerns the interaction
between facts and values; and the other, more interesting, one relates to the role
of language in transforming reality into the truth conditions of assertions. The
second muddle is the more subtle and is the result of failing to differentiate
between the *existence conditions* and the *truth conditions* of factual assertions.
Values may be critical in determining that a particular statement should be
made but they do not, of themselves make statements true (or false). When
these muddles are cleared up, little of the case against realistic facts remains.
The little that does remain disappears when one reflects that if telling were
not different from living, telling would be pretty pointless. When the case
against realistic facts collapses, the radical arguments against realistic fictions
that we have examined here also succumb. 'The truth of fiction' is a difficult
concept; but verisimilitude goes deeper than a mere confidence trick and cannot be dismissed as a mere *effet de réel*.

---

[21] *Rambler* No. 4, quoted in Damien Grant, *Realism* (London: Methuen, 1970) p. 46.

3

Has the Cinema Rendered the Realistic Novel Obsolete?

We have so far considered two arguments against realistic fiction. In the first chapter we refuted the argument that the supposedly unrealistic nature of contemporary reality makes it unsuitable for realistic treatment. In the second, we confronted the philosophically more radical claim that, in view of the inevitable differences between the structures of stories and the experiences recounted in stories, the former could never be true of or to the latter. In this chapter, we shall deal with the rather less sweeping assertion that, since there are better ways of revealing or expressing the real world than narrative fiction, the realistic novel is now obsolete.

This has been very forcibly expressed by Robert Scholes in *The Fabulators*, an influential and widely quoted book published nearly twenty years ago. In an often cited passage he wrote:

> The cinema gives the *coup de grâce* to a dying realism in written fiction. Realism purports – has always purported – to subordinate words themselves to their referents: to the things words point to. Realism exalts life and diminishes art, exalts things and diminishes words. But when it comes to representing things, one picture is worth a thousand words, and one motion picture is worth a million. In face of competition from the cinema, fiction must abandon its attempt to 'represent reality' and rely more on the power of words to stimulate the imagination.[1]

This passage is a striking act of compression; for to pack so many dubious assertions into such a small space is an extraordinary achievement. It is perhaps worth dealing with some of the minor ones briefly, before examining Scholes's main claim – that the cinema has superseded the realistic novel.

1 The claim, first of all, that written fiction is dying. This, as was discussed in the introduction to this book, is simply unfounded. The vast majority of novels written, published, sold and read attempt, with varying degrees of success, to be realistic. These include some first rate works – as well as, of course, a good deal of trash – so the continuing domination of the novel by realism cannot be explained simply by the triumph of commercial over literary values.

[1] Robert Scholes, *The Fabulators* New York, 1967.

2 Secondly, the claim that the realistic novel is concerned only (or even mainly) with representing *things*. This is also untrue. The remorseless accumulation of 'realistic' material detail is only one aspect of certain styles or phases of realism – for example of the Naturalism associated with the Medan School. But even in such cases, the physical details merely provide an essential background to action and to psychological and historical analysis. (The most determined attempt to represent *things* to the exclusion of thoughts, feelings, memories and other mental phenomena is to be found in the anti-realistic novels of Robbe-Grillet – with abominable and unrealistic results.)[2] As we shall discuss in Part III, it is a common mistake to confuse realism – understood as the attempt to capture a piece of reality for fiction – with certain techniques employed by particular novelists endeavouring to express reality in their fiction. I say 'expression', rather than 'representation' – and this brings me to the third and most important error in Scholes's muddled paragraph.

3 Even realistic fiction does not attempt to *represent* reality. Words are not representational signs: they are expressive, not mimetic. No realistic writer has ever thought otherwise. Realistic fiction, therefore, is not in competition with the cinema as a representational mode of signification. But we have now arrived at the main theme of this chapter.

A movie consists of a certain footage of film combined with a sound-track. No one has suggested, so far as I know, that the sound-track threatens the realistic novel. We have had spoken dialogue and sound effects in theatre for longer than we have had novels of any sort, never mind realistic ones. Rather, it is what the cameraman rather than the sound-recordist can do that is at issue.

The camera can render, by reproducing their visible aspects, portions of the physical world. Now, if the role of words in a novel were the same as that of the camera in film – namely to replicate the visible surfaces of parts of the world – then there could be no doubt that cine-photography, which copies visible surfaces with effortless precision and the instantaneous inclusiveness of the eye, would be indisputably superior to the pen as an instrument for achieving the aims of realistic fiction. The cameraman is better at reduplicating visible surfaces than the writer. But it follows from this that cine-photography has superseded descriptive or narrative prose, or that the cinema has rendered the realistic novel obsolete, only if reality is believed to consist essentially of visible surfaces.

It is hardly necessary to state that reality is *not* identical with the visible appearances of physical objects. Rather, it is the continuously evolving *sense* we make of the physical, psychological and social phenomena that present

---

[2] The case of Robbe-Grillet is, of course, rather difficult. His critics are divided as to whether he is attempting to present reality as it is, stripped bare of anthropomorphic narrative clichés; or whether he is bent on undermining the mimetic contract. See Chapter 7.

themselves to us. That sense is only in part fixed by the physical characteristics reality displays at a given moment. It is certainly not exclusively determined by the visible appearances or properties of the material entities surrounding the subject. For a start, reality has tactile, olfactory, thermal and other properties that cannot be represented visually. (The coldness of a frosty scene is *inferred*, not directly experienced, by the film-goer.) But even suppose reality *were* identical with purely visual reality, would cine-photography supersede the descriptive prose of the realistic novel?

The answer is again: No. And the reason for this is quite simple. Replicating the visual surfaces of a portion of the world is not the same as replicating, or even signifying, a moment in visual *experience*. And it is certainly not the same as replicating or signifying that experience infused, as visual experience always is, by knowledge from past visual experience. Even less is it like replicating or signifying a consciousness in which visual experience and knowledge are brought together in a subject imbued with a sense of self derived from past visual and non-visual experience.

At best, the camera renders sensibilia, not experiences or perceptions. It reveals visual surfaces laid out in space and cannot directly display visual perceptions that are also deeply interconnected in time. Pictures, even moving ones, cannot of themselves depict the *sense* even of visible things, in which experience and knowledge are dovetailed. (Words, in contrast, are able to express *only* the sense or meaning of things, rather than the things themselves.) If the cinema appears to present visual reality itself, this is because the cinema-goer provides the sense.

That there is an irreducible difference, an unbridgeable gap, between the replication of visible surfaces and the presentation of visual experience becomes especially noticeable when film-makers try to model the later on the former. The clumsiness of the tricks they use is more often embarrassing than amusing. For the elementary psychology of visual perception seems to be ignored by, or unknown to, film directors. Let me give some examples:

1 When I look about a room, I do not experience the vertigo that the camera, in trying to reproduce my scanning behaviour, inadvertently simulates.

2 When my attention on an object wavers, the object does not go out of focus in the way that the cameraman, either a literal swallower of the crude metaphor of 'focusing of attention' or a victim of the limitations of his instrument, often represents it as doing. When I lose interest in an object, it does not grow blurred edges – it simply ceases to be there in a way that cannot be *pictured*.

3 Some directors like to attach cameras to the moving bodies of protagonists engaged in intense physical activity in the hope of approximating the relevant visual experiences more closely. The results are usually unfortunate. The use of a hand-held camera to show the world apparently bobbing up and down around a running person or shimmying around someone driving a fast car,

with the intention of giving the authentic feel of running or driving fast, are cases in point. The visual experiences that we are thereby invited to participate in (which can be reproduced in daily life only by *abnormal* attention to the visual world as one runs or drives) are closer to the pathology than the psychology of vision. In the primitive world of the cinema, running seems to produce oscillopsia. Outside of the Odeon, this is usually associated with rare upper brain-stem lesions.[3]

That the world does *not*, under normal circumstances, appear to bob up and down when we run for a bus or whirl round when we turn our heads is due to afferent feedback, which permits the eye to compensate for the move-. ment of the head so that it does not misinterpret the relative movement of head and world as movement of the world. This specific explanation is important insofar as it supports a more general point: that we make continuous, on-line *sense* of our experience against a background of previous experience; that is to say, in the light of what we know. There is simply no way of *picturing* this.

The camera, then, cannot do justice even to *visual* reality because it cannot depict the knowledge that makes sense of visible appearances and which, except in certain comparatively rare syndromes of agnosia following damage to the cerebral cortex,[4] permeates all visual experience.[5] The belief that the camera is able to depict knowledge may be a consequence of taking rather literally the visual metaphors we often use for knowledge, though I suspect it is due mainly to a failure to think sufficiently deeply about these things.

There are potent metaphors linking vision and cognition. The overlapping connotations of 'viewpoint' may be responsible for much elementary confusion between camera angles, head or brain angles, and self angles. The physical, the psychological and the social are all assimilated in the naive world of cine-photography to the geometrical – a reduction that is comparable to locating the Cartesian *cogito* at 0,0,0 of Cartesian space. One result of identifying the many-layered concept of 'viewpoint' with its elementary realization in physical space – and the consequent inability to differentiate geometrical angle from self angle – is that the same panning movement may be used to show a landscape perceived by no one, that landscape perceived by *anyone*, and the same landscape being perceived by someone of especial importance to the story being filmed and presumed, at

[3] Gay, A.J. and Newman, N.M. Eye movements and their disorders. In *Scientific Foundations of Neurology*, ed. M. Critchley, J. O'Leary and W.B. Jennett. Heinemann, London (1972).

[4] These have been recently reviewed in Bechinger, D. and Tallis, R.C. *British Journal of Occupational Therapy* 1986.

[5] In this context, it is interesting – and revealing – how the very camera tricks used to try to simulate visual experience are also employed on other occasions to indicate pathological states – pathology of vision, of emotion of of social situation – and, by dull sophisticates such as Jean-Luc Godard, to 'subvert' the cinematic genre.

that juncture, to be in a particular state of mind and in the grip of certain preoccupations. The camera, unable to differentiate between *sensibile,* sensation, perception and viewpoint, can scarcely be expected to distinguish between a landscape revealed to no viewpoint and one revealed to a particular individual. In short, it cannot distinguish between physical and psychological aspects of 'point of view'.

We have already commented on how a change or loss of interest in an object is often represented on film by unfocusing. The shift from the physical to the mental, or from external objects to their inner representation, is often signalled in precisely the same way. The remembering or dreaming mind is apparently an eye in need of spectacles and therefore best represented by a poorly focused camera. (It would be unkind to pursue this further and ask to what extent human memory actually does take the form of visual images and whether, even if mental images *were* a central feature of most reminiscence, they would make sense by themselves.) The confusion between physical and social viewpoint is well illustrated by that cliché of the cinema, the tilt shot, in which the visual world of an oppressed or frightened person is recorded through a camera located round about somebody's feet.

The truth is that even purely visual perception has many more dimensions than the camera has degrees of freedom to depict. But even when it is conceded that, yes, the camera does have the limitations we have discussed, the concession is made only in order that the wrong conclusions can be drawn. It is suggested that, because the camera can record merely the visible surfaces of things, i.e. some of their physical properties, it is therefore 'objective' or 'neutral' in a way that the spoken or written word could not be. But this 'objectivity' is, of course, a myth.

The cameraman or director selects, just as the prose artist does, those details which appear to be relevant to the story being filmed. It is then up to the audience to contribute its own knowledge, subjectivity, etc. to the displayed visible surfaces in order to make visual and narrative sense of them. If a moving picture *were* purely objective, it would be quite senseless; or it would require its sense to be supplied by the audience. This would imply total non-selectivity and a complete abdication of control by the film-makers. Any movement away from subjectivity by the director or cameraman will always be counterbalanced by an increased subjectivity and freedom on the part of the audience. If the film consists only of a record of what happened to fall within the field of the camera over a certain period of time, the boring result (and such films have been made) will probably stimulate the audience to exercise its freedom to leave the cinema. For the audience will resent having to provide so much in the form of knowledge and interpretation, in short *sense,* itself. Subjectivity is not replaced by objectivity but transferred from producer to consumer.

The loss of control associated with the apparently greater objectivity of the camera compared with the pen becomes especially evident when we consider one aspect of the supposed superiority of cine-photography over descriptive prose. Barthes[6] points out that the camera, unlike the pen, can not only present a great deal of the visible world at once but also, once it has been presented, can leave it before the viewers, to look after itself as it were. Because we have the hero's scarred face always before us, the 'narrator' (cameraman/producer) does not have repeatedly to refer to it in order to keep it before our attention. Is this necessarily an advantage? Repeated allusion to things – so that their presence is recurrent rather than continuous – may confer upon them the status of *leitmotif*. The blue flower in the buttonhole of Tonio Kröger's father, for example, is a narrative device of great poignancy. The impact of this *leitmotif* depends upon its being present only when the writer wishes to invoke it. The prose medium permits this degree of control. If, however, the film script indicates that 'so and so always wore a blue flower in his button-hole', then the camera is obliged to display the flower whenever that person appears on the screen.

The more general point underlying this example is that whereas descriptive prose may signify only those realities which are regarded as relevant at a particular moment, cine-photography is forced to entrain many things that are irrelevant. As already noted, apparently greater 'objectivity' is bought at the cost of loss of control. In the novel, nothing will be present except at the specific invitation of the author; whereas every shot in a film is cluttered with uninvited contents. This may be more faithful to the visible surface of things; but it is considerably less faithful to the *experience* of reality, where fluctuations of attention continually exclude the irrelevant and pick out the relevant; and less true again to our *sense* of the real.

A camera replicating the appearance of an object or a scene or a series of events is no more faithful to the 'truth' of these things than is a piece of prose. For truth is always a matter of the *sense* of a piece of reality and this will have to be inferred by an observer who looks at its cine-portrait or be discovered by him from the (necessarily verbal!) dialogue. Photography, being a representational mode of signification, simply duplicating one aspect of the signified, stops short of expression, that is to say, of embodying meanings that can carry truth values.

A *picture* of an ink bottle is not in itself either true or false unless it is additionally asserted (i.e. non-pictorially indicated by means, for example, of a caption) that this ink bottle actually exists or existed, that this is a portrait of a particular ink bottle that occupied a particular position at a particular time, or that it belongs to me. Pictures do not have truth values in the way that certain statements do because pictures cannot *assert* themselves or, rather, assert that what is presented in them is, in fact, the case. There is no way of indicating by purely pictorial means the difference between, say, a hypothetical possibility being entertained and an actual state of affairs being reported or between an abstract and a general statement. A picture does not of itself

[6] Roland Barthes, The Death of the Author, in *Image-Music-Text*, selected and trans. Stephen Heath, London: Fontana, 1977 p. 146.

have a determinable truth value because its meaning, and hence its truth conditions, cannot be specified except through non-pictorial modes of signification.[7]

If the claim that the camera cannot lie has a kind of limited truth, it is precisely for the reason that it cannot, by itself, tell the truth, either. These reasons are similar to those which make it impossible for a stone or a cup of tea to tell, or to be, a lie.[8] (Any of these things may, of course, be used to complete or to substantiate a lie that has been set up in an expressive mode of signification.) Physical reality is in itself neither true nor false; neither are its representations, those signs which replicate part of its physical appearance. Only modes of signification which *express* it through materializing one of its *senses* which can then be asserted, are able to generate truth values.[9]

Replication is not expression.[10] Film cannot therefore *express* the 'real' world better than the descriptive prose of a realistic novel. This observation is powerfully supported by the continuing popularity and cultural centrality of the novel as an art form. The advent of the cinema has not meant the eclipse of the novel; indeed, the novel has not merely survived, but flourished. And this despite the disadvantages the novel labours under with respect to its conditions of consumption compared with the cinema. The cinema imposes an uninterrupted, complete viewing while novels are usually read in distracted snatches. (This advantage will be eroded by the wider availability of video-cassette players; increasingly films will be watched under the kind of adverse conditions which surround the reading of novels.)

It cannot be denied that moving pictures provide an alternative method to the presentation of reality nor that it is possible to achieve things in film that are beyond the reach of descriptive prose. The cinema and writing have different capabilities and limitations. But if there are many things that a camera can do which are beyond the reach of a pen, there are many other things which can be achieved by the pen and not by the camera. The latter has not rendered the former, even as a tool of description, obsolete. This becomes abundantly clear when one sees the usually dismal and sometimes downright embarrassing results of attempts to film great realistic novels.

---

[7] cf. Wittgenstein's observation that 'The intention – the intentionality – never lies in the picture itself because, however the picture is constructed, it can always be meant in a different way.' This insight, which was central to his rejection of his own picture theory of propositions, is quoted in Anthony Kenny, *Wittgenstein*, Penguin, London: 1975.

[8] For a more detailed discussion of this, see Chapter 2.

[9] See *Not Saussure*, ch. 4.

[10] The failure to appreciate the radical heterogeneity of linguistic and pictorial modes of signification was probably behind the once-fashionable search for literary equivalents of non-representational painting. After Kandinsky, after Mondrian, fiction, too, should, it was argued, be 'non-representational'. If novelists are going to keep up with painters, then we must have Abstract fiction. From this viewpoint, realism becomes analogous to chocolate-box painting. As if language, the home of abstraction, the matrix of all non-representational modes of signification, should have to be taught to keep abreast of non-representational developments in painting!

Is it scarcely unexpected, then, that the rise of the cinema has not meant the demise of prose realism, despite the contrary claims of those who feel it should have done. For the pen is arguably more adapted to signifying multi-dimensional human reality than film because consciousness is closer to language than to pictures. Realism remains the great unfinished adventure of the novel and the realistic novel an immensely powerful instrument for furthering human consciousness and self-consciousness. It has not been superseded by the cinema; even less has the latter given it the *coup de grâce* on its death bed.

Althusser and the 'Ideological' Arguments Against Realism

4

Realism and the Idea of Objective Reality

Realist art or literature is seen as one convention among others, a set of formal representations, in a particular medium to which we have become accustomed. The object is not *really* lifelike but by convention and repetition has been made to appear so. This can be seen as relatively harmless or extremely harmful. To see it as harmful depends on a sense that . . . a pseudo-objective *version* of reality (a version that will be found to depend, finally, on a particular phase of history or on a particular set of relationships between men and between men and things) is passed off as *reality*, although in this instance at least (and perhaps more generally) what is there has been made, by the specific practices of writing, painting and film-making.[1]

This bourgeois genre [the novel] has always been felt to be related to the economic world; it has contributed largely in developing the kind of cultural consensus necessary to the growth of modern capitalism.[2]

All ideological State apparatuses . . . contribute to the same result: the reproduction of the relations of production, i.e. of capitalist relations of exploitation.[3]

4.1 Reality as Artefact

I have already discussed how articulated or factual reality is in an important sense *artefactual* reality; how even remembered reality, inasmuch as it is structured differently from current experience, is an artefact of the remembering

[1] Raymond Williams, *Keywords*, (London: Fontana, 1976), pp. 219–20. The essays in this book, erudite and penetrating, are marvels of concision.

[2] Maurice Couturier and Regis Durand, *Donald Barthelme*, (London: Methuen, 1982), p. 69. One could argue with equal (that is to say as little) plausibility that the work ethos lies behind *both* the growth of modern capitalism *and* the writing (and even the reading) of long books. That is, in other words, the novel is a product or symptom of 'the consensus necessary to the growth of modern capitalism' rather than a cause of of it. The images of Thomas Mann's Aschenbach and of Mann himself dramatize this Weberian interpretation that is at least as plausible as the Marxist implications of this quotation from Couturier and Durand.

[3] Louis Althusser, Ideology and Ideological State Apparatuses in *Essays on Ideology*, (London, Verso Editions 1984), p. 28.

consciousness.[4] I argued, however, that we were not entitled to conclude from this that factual and remembered reality are false. For if they were false, there would be no means of proving or knowing this. There would be no alternative, direct access to what is out there that would enable us to compare reality itself with those representations that are supposed to traduce it. As an argument against realism in fiction, therefore, the appeal to the observation that reality and fiction are differently *structured* seems to be self-defeating.

There is, however, a more radically sceptical position available to the critic of realism. It has inspired important trends in recent literary theory, being attractive to critics of both neo-Kantian and Marxist persuasions. It is suggested that we get reality wrong not only when we report and remember it but even as we *experience* it. What is experienced as 'reality' is not reality-in-itself but a distorted version of it that is related only indirectly (and rather problematically) to what is really out there, to 'how things really are'; for not only are facts, stories and memories artefactual but so also is current, on-line experience. Realism can then be criticized on the grounds that it fails to acknowledge or deal with this and consequently (consciously or unconsciously) colludes in the process by which the artefactual nature of reality is overlooked or even concealed. In this and the next two chapters, I shall examine these arguments – in particular as they have been used by Marxist critics influenced by Louis Althusser.

In what respects is reality an artefact, a human construct rather than a collection of natural objects or a series of natural events? In what respects is it not 'simple there' to be encountered by us but *made* by us; *created*, rather than passively received?

The most obvious sense in which reality is a human construct, historically derived rather than naturally given, is that our environment is almost entirely man-made: we pass much of our lives either using, or literally enclosed in, human artefacts. Even where we appear to have direct contact with, or actively seek out, 'Nature', that experience has a social framework: the transhuman weather in the streets has an adjectival or adverbial relation to the urban scene; a 'natural' landscape is framed by a window; a country walk is more immediately related to its recreational genre and a variety of pastoral traditions than to undifferentiated matter ('the soil') or unmediated physical reality. When we eat, it is processed Nature that we consume: even 'unprocessed' consumables are *commodities*; and as such, they are part of the social nexus rather than pieces of nature. ('Natural' foods are as natural as their polythene wrappers). When, finally, we die and are ingested by Nature, the process of dying is socialized to the very edge of oblivion.

So much is obvious. But there are less obvious senses in which reality is a social or, to use the term that will bulk large in these chapters, an ideological, artefact; and it is these less obvious senses that are germane to the 'political' arguments against realism in art and, in particular, realistic fiction.

[4] See Chapter 2.

We do not confront reality as isolated individuals but as members of collectives. The encounter between the individual and what is 'out there' is mediated by the other individuals who constitute those various collectives. For what is 'out there' is not simply matter-in-itself but what is *acknowledged* to be out there; pieces of matter are 'there' not simply in virtue of their existence but because they matter to someone. Reality is what counts as real to *someone* – or, more precisely, to someone representing or adopting the viewpoint of a group or somehow under its influence. Reality, in other words, is what 'they' – or 'I' insofar as I am they – acknowledge. Even apparently directed or uncontaminated sense perception is social in its essence; and so *a fortiori* is the judgement, based upon perception and conception, that something or other is 'real'. There will be competing *versions* of, but no direct or unmediated or unbiased access to, reality.

Not everyone will be impressed by this as an argument against the idea that there is a 'given' reality and some will be moved to point out that our idea of 'reality' is based at least in part upon a direct confrontation between a socially innocent sensorium and raw (or indeed processed) matter or Nature. Is it not this that, in the end, tethers our conceptions of reality to the realities of our (bodily) existence? Experience after all is ultimately physiological and the body constitutes that literal view-point in relation to which all other viewpoints are merely metaphorical. Through our bodies – which are natural objects whatever human constructions we may place upon them – we gain direct access to reality: this indeed is the condition of bodily survival; that is to say of survival. Reality is therefore ultimately defined in relation to 'natural' bodily needs and only secondarily determined by what the collective will acknowledge as being 'out there'. The starving body knows that what is 'out there' is not negotiable, is not amenable to limitless reinterpretation.

There are important truths in these observations but they are not relevant to the discussion about the constructed nature of reality insofar as the latter has a bearing on the status of literary realism. For the reality that the realistic novel attempts to report is not composed of the *sensory* experiences of organisms but of the social experiences of persons. 'Pure' sensation lies beneath language: explicit, communicated experience will be woven in with language and so be socially mediated at a high level. Moreover, a novel that claims – or seems to claim – that 'this is how it was for such and such a type of person in such and such a place' must have a scope that far exceeds the actual or indeed the possible experiences, sensory or social, of any individual. Fiction is interesting – and is counted as 'serious' – insofar as it seems to report on a 'typical' or 'representative' reality and so to tell us about a larger reality than that of the actual observed moments of a few characters' lives. The reality presented in a 'literary' novel is, by implication, an extended synecdoche of a much larger reality that is not directly available to a solitary, 'innocent' sensorium. The reality that realistic novels deal with or speak for is an object of higher-order knowledge rather than an intentional object of an individual's sensations.

Our sense of the world 'out there' is based mainly upon what we have been told, read or have seen on film. As we noted in Chapter 2, the world we know is constituted largely out of 'knowledge by description' rather than 'knowledge by acquaintance'.[5] '*The* world' is *a* world of facts reported to us; the reality we are situated in is not only a constellation of material objects set out in space and a sequence of personal experiences but also a susurrus of rumours. Some of these may be true and a greater number false; the vast majority of them, however, cannot be evaluated by the individual who hears – and may act upon – them. We have to take most of 'our' world on trust.

4.2 Artefact and Ideology

Reality at the level addressed by the novel, then, is undeniably what *counts* as real; and what counts as real is what is *acknowledged* by the group to which the individual belongs at a given moment or the group consciousness that is operating through him – what 'they' count as real; or what is generally accounted real. There are therefore potentially many competing versions of what counts as reality; but in practice there is considerable consensus: much appears to be 'indisputable' and 'obvious' and is consequently 'taken for granted'. This consensus is – according to those many philosophers for whom power and politics are the ultimate social realities – the achievement of ideology.

Ideology in this extended sense is that in virtue of which one account of, or one part of, reality becomes reality *tout court*; or a historically derived reality presents itself as eternal and extra-human, as given rather than made, as objectively sensed rather than intersubjectively constructed. Ideology 'privileges' one version of reality over all others and suppresses any suspicion that things might be ordered or perceived differently. (Controlling the order of things and controlling the way that order is perceived are separate tasks; but it will be obvious from the discussion so far that they are not easily separable, especially as the latter is essential to the former.) Ideology is the medium or mediator which ensures that the individual identifies himself with the dominant group and that his version of reality coincides with their version of reality; so that *I* construe reality as 'they' construe it or we all intuit the world 'out there' as 'one' intuits the world out there.

What counts as 'reality', then, is a privileged version of what is out there and is at least in part an *outcome* – of a struggle between rival experiences of the world, related to competing needs and conflicting interests. It is defined, according to mainstream Marxist thought, by those who have control over the means through which realities are given public acknowledgement – by, that is to say, the ruling class. Itself privileged, it assists in maintaining the

[5] Bertrand Russell, Knowledge by Acquaintance and Knowledge by Description in *Mysticism and Logic*, (London, Pelican Books 1953).

privileged position of those who endorse it. The most potent way of endorsing a version of reality is by articulating it and then embodying it in the comparatively permanent form of written discourses. Reality is therefore sustained by, as well as importantly defined by, that which is written down. 'Reality' will be identified to a lesser or greater extent with that version of the world endorsed by the self-legitimating writing of those who already have power. The victors in the ideological struggle will be well placed to perpetuate the version of the world that will keep them in power.

If the idea that 'reality' is defined in this way seems implausible this is precisely (it would be argued) because it is of the essence of ideology to efface itself and to conceal all evidence of the struggle whose outcome it influenced so decisively. Reality will carry few marks of the processes by which it was derived or produced. It will appear to be simply, incontestably irrefutably 'there': the historical and transient will seem natural and permanent. Indeed, it is the central task of ideology to naturalize social phenomena and to confer upon them the objectivity of material world, to make that which has been constructed by human beings seem to confront them as naturally given. 'This tree has green leaves' and 'This tree belongs to Lord Jones' become two equally obvious 'facts' about the tree. Behind the second 'fact' are many assumptions which could be questioned: that trees can belong to individuals; that whatever grows on someone's land belongs to that person; that a person shall own whatever has been bequeathed to him; that ownership confers certain rights; and so on. All of these facts – and the conflict hidden in certain sorts of ownership – will be obliterated in a bald, positive statement of how things are that implicitly naturalizes ownership.

4.3 Althusser on Ideology

These are the familiar arguments. In the 1970s they were rejuvenated by Marxist literary critics writing under the influence of Louis Althusser and in particular his seminal article Ideology and Ideological State Apparatuses (referred to henceforth as IISA).[6] It will be useful to summarize the argument of this essay before examining the application of its theses to the critique of realism.

Althusser begins his essay by reminding us of the Marxist doctrine that the primary task of the State is to ensure the reproduction of the conditions of production. Without this, there would be no further production and the social order would collapse. Since the conditions of production are not to the benefit of everyone, the State is obliged to be

> a 'machine' of repression, which enables the ruling classes . . . to ensure their domination over the working class, thus enabling the former to subject the latter to the process of surplus-value extortion (i.e. to capitalist exploitation) (IISA p. 11).

[6] See note 3 for the reference. See also Appendix to Part II.

How does the State stabilize a situation which, being disadvantageous to most of its subjects, should be highly unstable? By means of certain 'State apparatuses'. The obvious instances are the 'Repressive State Apparatuses' (RSAs) that function predominantly 'by violence': the Army, the Police, the Courts, the Prisons, etc.[7] But these are insufficient in themselves to maintain the status quo and require further support in the form of the Ideological State Apparatuses (ISAs).

ISAs operate by 'ideology' rather than by violence and differ from the RSAs in that they are not confined to what is usually regarded as the political arena; for they include the family and even leisure activities (such as Literature, the Arts and sports). Indeed, Althusser's list of ISAs (IISA p. 17) makes their presence co-terminous with all social activity. Despite their superficial diversity, and even their contradictions, they are 'unified beneath the ruling ideology which is the idea of the ruling class'. Football and breast-feeding, novel-writing and church-going are all committed in some way to preventing individuals from realizing the extent to which they are caught up in a productive process that benefits the few and exploits the many. For

> no class can hold State power over a long period without at the same time exercising its hegemony over and in the State Ideological Apparatuses (IISA p. 20, Note 8).

If you can win the minds and hearts of the people so that they collude in their own oppression, then the business of oppressing them becomes a good deal easier. It is easier still if neither the oppressors nor the oppressed know what is going on: the former will not feel guilty nor the latter aggrieved; and the social order will seem natural, inevitable, obvious, beyond criticism, and as little open to human influence as the course of the stars or the sequence of night and day. Continuing domination is thus assured to those who win the ideological battle.

But what, precisely, *is* ideology? For the early Marx

> ideology is the system of ideas and representations which dominate the mind of a man or a social group (IISA p. 32).

But this is not adequate to Althusser's vision in which ideology is seen to be much more pervasive. For Althusser, ideology is that which

> represents the imaginary relationships of individuals to their real conditions of existence (IISA p. 36).

Ideologies 'constitute an illusion'. They do, however, 'make allusion to reality'. And so

---

[7] RSAs include the Government and the Administration. In the case of the latter, the violence by which they function may take 'non-physical forms'. (Could it be that Althusser is here alluding to those forms that have to filled out in triplicate and other repressive bureaucratic constraints? These are of course not only violent in themselves but may predispose the oppressed citizen to violence.)

[8] For a brief discussion of this claim, see Appendix to Part II.

we arrive at the conclusion that in ideology 'men represent their real conditions of existence to themselves in an imaginary form' (IISA p. 37).

'All ideology expresses a class position' (IISA p. 33) – while at the same time concealing this – and it

> represents in its necessarily imaginary distortion not the existing relations of production (and the other relations that derive from them), but above all the (imaginary) relationship of individuals to the relations of production and the relations that derive from them. What is represented in ideology is therefore not the system of the real relations which govern the existence of individuals, but the imaginary relation of those individuals to the real relations in which they live (IISA p. 38–9).

Ideology must not be thought of merely as a set of ideas or mental phenomena: 'Ideology has a material existence' (IISA p. 39). This proves a very tricky thesis for Althusser to sustain and, in the end, he merely begs us to

> 'be favourably disposed towards it, say, in the name of materialism' (IISA p. 40, Note 9).

'In the name of materialism', then, we have to accept that

> an ideology always exists in an apparatus, and its practice, or practices. This existence is material (IISA p. 40).

More precisely, an individual's (ideological) ideas

> are his material actions inserted into material practices governed by material rituals which are themselves defined by the material ideological apparatus from which derive the ideas of the subject (IISA p. 43).

Ideas 'disappear'

> to the precise extent that their existence is inscribed in the actions of practices governed by rituals defined in the last instance by an ideological apparatus (IISA p. 43–4).

Ideology is so potent and inescapable *because* it is invisible; *because* it does not consist of a set of ideas that çan be debated, tested, opposed but is *implicit in practices*. One such practice is that of writing literature, in particular realistic novels.

We shall leave Althusser's essay at this point in order to see how the ideas presented so far have been used in the attack on the realistic novel. We shall return in Chapter 5 to examine the Althusserian concept of the Subject and its use in the attack on realism.

---

[9] Althusser's polemic methods are touched on in Appendix to Part II.

4.4 The 'Neutrality' of Realism

The thesis we must examine then, is that the realistic novel, by working with 'the given', by taking for granted what is usually taken for granted, by replicating, or attempting to replicate, reality without really questioning it, collaborates in the work of ideology: the naturalization of the social, the eternization of the historically derived, the installation of but one version of reality as reality itself. For realistic novels are realistic – or seem realistic to their readers – precisely because they do not question what is customarily taken for granted. Consciously or unconsciously (usually the latter – the realistic novelist is considered to be naive rather than opportunistic), realism sides with the victors in the ideological battles that underlie current definitions of reality. Writing that does not challenge what counts as 'reality', and that fails to dismantle the artefact, does the work of ideology and sides with the powerful who will inevitably articulate what is there in a way that is at least self-centred and self-serving. Moreover, in virtue of its claim to stand for more than the particulars it describes – *Middlemarch* is not just about a particular group of people in a particular nineteenth-century provincial town – 'literary' realistic fiction gives an especially powerful endorsement to the reality it fails to question. The very claim of realistic writing to 'reflect' reality, simply to uncover what is typically 'there', ensures that it uncritically reproduces the bias and prejudice embodied in the conventional conception of reality. The myth that it describes reality dispassionately and objectively only embeds the realist enterprise more deeply in the reality it mistakenly believes itself to be outside of. Its pretence to be outside of reality, when it is in fact inside, makes it ideologically more potent, a more effective weapon in the hands of those who have already won the ideological struggle.

The 'ideological' case against realism is well presented in Catherine Belsey's *Critical Practice*.[10] The essence of Belsey's Althusserian critique is that realism does not, and indeed cannot, question the process by which either reality or the realistic texts that purport to represent it are produced. It takes 'the obvious' for granted and imagines itself to be a transparent window on reality. It is therefore doubly naive and this is especially harmful because the claim to objectivity gives the realistic novel such prestige. Realism, which overlooks or conceals its own uncritical acceptance of an ideologically derived version of reality, endorses that reality by seeming to describe it from without. By stopping at 'the facts' without considering how they came about – the history behind 'the order of things', the process by which the order of things was articulated into facts, into *the* facts – realism colludes in

---

[10] Catherine Belsey, *Critical Practice*, (London and New York: Methuen, 1980). The enormous debt that I owe to this lucid and succinct account of some of the 'ideological' arguments against realism is in no way diminished by my disagreement with most of its premises and nearly all of its conclusions. Ms Belsey in her turn acknowledges her debt to the ideas originally put forward by Colin McCabe (Realism and the Cinema, *Screen*, 15, No. 2, 1974).

the process, central to the work of ideology, by which history becomes nature, and one possibility becomes and remains inescapable actuality. The 'revealing' objective gaze of realism actually conceals the power struggles that lie behind the construction and definition of reality. The master myth of realism – '*Je ne propose risen; je n'impose rien; j'expose*' – is in fact the hidden motto of all ideology. Just as it is the essence of ideology to conceal itself, so it is the essence of realism to conceal its own constructedness and that of the reality it purports to reveal impartially. By this means it is able to support the epistemological, economic and political status quo. The realistic novel, seemingly effacing itself before the reality it impartially exposes, is politically all the more powerful for keeping its politics invisible; for pretending that it is a mere window which permits an objectively observed objective reality to be transmitted with minimal distortion from one consciousness (that of the author) to another (that of the reader). Realistic fiction is therefore an important component of the Literary State Apparatus that works to ensure the reproduction of the means and relations of production.

4.5 Realism and the Contradictions of Capitalism

Such are the general arguments implicating realism in the process by which the status quo is maintained and the oppressors are permitted to continue oppressing the oppressed. Like Althusser's views, from which they are derived, they are of such enormous scope that they are hardly amenable to critical examination. They are utterable but literally unthinkable: one cannot get outside of them to see whether or not they are the case. (As we shall discuss in Chapter 6, ideology as Althusser seems to envisage it is co-terminous with intelligibility.) In order to assess these arguments, therefore, we need to look for specific consequences that might be expected to flow from them and the features of realism that it is claimed result from, or reveal, its ideologically compromised state.

If reality is the product of a conflict whose victors will shape reality and define what counts as real, the alternative viewpoint of the losers, the oppressed, will be suppressed when the battle has been lost and won. To adapt the familiar Marxist slogan, the ruling vision will be the vision of the ruling class and the whole world will seem to be intelligible from a single (privileged) point of view. The contradictions implicit in capitalist society, which exploits the many to the benefit of the few, will be rendered invisible. Realistic writing, which is in complicity with the dominant ideology, will consequently be unable to tolerate multiple versions of reality. Accordingly, classic realism,[11] as Belsey asserts, 'cannot foreground contradiction' (Belsey,

---

[11] 'Classic realism' proves to be a very broad category indeed. For Belsey it has the same extension as for McCabe (*op. cit.*, p. 212):

> The category of the classic realist text lumps together, in book and film, *The Grapes of Wrath* and *The Sound of Music*, *L'Assommoir* and *Toad of Toad Hall*.

p. 82) and 'heterogeneity – variety of points of view and temporal locations – is contained in homogeneity' (Belsey, p. 78).

At first sight, this charge would seem to be at odds with obvious fact. Who could doubt the power of the realistic novel to dramatize genuine conflicts of interest within a supposedly unified social order? The collision between the old order and the new, the governors and the governed, the oppressed and their oppressors, the centre and the fringe, the majority and the minority, the individual and society – are these not the very stuff of realistic fiction? The processes by which one group within society attempts to further its vested interests under the cover of a rhetoric about what is indisputably morally or theologically right, naturally just or simply natural, obviously true or simply obvious, have surely been major themes in realistic fiction. The fictional case studies of the Law and of the Church in Dickens – to reach for an obvious example – showed how the law may be used to further the welfare of the well-heeled few against the impoverished many and how ecclesiastical rhetoric may be employed to give a legitimating veneer of spirituality to human greed. The realistic novel has contributed in no small part to our understanding of the devious ways of ideology and above all its tendency to conceal itself. And if most people are aware that even the most seemingly stable social consensus is riven with conflict and contradiction and that the State is not one big happy family but the scene of an eternal struggle between conflicting points of view and warring interest, surely this is in no small part due to the experience of reading realistic novels.

4.6 The Hierarchy of Discourses

To argue along these lines, however, is to miss the point of the Althusserian critique. Of course realistic novels present different, often conflicting, points of view; of course realism can show contradictions within society – especially between the rhetoric of the ruling classes and the needs and experiences of those whom they govern and whose welfare they pretend to have at heart. But it cannot acknowledge that reality is *irreducibly* polycentric. A realistic novel can highlight contradiction within capitalist society but it does not accept its inevitability: contradiction is there but it is not 'foregrounded'.

According to Catherine Belsey, contradiction is overcome in classic realism by the deployment of a 'hierarchy of discourses'. Warring voices, mutually incompatible points of view, conflicting worlds, etc., evident at one level, are resolved by being gathered up into the homogeneous and unified discursive space of a higher-level authorial voice and standpoint. The very

---

The term is a rather blunt instrument used for castigating all texts that aim to produce the 'reality effect', to sustain the illusion that they 'show things as they really are'. As Terry Lovell has pointed out (*Pictures of Reality*, London: BFI Publishing, ;1980), a hostile attitude to realism so broadly defined leaves fiction very little to do other than to reflect, somewhat narcissistically upon its own processes of signification. Hardly the recipe for the popular texts that will ignite the revolution.

tense in which realistic stories are told seems to confer a privileged viewpoint upon the teller. And Belsey argues that this privilege extends to the reader:

> the conventional tenses of classic realism tend to align the position of the reader with that of the omniscient narrator who is looking back on a series of past events. Thus, while each episode seems to be happening 'now' as we read and the reader is given clear indications of what is already past in relation to this 'now', nonetheless each apparently present episode is contained in a single intelligible and all-embracing vision of what from the point of view of the enunciation is past and completed (Belsey, pp. 77–8).

The novel may present two conflicting realities – between servant and master, for example – but the author will be unable to resist adjudicating between them or reconciling them in a third 'objective' version of reality. The plurality of realities will be subsumed under his unifying, omniscient gaze. Alternatively, conflict may be 'handled' and effectively suppressed by the seemingly inevitable evolution of the events towards the harmony of an aesthetically satisfying closure. The sense of ending will over-ride and heal the intuition of a reality riven with conflict.

Referring to the end of *Jane Eyre*, Belsey comments

> Harmony has been re-established through the re-distribution of the signifiers into a new system of differences which closes off the threat to subjectivity, and it remains only to make this harmonious and coherent world intelligible to the reader, closing off in the process the sense of danger to the reader (Belsey, pp. 75–6).

All's well that ends well; or, rather, all's well that ends – or at least gives the appearance of ending. Viewpoint A and viewpoint B are reconciled in a final duet which gathers up the conflicting voices in a third voice that seems to stand for an imaginary viewpoint C in which the warring visions and interest are reconciled.

Belsey examines the operation of 'the hierarchy of discourses' in *Bleak House*. At first, the novel seems to acknowledge the contradictions in the society it examines:

> The story itself concerns social and ideological contradictions – that the law of property set up in the interests of society benefits only lawyers and destroys the members of the society who invoke it in their defence; that the social conception of virtue promotes hypocrisy or distress (Belsey, p. 79).

Moreover, the novel has two narrators and at the beginning of *Bleak House* these form 'a striking contrast'. The reader, however, is quickly put into a position where he feels that he transcends the viewpoint of these two narrators and so the conflict between them. He 'is constantly prompted to supply the deficiencies of each narrative'.

Thus, a third and privileged but literally unwritten discourse begins to emerge, the discourse of the reader which grasps a history and judges soundly (Belsey, p. 80).

Gradually the three discourses converge 'to confirm the reader's apparently extra-discursive interpretation and judgement' (Belsey, p. 81). By this means

> *Bleak House* constructs a reality which appears to be many-sided, too complex to be contained within a single point of view, but which in fact is contained within the single and non-contradictory invisible discourse of the reader. . . . By thus smoothing over the contradictions it has so powerfully dramatized in the interests of a single, unified coherent 'truth', *Bleak House*, however critical of the world it describes, offers the reader a position, an attitude which is given as non-contradictory, fixed in 'knowing' subjectivity (p. 81).

The classic vice of classic realism becomes apparent: it cannot resist setting up the reader (or at least the author himself) as a position 'from which the text is most obviously intelligible'.

4.7 The Hierarchy of Readers

This at first sounds plausible – until we ask ourselves how Belsey came to know what she has pointed out to us. How has she become aware of the contradictions that she claims are being smoothed over, indeed obliterated? The contradictions presumably originated from Dickens's novel; and unless he had himself 'foregrounded' them, or his intention to conceal them had been roundly defeated, they would presumably have not been evident to her. Belsey's critique itself seems to show that it·is at least open to the reader to resist being placed in a position from which the text becomes intelligible and the contradictions it alludes to are reconciled, smoothed over, effaced, denied, etc. Belsey's worry is, surely, therefore, groundless.

It will have become clear that the reader for whom she is so concerned is not someone like herself but 'the ordinary reader'. *She* is able to lift the carpet and see the contradictions that have been brushed beneath it: that is what puts her in a position to be able to criticize Dickens for concealing the very reality he has in fact revealed to her. But she is in a privileged position *vis-à-vis Bleak House*; other readers may not be so well placed. Her criticism of the novel takes its rise from a concern for readers – average readers, or average bourgeois readers – who are postulated to be less intelligent, or more easily taken in, than herself.

Behind her critique of *Bleak House*, therefore, is an unexamined assumption which goes against the radical premises of her political position. She takes for granted the existence of a hierarchy of readers and her own place at or near the top of the hierarchy. Her own analysis of *Bleak House* adds a further tier to 'the hierarchy of discourses' she has identified within the novel; in this top tier, the tendency of the other discourses to readers less well trained, or less gifted than herself is made plain. At the top of the hierarchy of discourses are available confident, monosemic, readings of novels – and of their rather dim readers.

Belsey, then, accepts quite uncritically a contempt for the average reader that is not uncommon amongst academic critics – hardly surprisingly as without the idea of the (comparatively) stupid average (untrained) reader, the kind of criticism which aims to unmask literature would lose a good deal of its implicit purpose. The relative stupidity (insensitivity, ignorance, etc.) of the average reader is of course pre-supposed in much modern criticism, where the critic's job is to mediate between the untrained public and the opaque and baffling modern or postmodern text – as we shall discuss in Part III; but, by a strange irony, it is most evident in the case of critics who express their radical (often egalitarian) political sentiments in the deployment of radical ideas in literary criticism. The ideological critics, in particular, imagine themselves as the somehow awakened able to speak to readers who are still lost in the collective ideological dream. By a further irony, it is always those who grant ideology its widest scope, so that it is almost co-terminous with intelligibility, who consider themselves most able to speak confidently of its pernicious influence.[12]

Lest in speaking of 'contempt' for the reader[13] I be accused of exaggeration, consider this passage from *Critical Practice*

> The success with which the Sherlock Holmes stories achieve an illusion of reality is repeatedly demonstrated. . . . According to *The Times* in December 1967, letters to Sherlock Holmes were then still commonly addressed to 221B Baker Street, many of them asking for the detective's help (Belsey, p. 113).

The appreciative reader of realistic novels, it seems, is in grave danger of confusing fiction and life at a very elementary level indeed. He or she is like the child who writes to Father Christmas or the fully paid up member of the Munch Bunch Club who expects to be visited by Rosy Raspberry or Pete Pepper.[14] No wonder critics have to be alert, watchful and wakeful among the sleeping, if readers not only imbibe the implicit ideology of the novels they read but imagine that what they read is factually true as well as fictionally plausible!

---

[12] See also Chapter 6. In the meantime the following quotations may support my point: 'As I have argued, meanings circulate between text, ideology and reader, and the work of criticism is to release possible meanings' (p. 144). 'In producing knowledge of the text, criticism [is] no longer the accomplice of ideology' (p. 138). 'Criticism is the science which offers finally a knowledge of history' (p. 138).

[13] The theme of the 'contempt for the reader' is really deserving of a book in itself. It will be touched on again in Part III.

[14] This point is also made by Lovell (*op. cit.*)

> . . . it is true . . . that the boundaries between reality and representation are sometimes confused. When Len and Rita married in the British television soap opera, *Coronation Street* they were showered with wedding presents from

4.8 Foregrounding Contradiction

There is of course no reason whatsoever why realistic fiction should not 'foreground contradiction'. Nor is there any reason why it should not unmask the workings of ideology by which by which 'Nature is passed off as History' and the mystification which 'transforms petit-bourgeois culture into a universal nature' – just as Barthes did or attempted in the realistic essays in *Mythologiques*:

> The starting point of these reflections was usually a feeling of impatience at the sight of the 'naturalness' with which newspapers, art and common sense constantly dress up a reality which, even though it is the one we live in, is undoubtedly determined by history. In short, in the account given of our contemporary circumstances, I resented seeing Nature and History confused at every turn, and I wanted to track down, in the decorative display of *what-goes-without-saying*, the ideological abuse which, in my view, is hidden there.[15]

It would be difficult to imagine a better starting point, and more effective irritants to trigger a serious realistic novelist, than that 'impatience', that 'resentment'! A realistic novelist can, like a realistic essayist, dismantle reality by exposing realistically how it is put together, dramatizing the mechanisms that are employed in constructing it.

The fact that reality has been constructed and is historically derived makes it no less realistic, no less a condition of and constraint upon the lives of individuals and no less the theatre of the actions for which they are to a different degree responsible. The taken-for-granted, if it is visible to a literary critic, will also be available for questioning in realistic fiction, for unmasking by those who are oppressed by the oppressors. Realistic fiction can assume the viewpoint of the oppressed, can show how people seize power and legitimate their positions by shaping their own versions of what reality is. It can show how epistemological domination reinforces social, economic, moral and sexual oppression. As the following excerpt from *Jane Eyre* (quoted by Belsey) illustrates, it can vividly realize the terror of non-reciprocity in the relations between those who (to use Sartre's terms) 'merely live in the world' and those 'who have the use of it'. Jane is presented to Mr Brocklehurst

> I looked up at – a black pillar! – such, at least, appeared to me at first sight, the straight, narrow, sable-clad shape standing erect on the rug: the

---

viewers. But neither naturalism nor realism depends upon this type of confusion. Most viewers, most of the time, are well aware of the difference between 'The Rovers Return' and their local pub, even though they may well assess the former as a realistic representation of the latter. They are also much more aware than conventionalist critics suppose, or than they themselves can articulate, of the rules which govern this type of representation. The critics 'or the viewers' naive complaint that such and such is 'not realistic' frequently masks a complaint that the rules have been broken (Lovell, p. 80).

[15] Roland Barthes, *Mythologies*, trans. Annette Lavers (London: Paladin, 1973), p. 11.

grim face at the top was like a carved mask, placed above the shaft by way of capital (quoted in Belsey, p. 76).

There is no obligation upon the realistic novelist to renegue on that vision, to resolve all conflicts in a harmonious closure. Nor is she or he obliged to subsume all the voices and viewpoints of the characters under an over-riding voice, an omniscient authorial viewpoint in which the partial intelligibility of the characters' different worlds is rounded off.

Pirandello's story *Signora Frola and Her Son-in-Law Signor Ponza*[16] is a superb example of a realistic story in which two utterly irreconcilable points of view are presented as equally plausible and there is no attempt to adjudicate between them. There is no way of telling which of the protagonists is mad but the interpretation of the entire story – which is realistic throughout – depends crucially upon this. At the end of the tale, none of the inhabitants of the town of Valdana knows whether it is Signora Frola or her son-in-law who is insane. Neither does the narrator, nor does the reader. The narrator begins with his own anguish; by the end of the story, the reader, like the citizens of Valdana, is unable to say 'where the fantasy is, and where the reality'. He does not transcend, nor is inclined to feel superior to, their anguish, nor that of the narrator.

I think enough has been said to carry the point that just because realistic writers in the past may have been concerned to resolve conflict in a final harmony, a central over-riding intelligibility, it does not follow that future realists are obliged to do this. Or not unless one makes the (admittedly common) error of identifying realism not with an *aim* but with a particular historical *method* of achieving that aim. The realistic novel can present a polycentric universe, tossing the reader from consciousness to consciousness without adjudication, closure or spurious resolution. It need not be fatally tempted by the wish to gather up everything into the fatherly, benign, 'detached' gaze of the omniscient and disinterested author, or an implied voice transmitting a received wisdom and neutralizing the real conflicts it pretends to be about.

Equally, although realistic fiction has historically been dominated by a European, middle-class male viewpoint – as indeed have other forms – it does not follow that this must continue in the future. The form is there to be used by anyone who is willing to meet the challenges that it presents. Realism may be expropriated by the oppressed on behalf of the oppressed (as indeed is happening in South Africa) to express their condition – to express the reality that faces them.

But in talking of 'the reality that faces them' I open up a new set of questions. Supposing that not only reality but also the subject who experiences or faces it is an ideological construct? What then? This brings us back to Althusser.

---

[16] In *Luigi Pirandello Short Stories*, trans. Frederick May (Oxford: Oxford University Press, 1975).

5

Realism and the Subject

5.1 The Subject as Artefact

We have examined the view that 'objective' reality is not given to, but constructed by, the historical subject; that what confronts us is not the raw material served up by nature but the highly processed stuff evolving through history. We discovered, however, that the implications of this for the novel were not as radical as had been suggested by, for example, Marxist critics impressed by the historical nature of reality. A sophisticated awareness of the historically derived or socially mediated nature of even the most brutish of brute facts is not incompatible with commitment to realism.

There is, however, a yet more radical claim: that not only the reality facing the subject but also the subject who faces that reality is socially and historically constructed. While the position discussed in the previous chapter could be construed as a watered-down and politicized neo-Kantianism – with the (transcendental) subject constructing its socially and historically mediated world – the position to be discussed here draws the subject itself into historical and social processes, emphasizing the extent to which the subject is *not* self-constructed.

Although as Fichte said, the 'I' is not a fact but an act, it is not sovereign since the act by which it is constructed does not originate from within itself. Far from being self-determining, an originary point of synthesis that confects the world in which it finds itself, the 'I' is a *product*, a result, on all fours with the reality that confronts it. the 'I' is part of, rather than the source or the user of, the system through which the world is organized and rendered intelligible to its inhabitants. The subject, far from subjecting all things to itself as its objects, is itself subjected. It is not the *centre* of its or the world, a Cartesian 0,0,0 at the heart of a private reality, a principle of synthetic unity by which reality is made coherent.

The belief that the subject is the constitutive centre of its world is therefore an illusion; but this is an illusion which, according to many contemporary critical theorists, realism cannot escape. Realism cannot accept or acknowledge the 'de-centred' self. In classic realism, the self presupposed is the centre and source of meaning, distinct from the society in which it operates and engaging with it as a free and independent agent furnished with its own principle of coherence and unity. In accordance with this false, idealistic (in the philosophical sense) view of the subject, realism

(a) presents the reader with intelligible, consistent characters;
(b) implies a coherent entity called 'the author' whose imagination is the source of these characters and whose authority determines and endorses the meaning of the narrative; and
(c) reinforces the reader's erroneous views about his own subjectivity by presenting him to himself as a privileged position from which events and characters are uniquely intelligible.

The attack on the centred self, on the sovereignty of the ego and ordinary daylit consciousness, has been mounted from different directions:

> The researches of psychoanalysis, of linguistics, of anthropology have 'decentred' the subject in relation to the laws of its desire, the forms of its language, the rules of its action, the play of its mythical and imaginative discourse.[1]

And to this, one might add Nietzsche, 'under the sun of whose great search' Foucault conducted his own researches.

The paramount influence, however, has been post-Saussurean linguistics with its shift from an item-centred to a system-based analysis of both language and discourse. Just as words do not have meaning in isolation but owe their meaning to their relations to other words, to their positions in the system of differences to which they belong, so selves are not independent atomic constituents of society. The self is merely a set of social relations and these in turn refer to a larger, indeed infinite, system of relations which operates through the self but is largely unknown to it. When I speak, I do not use language and subordinate it to my own purposes; rather it speaks through me: I am not a fount of meaning but a conduit through which linguistic meaning passes; a linguistic site where differences play. Likewise, when I act, I do not operate as free agent upon the social reality outside of me but rather *I* am operated upon by *it*; for my actions have meaning only insofar as they realize positions in a system of which I have scarcely any knowledge. My own consciousness of the intended meaning of my verbal and non-verbal acts is almost irrelevant:

> . . . once the conscious subject is deprived of its role as a source of meaning – once meaning is explained in terms of conventional systems which may escape the grasp of the conscious subject – the self can no longer be identified with consciousness. It is 'dissolved' as its functions are taken up by a variety of interpersonal systems that operate through it.[2]

[1] Michel Foucault *The Archeology of Knowledge* (London: Tavistock, 1972), p. 22.
[2] Jonathan Culler, *Structuralist Poetics* (London: Routledge & Kegan Paul, 1975), p. 28.

5.2 The Subject as Linguistic Artefact

The arguments leading to the linguistic decentring of the self are put forward by Emile Benveniste, for whom the Fichtean act that constitutes the 'I' is a linguistic act. Belsey summarizes his position as follows:

> it is language which provides the possibility of subjectivity because it is language which enables the speaker to posit himself or herself as 'I', as the subject of a sentence. It is through language that people constitute themselves as subjects (Belsey, *ibid*, p. 59).

Since individuals do not invent the language that they use (and are anyway used by, rather than users of, it) they are constitut*ed* rather than constitut*ing*. The 'I' is consequently caught up in the play of difference that is the essence of language, a play of which no one is master.

Benveniste's arguments are extraordinarily muddled and he manages to pack an impressive amount of self-contradiction into the short essay in which he argues that the self is produced by or in language.[3] He begins by pointing out that discourse consists essentially of an *exchange* and states that the ability of speech to act as a vehicle of communication must be due to the properties of language itself – of the system rather than of individual speech acts. He jumps from this claim – the basis of which is not very clearly established – to the conclusion that

> It is in and through language that man constitutes himself as a *subject*, because language alone establishes the concept of 'ego' in reality, in *its* reality which is that of the being (Benveniste, p. 224).

It is, of course, difficult to be sure precisely what this means: 'constituting oneself as a subject' could imply putting oneself forward in society as a subject (i.e. as someone who is to be taken account of by others, whose rights are to be considered); perceiving oneself as set off from the rest of the world which is then constituted as 'object', 'other'; or being aware of oneself as coherent, continuous, unified – as a homogeneous 'thing'. Benveniste's further assertions do not fully elucidate his position.

> Now we hold that that 'subjectivity', whether it is placed in phenomenology or in psychology . . . is only the emergence in the being of the fundamental property of language. 'Ego' is he who *says* 'ego'. That is where we see the foundation of 'subjectivity', which is determined by the linguistic status of 'person' (Benveniste, p. 224).

Subjectivity, however

> . . . is not defined by the feeling which everyone experiences of being himself (this feeling, to the degree that it can be take note of, is only a reflection) (Benveniste, p. 224).

[3] Available in: Emile Benveniste, *Problems in General Linguistics*, trans. by Mary Elizabeth Meek, Miami Linguistics Series No. 8, Coral Gables, Fl: University of Miami Press, 1971. See especially 'Changes in Linguistics' and 'Man and Language', in particular the essay Subjectivity in Language.

The linguistically constituted subjectivity, however, accounts for the self as 'the psychic unity that transcends the totality of the actual experiences it assembles and that makes the permanence of consciousness' (p. 224); and the 'establishment of subjectivity in language creates the category of person both in language and also . . . outside of it as well' (Benveniste, p. 227).

It would appear, then, that according to Benveniste, being a subject, and some aspects of feeling that one is a (unified) 'self', result from one's entry into language as a speaker. More specifically, it his engagement in dialogue that constitutes him as a person. Conscious selfhood, or personhood, is the inner reflection of the oppositional status the speaker has when he engages as an 'I' in dialogue:

> Conciousness of self is only possible if it is experienced by contrast. I use *I* only when I am speaking to someone who will be a *you* in an address. It is this condition of dialogue that is constitutive of a *person*, for it implies that reciprocally *I* becomes *you* in the address of the one who in his turn designates himself as *I* (pp. 224–5).

The physically differentiated individual becomes *I* by positing himself as 'I' opposed to '*you*'.

This is a very vulnerable argument. Even if one allows that the self is experienced not positively but only differentially, that it exists by contrast with the not-self, it does not follow that it is experienced, or exists, only in opposition to the (verbal) 'you'. For the not-self includes non-verbal objects (material things outside of its body) as well as entities apprehended verbally. Even if one interprets the 'I' as a grammatical subject and assumes what has to be proved, the purely oppositional and commutative relationship that Benveniste refers to is not confined to *you*. For 'I' may also be opposed to *it, he, we, that (over there)*, etc.

It seems that Benveniste *does* at times intend the 'subject' to be construed in the narrower sense of the *grammatical* subject. It is, of course, easy to decentre the self linguistically if one either *begins* with the assumption that the I is a linguistic entity; or if one takes it for granted that the self is to be identified with the grammatical subject. The assertion that it is through language that people constitute themselves as subjects is a mere tautology if the term 'subject' is employed merely to indicate the grammatical subject of a sentence. You couldn't make yourself the subject of a sentence if there were no sentences. In this narrower sense of 'subject', it is obvious that being a subject must depend upon being referred to linguistically.

The uncertainty is compounded rather than resolved when Benveniste suggests the mechanism by which language establishes the basis of subjectivity. He notes that personal pronouns are a universal characteristic of all languages. The apparent absence of these grammatical forms in certain languages can be explained away as being due to conventions of politeness which dictate deliberate suppression of such pronouns; and he declares that a 'language without the expression of person cannot be imagined'. He then points out that personal pronouns refer neither to a concept nor to an individual. This is obviously true of 'I' which is what Jakobson called a deictic shifter: its referent will depend upon who is uttering it; and establishing that referent will require referring to the very speech act in which it is uttered. It is this which provides the deictic co-ordinates necessary to identify the referent of 'I'. 'I' refers to whoever is saying 'I'.

Benveniste draws some surprising conclusions from the status of the first-person singular personal pronoun.

> What does *I* refer to? To something very peculiar which is exclusively linguistic: *I* refers to the act of individual discourse in which it is pronounced. . . . The reality to which if refers is the reality of the discourse. It is in the instance of discourse in which *I* designates the speaker that the speaker proclaims himself as 'subject'. And so it is literally true that the basis of subjectivity is in the exercise of language (p. 226).

It is of course untrue that 'I' refers to a particular linguistic act; on the contrary, it mobilizes the deictic co-ordinates in order to arrive at its true referent, which is the individual generating the act – the speaker. The conclusion that language itself is the referent of the pronoun is based upon a mistake widely perpetrated by Structuralist thinkers and accounts for many of the startling ideas associated with 'post-Saussurean' theory.[4] It takes the form of confusing *the referent of discourse* with *the means by which reference* is achieved. If the means of access to the referent of 'I' is confused with the actual referent, then it only requires the observation that the means of access is linguistic (the speech act itself), to draw the conclusion that the referent of 'I' is linguistic and that 'the basis of subjectivity is in the exercise of language itself'.

Benveniste's position seems, therefore, to be based upon an error. And this will come as no surprise to those who feel that whatever construction one puts on the 'subject', it seems implausible that the totally fortuitous and unexplained existence of handy pronouns used to refer to oneself should play such a central part in the creation of the self. The unconvinced will be puzzled as to how language – and especially dialogue – could arise in the absence of pre-existing subjects. Or how a speaker 'could appropriate to himself an entire language by designating himself as *I*' if he were not already a self. Benveniste himself seems undecided on this crucial point; for at one place in the essay he says that

> Language is possible only because each speaker sets himself up as a *subject* by referring to himself as *I* in his discourse (Benveniste, p. 225).

It would appear from this that the subject, far from being 'a tropological

---

[4] In fact it is difficult to be certain whether Benveniste can be accounted a Structuralist. It looks as if he would like to be and his commitment to the Saussurean perspective is unquestioning. Even so, some of his statements seem to cast doubt upon his credentials as a Structuralist, structuralist fellow-traveller or even as a post-Saussurean linguist.

construct',[5] the result or the product of language, is itself the source of language; for language seems to depend upon the subject 'referring to himself'. The speaker it seems is not only prior to the subject but also to language, and is, indeed, the very condition of its possibility. Language is predicated upon the pre-existence of speakers – a most curious state of affairs! Moreover, it is difficult to see how the subject could refer to himself – or want to do so – unless he or she existed in the first place: self-reference must presuppose some kind of pre-existing self to refer to.

The Benveniste circuit – language creates the self that creates language; self-reference generates the pronouns that in turn create the self that is referred to – illustrates the problems that arise when one wishes to dissolve the self entirely into a social system or institution such as language. For those systems and institutions would seem to require the interaction of subjects to bring them about and keep them in play; and such an interaction between subjects must imply that they pre-exist the system, however much they are bound up with or shaped by it.

For both Lacan and Althusser, the subject is mediated by language and specified within it, but nevertheless has some basis outside of language:[6] the 'I' is not merely a Benvenistean self-referring iotacist. According to Lacan, the subject is produced by the interaction between an initially shapeless *hommelette* and language in an unconscious that is consequently 'structured like a language'. It would be impossible to do justice to either the obscurity or the ingenuity of Lacan's arguments in a brief treatment and I have examined them at length elsewhere.[7] Suffice it to say that they seem marginally more plausible than those of Benveniste, insofar as he does not claim that the self has been created by the grammar of a pre-existing language. Rather he suggests that it is the product of the grammar of the interaction between a doomed quest for plenitude and language which provides the substrate of that quest. Lacan, however, is implausible for other reasons.

The interaction between *hommelette* and language seems to take place in a world curiously void of other events. Language does not serve any practical or even specific purposes, such as getting someone to pass the salt or to close the door. Such uses of language are not readily assimilated to the magical manipulation of the absence of the mother. Lacanian language, in other words, is ahistorical, indeed asocial. This does not trouble Lacan for whom 'the world of words creates the world of things'; but it does trouble others who find such radical nominalism difficult to swallow because they believe themselves to be inhabitants of a world not entirely or primarily constituted out of parts of speech.

[5] John Brenkmann, Narcissus in the Text, *Georgia Review*, 30 (1976), pp. 243–327. This paper is discussed in Jonathan Culler, *On Deconstruction* (London: Routledge & Kegan Paul, 1983), pp. 252–7.

[6] In practice, it is almost impossible to decide whether the Lacanian self has an extra-linguistic basis (*vide infra*).

[7] I have discussed Lacan's ideas and style in *Not Saussure* (London: Macmillan, 1987), (Chapter 5) and in The Strange Case of Jacques L. *PN Review*; 14(4) (1987): 23–6.

It is often unclear whether the shapeless *hommelette*, hotly but ultimately unhappily pursuing its own disappearing image (and/or its missing mother), hopelessly trying to recapture the primordial state in which it had enjoyed plenitude and had not experienced absence, comes into language from the *outside*. Derrida's attack on Lacan takes its rise from the assumption that the latter believed the self and language to have independent origins. And there are certainly places where the reader might be forgiven for thinking that Lacan sees the self as the product of the interaction between pre-linguistic unconscious desire and language.

But at least one poor soul – a disciple to boot – had his knuckles very severely rapped for suggesting such a thing. In a conversation with Anika Lemaire (reproduced in her book *Jacques Lacan*, trans. by David Macey, London: Routledge & Kegan Paul, London, 1977), Lacan

> states his trenchant opposition to the fundamental proposition defended by his follower Laplanche. [Laplanche] goes directly against the very point on which his own statements leave absolutely no possible doubt, namely that, on the contrary, language is the condition of the unconscious (Lemaire, p. 249).

This accords with Eagleton's interpretation (in *Literary Theory*, Oxford: Blackwell, 1983):

> and indeed for Lacan the unconscious is a particular effect of language, a process of desire set in motion by difference (Eagleton, p. 173).

On the other hand, there are frequent references to the developing infant's 'entry into the symbolic order' and it is surely not unreasonable to think that one can enter into something only from the outside.

Those who are bewildered by the Master's *Ecrits* may take comfort from Eagleton's assertion that, in Lacan, 'Language, the unconscious, the parents, the symbolic order ... are not *exactly* synonymous' [italics mine]. Presumably, they are sufficiently nearly so for our confusing them to be no cause for concern. Perhaps we ought to think twice in future before withdrawing the driving licence of a man who mistakes his father for a preposition or his sexual desires for a traffic light on green.

Althusser was strongly influenced by Lacan; despite this, his ideas about the self and the 'subject', though in the end no more plausible, are more interesting since they take account of the historical and political nature of the self and of language. They are central to the 'ideological' argument against fictional realism. We shall therefore return to Ideology and Ideological State Apparatuses.

5.3 The Subject as Political Artefact

The idea of the subject has two poles: that of the metaphysical subject (whose scope ranges from the transcendental ego to the perceiving subject who is the basis of viewpoint); and that of the social or civic being who is subjected to and is integrated into the social structure. The heart of Althusser's thesis is that this distinction is false – a symptom of the false consciousness that is the work of ideology. The unitary, pre-social 'metaphysical' subject is in fact a social construct. The process of its construction is mediated by the Ideological State Apparatuses (ISAs).

Ideology

> has the function (which defines it) of constituting concrete individuals as subjects (IISA, p. 45).

Ideology 'interpellates individuals as subjects' and in so doing constitutes them as subjects. We are individuals insofar as we have separate bodies but this is not in itself sufficient to make us into subjects. A subject is someone who 'works by himself' and contributes without radical question to the process by which the State ensures the reproduction of the conditions of production. Nurses, sewage workers, farm labourers are all caught up in this process:

> In fact, the State and its Apparatuses only have meaning from the point of view of the class struggle, as an apparatus of the class struggle ensuring class oppression and guaranteeing the conditions of exploitation and its reproduction (IISA, p. 58).[8]

This is inescapable because 'man is an ideological animal by nature' (IISA, p. 45).

> As St Paul admirably put it, it is in the 'Logos' that we 'live, move and have our being'. It follows that for you and for me, the category of the subject is a primary 'obviousness'. . . . it is clear that you and I are subjects (free, ethical, etc.). Like all obviousnesses . . . (including the obviousness of the 'transparency' of language), the 'obviousness' that you and I are subjects . . . is an ideological effect, the elementary ideological effect (IISA, p. 45).

Although we are entirely replaceable and the system merely uses us, we have the sense of being unique subjects because we are addressed or 'hailed' by ideology. Because we are allocated a place by and in it, because we have our allotted niche, society seems to be *for us*. Our situation as subjects in it is something that we cannot really question or stand back from:

> . . . you and I are *always already* subjects and as such constantly practise the rituals of ideological recognition, which guarantees for us that we are indeed concrete, individual, distinguishable and (naturally) irreplaceable subjects (IISA, p. 46–7).

> ideology . . . 'transforms' individuals into subjects by that very precise operation which I have called *interpellation* or hailing which can be imagined along the lines of . . . 'Hey, you there!' (IISA, p. 48).

---

[8] This greatly clarifies the function of street lighting, home helps, district nursing services, hospitals, fire brigades, school meals, public toilets etc.

We are recognized, picked out, and we respond to this by turning from individuals into subjects. The transformation is, however, a purely theoretical event because we are 'always-already' subjects, having been recognized from the moment we were conceived. Even as we are growing *in utero*, our father's name, a certain station and status, etc. is lying in wait for us along with Mothercare kit and a multitude of child-rearing practices. Nevertheless, Althusser chooses to illustrate the process of *post*-natal subjection by a remarkably unconvincing example. If an individual is hailed in the street, he reminds us, he will turn round.

> By this mere one-hundred-and-eighty degree physical conversion he becomes a *subject*. Why? Because he has recognized that the hail was 'really' addressed to him. . . . Experience shows that the practical tele-communication of hailings is such that they hardly ever miss their man: . . . verbal call or whistle, the one hailed nearly always recognizes that it is really him who is being hailed. And yet it is a strange phenomenon . . . (IISA, p. 48).

(In practice, hailing rarely homes so specifically on to its target: one driver presses his horn and *everyone* turns round – a dangerous situation which is recognized and warned against in the Highway Code. If hailings 'hardly ever miss their man' it is because they hit every man within hailing distance. Elsewhere, outside of the street, we are not so easily hailed: we do not automatically assume that things are addressed to ourselves – unlike the dog in Pavese's poem who imagines that every smell is addressed to him and to him alone. If we were not able to ignore most hailings, to filter out most of what goes on around us, we should never get on with anything. But grubby empirical details, even those that bear upon the examples they use to support their theories, may not be of pressing concern to Grand Theorists.)

Althusser then proceeds to argue, on the basis of the examination of a single instance in the Scriptures, that the interpellation of individuals as subjects 'presupposes the "existence" of a Unique and central Other Subject' – namely God. It is in the name of this Absolute Subject that subjects are interpellated; in being turned into subjects, individuals are *subjected* – they are subjected to the Subject. The price of 'recognition' as a subject is to be subjected, to submit to a higher authority, 'to be stripped of all freedom except that of freely accepting his submission' (IISA, p. 56). Thus subjected, the individual will 'work all by himself'.

5.4 The Social Psychology of the Self

Few would dispute the general thesis, developed most convincingly by Mead in the 20s and 30s that the differentiated sense of self comes from without rather than from within;[9] that even if the sense that one is a self is

[9] See, for example, G.H. Mead, *Mind, Self and Society from the Standpoint of a Social Behaviorist*, ed. C.W. Morris (Chicago: University of Chicago Press, 1934).

presupposed, the specific content of the sense of self comes from without. The formation of a self-image, even self-recognition, consists to some extent of locating ourselves on a grid of attributes, concepts, comparisons, judgements, etc. that belong to the collective consciousness. Self-recognition and being recognized or acknowledged by society at large are intimately, even dialectically related: self-awareness is a kind of other awareness from within. The self is in part constructed out of internalized glimpses of the Generalized Other. Some of our most personal, private and intimate decisions have a public or external origin; their intelligibility is a general intelligibility: falling in love is no more personal than getting married; and no one would have devoted himself to literature or to healing the sick if (to adapt LaRochefoucauld's aphorism) 'he had not read about it first'. The very process of 'searching for one's true self' is an activity whose origin, rules and destination are largely social. Most thinkers, too, would agree with the Durkheimian perspective that locates many apparently internal concepts outside of the individual psyche in 'collective representations'.

All of this may be granted without having to agree that self-presence, as the condition for differentiated self-awareness, is *entirely* social in origin; or (and this is more to the point here) that all thought and action, insofar as it is intelligible, is subordinated rather particularly to the process of reproducing the processes of production and consequently to perpetuating a situation in which the few exploit and oppress the many. Nor is one obliged to subscribe to a rather improbable world picture in which the metaphysical category of subjectivity may be replaced by the social and political one of abjectivity.[10]

We shall return to these more general questions (especially that of the scope of terms such as 'ideology') in the next chapter. For the present, let us see how the Althusserian vision of the subject as a socio-political artefact has been used against the realistic novel.

5.5 Subjected Subjects and Realistic Fiction

As before, our main witness is Catherine Belsey. She considers three sorts of subjects: (1) fictional characters; (2) authors; and (3) readers. We shall deal with these in turn.

5.5.1 Characters

According to Belsey, classic realism

> performs . . . the work of ideology . . . in its representation of consistent
> subjects who are the origin of meaning, knowledge and action (Belsey,
> *op.cit.*, p. 67).

---

[10] Lacan, whose influence over this essay Althusser has acknowledged, would be unlikely to approve of the narrowing of his concept of the big Other to that of the political Subject. According to Colin MacCabe (*The Talking Cure*, London: Methuen, 1981, p. 212), Althusser, by identifying the big Other with the political Subject, 'represses the Other as the heterogeneous site of language and desire'.

Elsewhere she refers to 'unity and consistency of character' as the 'obvious' basis of the intelligibility of classic realism and claims that, for example, James's *What Maisie Knew* illustrates the classic realist commitment to presenting the subject as unified and 'autonomous'.

Whatever may be true of 'classic realism' – and this is a term that in her hands seems to have enormous scope[11] – there is no reason why a non-classical realism should not represent realistically a character who is neither unified nor consistent. There are, of course, many examples in the literature: Dostoyevsky, Zola, Hamsun – to name three that come immediately to mind – have presented such characters with overwhelming convincingness. But perhaps more to the point (since he is not supposed to be mad or in any other way extraordinary) is Leopold Bloom, whom Joyce presents for the most part with painstaking realism.

The impression one has of Bloom is not merely of a divided person but of a consciousness reduced to a colloidal suspension of thoughts, reason, observations and responses. He is event-driven, 'menu-driven' from without. Insofar as he is credited with beliefs, they are given almost phenomenologically and are always on the verge of disintegrating into sentence-brief aspirations towards themselves. Bloom's self approximates at times the Valéry-esque: the self as a 'mere probability of recurrence'. Such recurrences also provide some of the *leitmotiven* of the narrative so that character and story share out a reduced basis of coherence, without either being accredited with an artificially high level of unity. Molly Bloom is another character presented with phenomenological realism. Her famous soliloquy could hardly be read a piece of writing supporting belief in a rigidly ordered, stable ego, or as endorsing the civic conception of the self. And finally, Gertie MacDowell's fantasies about Bloom on the beach – cast as they are in the romantic prose style of *Peg's Paper* – could be seen as exploring the 'inter-textuality' of even our deepest and most private feelings.

As a last-ditch position, those who oppose realism for colluding with the 'bourgeois' conception of the unified self might condemn the revolutionary realism of *Ulysses* on the grounds that since the monologues of the characters are attributed (albeit often implicitly), there is still an implied unity of self: the incoherent dialogue is tethered to a name. A genuine break with the unified self should lead to unmoored voices, floating without attribution across the page. This is, of course, possible; but it would scarcely be realistic. For actions, thoughts and feelings are attributed in everyday life and it is difficult to imagine a society in which no action was attributed to anyone. I shall require a good deal of convincing before I shall accept that I was as much the murderer of Rohm as Hitler was or that it was I as much as Paris who raped Helen and triggered the Trojan War.

---

[11] As we already noted in Chapter 4. For Belsey, it encompasses, for example, *The Hobbit* and *The War of the Worlds* and is not therefore confined to novels constrained by empirical probability.

To the unprejudiced mind, the case of 'Ulysses' illustrates how realistic representation of persons is not incompatible with a radical revision or questioning of the concept of character. It might be objected that this novel cannot be classified as belonging to realism. Of course it has its mythological dimension; but much of it consists of hyper-realistic writing. Indeed, Wyndham Lewis saw *Ulyssess*, in *Time and Western Man*, as the terminus or the *reductio ad absurdum* of realism. My case is not undermined by the fact that the realistic details are contained within mythological framework. Those who have exploited Joyce's techniques – the stream of consciousness presented through interior monologue, for example – have shown how his realistic presentation of character can be separated from his use of mythology.

It is simply not true, therefore, that realism is inescapably committed to presenting and developing consistent and unified characters. Indeed, the idea of character as *essence*, as *humour*, antedates and, indeed, is rejected by realistic writers. One can accommodate almost any degree of unity or disunity in one's characters within a realistic framework. That most realistic writers do *not* choose to make totally incoherent characters, is more likely to reflect an extra-literary belief that people cohere to some degree than a literary constraint to impose an artificial unity upon the creatures that people their fictions. Which observation brings us back to the argument that our extra-literary perception of individuals as being to some degree ordered or coherent is a reflection of the influence of bourgeois ideology upon our world picture.

In defence of anti-realistic fiction, Belsey quotes Brecht's characteristically crude assertion that 'nobody can be identically the same at two unidentical moments'. There is a trivial sense in which we are changing all the time; the man who is pulling on his socks is not the same as the man who has completed the operation; but this cannot be extrapolated to the conclusion that individuals are totally disjointed and that one moment of a person's life has no relation to any other. There are continuities in even the least coherent lives, short of total amentia. Even then, there is bodily continuity. After the head injury which has rendered him totally demented, Mr John Doe's transformed behaviour, his amented antics are still his, even if it is others who attribute them to him and attach his successive actions to his name. Moreover, there are *degrees* of coherence and incoherence in the self: the fact that the demented form a distinctive sub-population shows this clearly.[12]

It is interesting to speculate what political milage is thought to be gained by denying the continuity of the self. Clearly, it is attractive to to those left-wing thinkers who believe that the idea of a coherent self is inextricably caught up with an oppressive and repressive society. But it also poses

---

[12] For a careful and illuminating account of the relationship between the concept of the self and those of unity, causal connectedness and continuity, see Colin McGinn, *The Character of Mind* (Oxford: Oxford University Press, 1982), chapter 6. This and the subtle discussion between Sydney Shoemaker and Richard Swinburne, *Personal Identity*, (Oxford: Blackwell, 1984) should make certain critics who dabble *en passant* in metaphysics ashamed of their own naivety.

problems for such thinkers. For where there is no continuity of self, there can be no basis for personal responsibility and the great crimes of oppression could be as justifiably attributed to the oppressed as to the oppressors; and a life of greed or of suffering would be unattributable. The 'downtrodden' would not exist as an identifiable group of individuals; there would be a succession of unattached and unassigned moments that bore no relation to one another and would certainly not add up to a life.[13]

So the realistic novelist may believe, as even the most radical theorist in practice believes, in the identifiable individual whose identity is under-written at the very least by the spatial and temporal continuity of his body, without being committed to the dubious idea of an inwardly and outwardly unified character. Indeed, it would not be unfair to say that it was the realistic novel, with its commitment to empirical observation of actual individuals, that did as much as anything to break the literary idea of character as fixed essence and replaced it by the idea of character changing (unfolding or disintegrating) with time and as revealed (or destroyed) in action. The essentialist conception of the character as an *a priori*, unchanging subject merely *expressed* in action – the character as *humour* or as transcendental self – ante-dates and is antithetical to realism.[14] It was the realistic novelists who began the process of decentring the subject, both in the sense of displacing the self from the centre of the very events that constitute his own life and displacing the individual subject from the centre of history. The view that

> the human subject, the economic, political or philosophical ego is not the 'centre' of history – and even . . . that history has no 'centre' but possesses a structure which has no necessary 'centre' except ideological misrecognition.[15]

almost defines one version of the realist vision.

As Belsey herself points out, romanticism is committed to the idea of the transcendental subject and cannot acknowledge the constructedness of the

---

[13] We know how Brecht showed that the idea of the discontinuity of the self could be used in exploitative sexual relations. It was the constant alibi of those of his characters who chose to express their sexual appetites to the full and it legitimized the infamous refrain – the *leitmotif* of the complacent hero taking his smiling departure of an abandoned, howling, pregnant lover – 'I am a man upon whom you can't rely'.

[14] In this (as well as in other respects) many realistic novels are antithetical to romanticism; for they emphasize the role of accident, disease and oppression – in short external circumstance – in the construction of the individual. *L'Assommoir* is a savage critique of *Heinrich von Ofterdingen*. Realistic fiction has done more than any other literary form to undermine the quasi-religious conception of the self as pre-formed, unfolding from within, kissed awake by crucial experiences. Realistic novelists have been in the forefront of those who have discredited the essentialist conception of the self, and the idea of a person as something half between an empty metaphysical subject and a mystical soul.

[15] Althusser quoted by Belsey, *Critical Practice* (London and New York: Methuen, 1980) p. 132.

self – except at the superficial, individualist level of the Baudelairean Dandy. 'Much of Romantic poetry records a quest for a lost wholeness and transcendence of the imaginary . . .' 'The Romantic rejection of the "real conditions" is based on a belief in the autonomy of the subject'. (*ibid*, pp. 122–3).

It was a realistic novelist (Stendhal) who first consciously presented a de-centred account of a major historical event – the Battle of Waterloo. He showed such an event being experienced by its participants not as a coherent totality but as an often confusing and frequently unintelligible succession of smaller events. And this in turn inspired Tolstoy to de-centre history in perhaps the greatest nineteenth-century realist novel.[16] History, Tolstoy demonstrated, does not revolve around individuals, not even supposedly great individuals; nor does it turn on individual decisions; nor, even, does it consist of epochal occurrences with clearly defined outlines. The 'great man', 'decisive event', vision of history is an artefact of hindsight.

The incoherence of the self was accepted by realistic novelists long before it was 'discovered' by political philosophers, ideologists and (eventually) radical literary critics. The chaos of daily consciousness, the intermission of dreams, the flux of human relations – these have long been the stuff of realism and defended by the realist against the simplifying views of philosophers or political scientists or biologists who imagined that they could understand individual lives in crude metaphysical, politico-economic or physiological terms. If one wished to appreciate the decentred self and the fact that history itself appears to be without a centre, one would do better to read the realistic novels of John Dos Passos than the tortuously teased out speculations and simplifications of Marxist or Freudian writing. It may be the case that 'the ideology of liberal humanism assumes a world of non-contradictory (and therefore fundamentally unalterable) individuals whose unfettered consciousness is the origin of meaning, knowledge and action' (Belsey, p. 67); but it does not follow from this that the realistic novelist shares that assumption. He does not have to subscribe to the beliefs implicit in liberal humanism; in fact it is difficult to think of an example amongst the greatest of such novelists who has done so.

5.5.2 Authors

The character is not the only subject who, it is claimed, realistic fiction falsely endows with unity. There is also the author himself in whose invented unity

[16]   'I am in [Stendhal's] debt more than any other's. I owe my knowledge of war to him. Reread his account of the battle of Waterloo in *The Charterhouse of Parma*. Who, until then, had described war in such terms, that is, the way it really is?'

Quoted in *Tolstoy*, Henri Troyat, trans. by Nancy Amphoux (London: Pelican, 1970), p. 172.

the realistic novel persuades the reader to collude and whose artefactual status the ideology of realism attempts to obscure.

The classic expression of this claim is in Barthes's essay celebrating 'The Death of the Author':

> We now know that a text is not a line of words releasing a single 'theological' meaning (the 'message' of the Author-God) but a multi-dimensional space in which a variety of writings, none of them original, blend and clash. The text is a tissue of quotations drawn from the innumerable centres of culture.[17]

'We *now* know': the implication is the 'we' previously did not know and thought that the author was the 'absolute' origin of his 'absolutely original' novel, and that he created it *ex nihilo* in a vacuum that ensured his total isolation from all other past and present practitioners of his craft. The further implication is that the author, as the absolute origin of his work, is the absolute authority on it and that his work or works 'release a single "theological" line of meaning'. 'We' have grown or woken up out of this illusion, too; for the self-same Copernican revolution that decentred the self has also 'dethroned the author' though he still 'reigns in consumerist criticism as the source and explanation of the nature of the text' (Belsey, p. 134).

For the enlightened critic, the author does not use language to express his own subjectivity, his inner vision or his vision of the world. His subjectivity does not antedate language; for the latter mediates the ideology through which he acquires his subjectivity. If he did wish to *to express himself*, he ought at least to know that the inner thing he thinks to translate is

> only a ready-formed dictionary, its words only explainable through other words, and so on indefinitely (Barthes, p. 146).

The author, then, does not underwrite, authorize, or endorse a view of reality expressed in his books; and his books do not embody perceptions, experiences, concepts, ideas and views that are personal to, and in some sense originate with, him.

The myth of 'the Author' – the Absolute Subject of Literature – merely replicates the fallacy implicit in the unitary characters, the originary selves, those sources of action, knowledge and meaning, that supposedly populate realistic novels. A reader who imagines that the novel he is reading emanated from a unitary character named on the dust jacket and who, furthermore, believes that this character has a personal viewpoint expressed in the novel, merely demonstrates the extent to which he is the dupe of the ideological process by which he is himself centred in a subjectivity that serves only to hold him subject to the social formation in which the majority are exploited to benefit the minority.

---

[17] Roland Barthes in *Image-Music-Text*, Essays selected and trans. Stephen Heath (London: Fontana/Glasgow: Collins, 1977). p. 146.

It is a notable feature of much contemporary criticism that it claims to be attacking received ideas prevalent amongst the public at large when in fact it commonly derives its targets from theories of other critics. So it will come as no surprise that the attack on 'the Author' is hardly relevant to the author as he is commonly conceived by ordinary (unpaid) readers. Even without Barthes to warn them against doing so, few non-professional readers would subscribe to the idea that the 'text' is a line of words 'releasing a single "theological" message from an Author-God'. So Barthes's target is an extremely egregious conception of the Author – the kind of conception that might have once been current in certain critical circles but hardly popular amongst average readers. Nevertheless (and this is again a very common ploy), the attack on the manifestly absurd views of other critics is used to smuggle in a less well-founded attack upon the the commonsense views of more ordinary readers.

In killing off the 'Author', Barthes tries to deceive us into thinking that he has also killed off the 'author'. We are liable to imagine (because Barthes takes it for granted) that if the Author is not a God, releasing a single line of meaning, a 'theological' message, then he is incapable of originality at all: he cannot speak, only quote. If he has not invented the language he has used, the genre within which he is writing and the world about which he speaks, then he is merely an echo-chamber of intertextuality.[18]

No one, of course, is absolutely original: if he were he would be unintelligible. Many earlier critics, however, influenced by Romantic rhetoric about the artist's private vision, the creative impulse, etc., have exaggerated the extent to which great writers are original; as if their ideas sprang fully formed from within themselves, or from nature, or from nowhere. Such conceptions of originality are, of course, absurd. Nevertheless, there is such a thing as relative originality; there are degrees of originality. James Joyce was considerably more original than the thousand forgotten epigones who wrote stream-of-dreaming-consciousness novels in the wake of his *Wake*. Similarly there are degrees of quotation: my copying our Barthes's remarks about the

---

[18] Or, more deeply, an echo-chamber of phrases, words clusters, grammatical forms, phonemes.

> '. . . for us . . . it is language which speaks, not the author; to write is, through
> a pre-requisite impersonality, to reach that point where only language acts,
> 'performs', and not 'me'. (Barthes, *op.cit.* p. 143.)

We do not invent the rules of language; speech and writing are *institutions* composed entirely of conventional relationships between arbitrary signs. Language therefore speaks us and not the other way round.

This kind of consideration could be applied to *any* rule-governed activity. We could, for example, argue that Kevin Keegan does not play football but rather that football plays Kevin Keegan; that it is the system, the rule book, the Cannon League, that kicks the ball and scores the goals. If this seems absurd (cf. the classical example of the ill-formed sentence *'Golf plays John'), how much more absurd when it is applied to a form of behaviour that, unlike football, engages basic needs.

death of the Author is less original than Barthes's thinking them up in the first place. Barthes is indubitably the author of 'The Death of the Author'; the views expressed therein originated from him; in that sense, they were original even if wrong. I wouldn't, however, be tempted to speak of 'The world of Roland Barthes'; but many critics – not, I repeat, ordinary readers – might be tempted to do so. For critics not uncommonly believe that a writer who shows any degree of talent and/or originality has a 'unique world or voice or sensibility' and that his works correspond to an idiosyncratic vision or a very different, personal reality. 'The World of Dickens', 'The Moral Universe of Joseph Conrad', 'Faulkner Country' are perceived by professional readers and not by the amateurs.

The process by which such doubtful entities as 'The Moral Universe of Joseph Conrad' are created involves concentrating upon idiosyncrasies to the exclusion of all else – as if a writer consisted entirely of what differentiated him from other writers, when writers have much more in common than they have differences. 'The Moral Universe of Joseph Conrad', in other words, is an artefact of analysis, generated by what the electronic engineer would call common mode rejection, enabling a signal to be enhanced by eliminating that which it has in common with its background. If these entities, created by professional readers, are subsequently referred to by unpaid readers, it is because they feel that a deference is due to experts.

In short, it is less often the author than the critic who releases a single 'theological' meaning. If authors have been set up as gods, it is perhaps because critics have set themselves up as priests and have in many instances oppressed other readers – and each other – by insisting that the work has a meaning which it is only within their power to reveal. The awful truth – one which few critics seem to acknowledge – is that sometimes readers fail to remember even the names of the authors of many of the books they have read and are therefore unlikely to build up a theological conception of them. The author is not merely invisible but forgotten.

It might be argued that the invisible or forgotten author reinforces his authority by his very invisibility: the narrative voice becomes the voice of pure knowledge; and the status of the text as artefact – as something somebody made, indeed made up – is concealed. The force of this argument depends upon a rather low view of the reader as someone who attributes objective truth of reality to whatever he reads.

When in the anonymously written TV soap opera *Dallas*, J.R. Ewing was shot, the identity of his assailant was kept secret for several months and it became the focus of intense speculation. A certain amount of status accrued in some circles to those who had been to America and had watched an earlier showing of a vital episode where all was revealed. It was obvious to everyone concerned that the choice of hit-man would be so manipulated as to extract the maximum mileage from the event; that the hit-man's identity was a matter of scripting, not of a naturally occurring reality. Although interest was intense, this was a reflection of a willing suspension of disbelief and not of a confusion between fiction and reality. At any time, those such as myself who were interested to know the 'facts', the 'truth' 'behind' the assassination attempt, were at liberty to dismount from the charade. We were not at any time in doubt about whether or not J.R. Ewing was a real person. Although the authority of the scriptwriters to have the last word on the 'true identity' of the assailant was never in doubt, neither was the artefactual nature of the script. This is a kind of situation that average readers – or viewers – are used to dealing with; but many critics seem to find it very hard to accept that this kind of sophisticated response to a 'text' is quite routine and is available to a child from about the age of five onwards (See also Chapter 4).

The death of the author, then, is simply the death of one, rather odd, conception of the author, developed for readily appreciated socio-economic reasons, by certain literary critics. The author with a small 'a' meanwhile remains alive and well. Barthes and not I was the author of 'The Death of the Author'; and neither of us wrote *War and Peace*.

5.5.3 Readers

As for the reader, we have covered most of the relevant points already. For Barthes, the death of the author signalled the birth of the reader:

> a text is made of multiple writings . . . but there is one place where this multiplicity is focused and that place is the reader, not, as was hitherto said, the author. The reader is the space on which all the quotations that make up a writing are inscribed without any of them being lost; a text's unity lies not in its origin but in its destination (Barthes, *op. cit.*, p. 148).

Clearly, 'the reader' cannot mean the average reader. There can be few non-professional readers who have the time or the ability to be a 'space on which all the quotations that make up a text are inscribed without any of them being lost' – especially since, as Barthes himself tells us a couple of pages earlier, the text is a tissue of quotations drawn from '*innumerable* centres of culture' and is 'an imitation that is lost, infinitely deferred'.

In the eyes of many critics, the average reader is, as we already know from previous discussion, the reverse of the Jamesian author; for he is one upon whom *everything* – even the distinction between truth and fiction – is lost. Belsey, who quotes other pages of Barthes's essay with approval, would find it difficult to rejoice at 'the birth of the reader', unless the reader thus generated were a post-Saussurean critic. For in her view, giving birth to readers is one of the classic vices for which classic realism is abhorred:

> Classic realism . . . performs . . . the work of ideology not only in its representation of consistent subjects who are the origin of meaning, knowledge and action, but also in offering the reader, as the position for which the text is most readily intelligible, the position of subject as the origin both of understanding and of action in accordance with this understanding (Belsey, p. 67).

Classic realism

> 'interpellates' the reader, addressing itself to him or her, offering the
> reader a position from which the text is most 'obviously' intelligible, the
> position of the subject in (and of) ideology (*ibid*).

This is an offer which an orthodox Althusserian would find almost impossible to refuse. As we observed in Chapter 4, however, Belsey's own critical
practice showed the offer in the very process of being refused. While she is no
mere plot-follower drowsing over a best-seller on a train, it seems rather less
than probable that her metaphysical status, or her awareness of herself in
everyday life is utterly different as a result. Refusing the offer made by classic
realism does not imply as ability to resist a sense of oneself as subject; nor does
acquiescing in the position offered by a reading of a realistic novel imply
acquiescing in that sense.

It would seem as if Belsey's central claim were that the unified coherent
world of certain realistic novels retro-acts upon the reader to confirm him or
her in his or her unified and coherent self. The novel colludes in the
ideological processes whereby the acentricity of reality and the decentredness
of the self are concealed in the name of a society cohering around the needs
and objectives of the privileged and the powerful.

> Initially (and continuously) constructed in discourses, the subject finds in
> the discourses of classic realist text a confirmation of the possibility of auto-
> nomous subjectivity represented in ideology as 'obvious' (Belsey, p. 63).

This seems (to put it mildly) to exaggerate the influence of realistic novels. It
takes little or no account of the conditions under which they are actually read.
Except where a novel is being read for a living, the reading is liable to be
repeatedly interrupted by unscheduled events of a diverse, even heterologous
kind. And even those who enjoy the privilege of reading without interruption
are able, as the example of Ms Belsey shows, to come through the experience
metaphysically unchanged. We may be 'hailed' by books; but we do not have
to turn round; and even if we do, the process of turning round through 180
degrees does not turn us into subjects or embed us more deeply in a false sense
of internal coherence.

Appendix to Chapter 5

Barthes's views do have a momentary appeal as a corrective to the
'biographism' that perpetually tempts certain literary critics. There seems to
be no limit to the lengths to which some critics will go to correlate the
writer's personal history with the form and content of his work.

Consider this passage from Walter Benjamin's essay on Proust (cited with
admiration by, amongst many others, that 'advanced' critic and fellow travel-
ler of post-Saussurean thought, Frank Kermode)

> Proust's syntax rhythmically and step by step reproduces his fear of
> suffocating. And his ironic, philosophical, didactic reflections

> invariably are the deep breath with which he shakes off the weight of memories. (*The Image of Proust* in *Illuminations*, Edited by Hannah Arendt. trans. Harry Zohn, London: Collins/Fontana Books, 1973, p. 216.)

The Mimetic Fallacy can rarely have been so arrestingly illustrated. The 'step by step' is particularly interesting. One wonders how many steps a fear of suffocation – or come to that a writer's syntax – has. The category error in the second sentence is also revealing: it is typical of the kind of absurdity biographism inevitably leads to.

An author's relationship with a distant, disapproving father may explain why he tried so hard to be a success in life, but not why he wrote books nor why he wrote such good books. Many have had similar relationships with their fathers and done neither. Nor would the unresolved Oedipus complex explain why the author chose verse rather than prose, why he had such a way with anapests and why he wrote about daffodils instead of badgers.

Barthes's views might also be useful against the cheap historicism of much biographically orientated literary interpretation where individual writers and even individual works are 'explained' on the basis of a *1066 and All That* version of history that establishes their 'historical situation'. (I am thinking in particular of Goldmann and Lukacs.) If such 'historical situations' exist, they hardly explain individual writers. For historical situations – that of being a nineteenth-century *rentier* (Lukacs on Flaubert), or a member of the *petit noblesse* at the court of Louis XIV (Goldmann on Racine) – are, by definition shared by many other individuals who may have written in a totally different manner or, more commonly, not at all.

Barthes, in other words, reminds us of the extent to which, what, and how an individual writes is influenced by things other than his collective and even personal experiences. An author writes within (or consciously against) a framework laid down by genre and the wider framework of the current practice of 'literature'; and when he writes, he does not create the world he writes about as if from scratch. He does not spin it out of his own inner tissues. Nor is his literary response to the world that of an isolated or independent consciousness or of one who brings only his own experience to bear on his interpretation of the world. There are conventions in both the practice of literature and the perception of the world. So the writer's voice is not entirely his own, his opinions are often 'their' or 'one's' opinions, and the language he uses has come to him from the outside. To appeal to his biography for a complete understanding of his books is therefore misguided.

Barthes has usefully emphasized these points. Nevertheless, one cannot ignore the biographical element in the formation of the writer and the influence of the particular occurrences of his life in determining the things he writes about and the manner in which he treats them. And also the success or otherwise with which he treats them. Barthes himself was able to write astutely about Parisian culture because he was French. His book about the Japanese culture, however, was a piece of crude orientalism – for the same reason. An African in Africa is more liable to write – and to write well – about Africa – the real Africa, not a Roussellian 'Africa of the mind' – than an Englishman who has never travelled abroad. One's location, the major events of one's life, will be vital determinants – though not the only ones – of the content and tone of one's writing.

It is interesting to observe how this obvious fact is accepted by Barthes's admirers when they discuss Barthes himself. Jonathan Culler tells us (*Structuralist Poetics*, London: Routledge & Kegan Paul, 1975, p. ix) that 'It is no doubt significant that Roland Barthes's linguistic "initiation" took place in Alexandria through the good offices of A.J. Greimas and that he read Viggo Brondal before he read Saussure'.

And Susan Sontag's remarks about Barthes (whose work she believes most likely to endure 'of all the intellectual notables who have emerged since the Second World War in France') are interesting. She suggests that 'perhaps the most striking difference between Sartre and Barthes is the deep one of temperament' (Introduction to *Barthes: Selected Writings*, p. xxi.) And later, speaking of Barthes's final writings, she writes that 'Barthes's voice became steadily more intimate, his subjects more inward'. She refers to Barthes's 'spiritual strivings that could not be supported by his aesthetic position'. And she tells us that 'at the end his temper, style and sensibility had run its course' and speaks of 'those "late" ways of experiencing, evaluating, reading the world; and surviving in it, drawing energy, finding consolation (but finally not), taking pleasure, expressing love'. All of this in the face of Barthes's own claim that 'the scriptor no longer bears within him humours, feelings, impressions. . . .' Even his admirers, it seems, don't believe his views when they are not actually expounding or advocating them or denigrating the contrary opinions. But then it is possible, as I know from my own experience, to admire Barthes without necessarily taking his ideas too seriously.

6

Realism, Ideology and the Contradictions of Capitalism

6.1 The Idea of a Dominant Ideology

The various arguments against realism examined in the last two chapters are centred on a common thesis: that realism overlooks the constructed nature of reality, presenting it, by implication, as objectively given rather than as the product of historical conflict and as coherent rather than riddled with contradiction. Conscious or deliberate falsification of reality, as in fantastical or romantic fiction, is comparatively harmless because the texts in question – and the worlds portrayed in them – wear their artefactual status on their sleeves. The distorted reality of realism, however, is potentially more dangerous. Realistic writers and certainly their readers, it is argued, *overlook* the divergence between the reality inside and that outside the novel. The former is consequently passed off as, or confused with, the latter. Indeed, the prestige of 'literature' may confer such authority upon 'serious' realistic fiction that it may over-ride other, possibly truer, versions of reality. At the very least, 'classic realism' contributes to the ideological process whereby the consciousness of the individual is manipulated in such a way that he is unable to think critically about and interrogate his world. He is confirmed in his delusion that reality as it is refracted through the dominant ideology, that of the ruling class, is reality itself, rather than merely one tendentious version of it.

The question Althusser addressed in *Ideology and Ideological State Apparatuses* is, Eagleton tells us

> How it is . . . that human subjects very often come to submit themselves
> to the dominant ideologies of their societies.[1]

The immediate answer is that if they didn't then the ideologies in question wouldn't be dominant. But this is to misconstrue the problem and, more important, to overlook the assumption implicit in the way it has been posed: that there *is* a dominant ideology and that it has the properties, functions and powers that Althusser and other Marxist writers attribute to it.

The first thing that strikes the unpersuaded reader as odd in Althusser's picture of society is the extent to which he *assumes* that the process of

[1] Terry Eagleton, *Literary Theory* (Oxford: Blackwell, 1983), p. 171.

socialization is part of the process of politicization as opposed to the other way round and the second is the ease with which the goals of politicization can be summarized. For Althusser, the acquisition of a sense of self and of a world picture are inextricably entwined with acquiescence in the political status quo. The very process of becoming a subject in the metaphysical sense entails subjecting oneself to 'the Subject' and involuntarily supporting a repressive state. It seems extraordinary that being co-present with others – indeed, being 'worlded' and even 'selved' – should have such a specific and readily defined character.

Now Althusser's question is certainly an interesting one. And it would also be valid if it had been posed somewhat differently. It touches on the fundamental mysteries of psychology and philosophy: How is a coherent inter-subjective world possible? And how are new, individual consciousnesses inducted into that world so that it shall be continued in, by and for them?

The very posing of this question forces one to acknowledge the necessity of invoking some kind of supra-individual orchestration of individual consciousnesses to ensure the continuous existence of a co-ordinated, coherent intersubjective reality. It is clear that no individual could gain access to the world through, or piece it together solely out of, sense data. The dismal failure of logical positivism to ground genetic psychology in the individual's empirical discovery of reality through perception has shown this only too clearly. Furthermore, most thinkers would agree with Durkheim's critique of the 'concept' as an intra-psychic entity abstracted from private perceptions and his locating their origin outside of the psyche in 'collective representations'.[2] And there must be few diehard romantics nowadays who would dissent from the perspective of social psychologists such as Mead for whom the organized, higher order, sense of the self comes from outside, in social interaction. That self-recognition and being recognized by society at large are intimately connected, even dialectically related, so that self-recognition is a kind of other-recognition from within, is generally accepted by most philosophers as well as psychologists. Even at the deepest level, the very process of being 'worlded' is socially mediated.

Once one abandons religious explanations – a pre-established harmony of perception, individual minds cohering in the mind of God and so on – then one appears to be faced with an inexplicable coincidence or dovetailing of literally millions of different viewpoints. We are obliged, therefore, to postulate that there are 'social forces' ordering the developing consciousness so that it may participate in, understand and operate within, the intelligible order that has been agreed upon by the collective. It does not, however, follow that the forces combing consciousness to self-intelligibility and socializing its world picture can be expressed entirely in narrow political terms or summarized so easily as as Althusser seems to imagine. It seems unlikely that

[2] Emile Durkheim, *The Elementary Forms of Religious Life*, trans. Joseph Swain, (London: George Allen & Unwin, 1915), pp. 432–9.

the fundamental process of establishing and maintaining an inter-subjective reality can be encompassed by the class struggle. After all, the idea of a common world, of a shared or public reality, must be logically prior to the dimmest intuitions of class interest, not to speak of the idea of oppression, justice and relative poverty or wealth in that world.

6.2 The Scope of Ideology

Totalitarian thinkers have a standard rejoinder to those who express doubts about the all-embracing nature of the class struggle. 'You are unable to grasp the scope of political brainwashing precisely because it is so successful. Your very rejection of the Althusserian (or Marxist) viewpoint is itself a measure of the triumph of ideology preventing you from looking past its version of reality to see that there are alternative versions which you are being prevented from considering.' This response (which *mutatis mutandis* is the defence used to render psychoanalytic theories immune from testing) unfortunately creates difficulties for those who hope that their writing might have revolutionary implications. For the Althusserian critique makes ideology inescapable and his own critique impossible.

This has been acknowledged even by sympathetic critics. If the price of being a subject is that one is subjected to the Absolute Subject, then, Colin McCabe points out,

> there is no *theoretical* perspective for ideological struggle in the face of dominant ideologies for there is nothing which escapes or is left over from the original production of the subject by the Subject.[3]

And McCabe's observations on Pecheux are equally applicable to Althusser:

> [He] remains committed to a *general* description of ideology and bourgeois politics with the result that ideology and bourgeois politics become the eternal Hell to which we are subjected and their alternatives are only momentary displacements into a better world. Ideological subjection thus becomes a feature of language [itself] while science and proletarian politics are transformed into ephemeral agents of grace which fleetingly rescue us from the sin of the subject position into which we inevitably relapse (MacCabe, p. 217).

If ideology were inescapable to this degree, it is difficult to see how it could have been *noticed* never mind resisted unless, to use MacCabe's apt phrase, we postulate an 'agent of grace' descending upon certain fortunate political thinkers.

In view of this, it is extraordinary that critics such as Belsey should claim, without apparent embarrassment, that criticism should be aimed at liberating the reader from the spell of the dominant ideology. Nevertheless, she asserts precisely this:

[3] Colin McCabe, *The Talking Cure* (London: Macmillan, 1981), p. 212.

> The task of criticism, then, is to establish the unspoken [ideology] in the text, to decentre it in order *to produce a real knowledge of history* (Belsey, p. 136).

We are all drowned in ideology and its imaginary versions of history except for those happy few who have somehow managed to surface and are consequently able to articulate the distorting ideology that interposes itself between the subject and true representations of himself, of society, of nature and of history. Belsey even concludes (from her discussion of Macherey) that criticism is *the* science which offers a knowledge of the mode of production of works of literature 'and so of history itself' (Belsey, p. 138).

These are wild claims and made all the wilder by the very position out of which they arise. If their implicit megalomania commands temporary assent, it is because of a largely unconscious ploy used widely in radical criticism – as well in radical political theory. The ploy consists of changing the scope of a key word – in the present case 'ideology'.[4]

Where it is a question of developing a radical condemnation of realism, 'ideology' seems to be almost co-terminous with intelligibility; but where it is a question of advocating alternative fictional genres (or of explaining the role of writers – and in particular critics – who will point the way to them), 'ideology' shrinks dramatically until it is merely a feature of political views or literary styles the critic dislikes. At any rate, 'ideology' becomes something *focal* rather than global, so that it can be observed, assessed as undesirable, criticized by an awakened consciousness, and even avoided.

Let us follow the fortunes of ideology. On p. 56 of Catherine Belsey's book we find ideology in the middle of its scope and power. There ideology is constituted out of

> the myths and imaginary versions of real social relationships.

Lest we take refuge in the comforting reflection that even myths and imaginary versions of reality may embody a certain sort of symbolic or even twisted truth, we must remember Althusser's essay where we are told bluntly that 'ideology = misrecognition/ignorance' (IISA,p. 57). And Belsey quotes, with apparent approval, Althusser's assertion that

> what is represented in ideology is not the system of real relations which govern the existence of individuals but the imaginary relations of those individuals to the real relations in which they live (IISA, p. 39).

The problem with ideology, however, goes even deeper:

> Ideology represents not the real nor a distorted reflection of the real, but the 'obvious'. What it suppresses is its own signifying practice (Belsey, p. 148).

---

[4] For a characteristically succinct and reliable account of the changing meaning of 'ideology' see Raymond Williams, *Keywords* (Bromley, Kent: Fontana/Glasgow: Croom Helm, 1976).

Worse still, ideology is not merely implicated in the creation of the obvious but, as Eagleton explains,

> it is the very medium in which I 'live out' my relation to society, the realm of signs and social practices which binds me to the social structure and lends me a sense of coherent purpose and identity (Eagleton, p. 172).

The price of extricating oneself from ideology must therefore be to drop out of society and its signifying practices altogether and to lose one's sense of coherence and identity. This is a price that neither Eagleton nor Belsey (authors of passionately argued books that they must have taken great pains to write and to get published, individuals who have remained very much in the midst of society) – nor, even, until perhaps latterly – Althusser, has proved willing to pay. But, surely, to convince others that ideology is both global in its scope and uniformly misleading, one should at the very least be one of the misled, so long as one remains within society. The impression these writers would like to convey, however, is that they are *not* misled, even if in this respect they are numbered amongst a happy few. They therefore fall victim to the Paradox of the Liar – and at a deeper level than even the Theban Liar.

For the latter claimed only that what *Thebans* said was untrue. He didn't try to persuade us that the very act of speaking and making sense was woven in with lies. Super-Theban Belsey, however, informs us that

> on the basis of Saussure's work it is possible to argue that insofar as language is a way of articulating experience, it necessarily participates in *ideology*, the sum of the ways in which people both live and represent to themselves their relationship to the conditions of their existence (Belsey, p. 42).

Taken in isolation, this passage would seem fairly unobjectionable: *Of course* language participates in ideology if you define ideology in that way. But it becomes an extraordinary claim when it is combined with the Althusserian premise that 'ideology = misrecognition/ignorance'. If, furthermore, we accept Belsey's statement that Saussure's 'discoveries' have the implication that it is only in virtue of language that the world is made intelligible – 'by differentiating between concepts' (Belsey, p. 59 and note 5) – ideology becomes co-extensive not merely with language but with intelligibility itself. Insofar as anything makes sense, the individual for whom it makes sense implicitly acquiesces in ideology – in that misrepresentation of reality which is necessary to ensure the reproduction of the conditions of production and the oppression of the many by the few. All recognition is misrecognition; all knowledge is ignorance.[6]

---

[5] See also p. 61:

> It follows from Saussure's theory of language as a system of differences that the world is intelligible only through discourse.

[6] This goes further than Althusser himself, as we shall discuss presently.

This conclusion is, as I have already intimated, awkward rather than helpful for those who would condemn realism on political grounds. If the very process of making sense of the world, or of making any part of reality intelligible, involves entry into and implicit support for the reigning ideology, there can be no way out except into unintelligibility. The awakening from ideology must be into senselessness; or into some kind of pre-linguistic asocial, or even asemic, awareness. From which it must follow that there can be no work of literature – or of literary criticism – that can stand outside of ideology. There is, therefore, nothing especially politically reprehensible about realism: *all* discourse, inasmuch as it is intelligible, is steeped in ideology. If, as Eagleton informs us, ideology encompasses everything from the practice of letting women go through the door first to 'my deeply unconscious images of myself and others', it must certainly enter the complex social act of producing and distributing a work of literature, *whatever* its genre. Romanticism, fantasy and anti-realism are as compromised as realism; Bertholt Brecht as much as Arthur Hailey. Even nonsense verse, such as this line from Isador Isou

M dngoun, m diahl thhna iou,

must collude in the dominant ideology because, if it makes sense at all, it does so by referring implicitly to the conventions of expressive verse and transgressing the expectations of sense set up by experience of the latter. Its having any meaning – as for example an escape from the tyranny of literary meaning – depends, in an inverted way, upon those more conventional modes of writing that are inevitably steeped in ideology. It seems as if '*Il n'y a pas de hors ideologie*' – except via a bash on the head; or, if that seems insufficiently radical (since even in coma there may be lucid dreams), decapitation.

6.3 Escaping both Contradiction and Self-Contradiction

For some critics, Pierre Macherey's approach to literature, as elaborated in *A Theory of Literary Production*,[7] seems to offer a way out of the impasse. Ideology is inescapably present in any text but it can be handled, put at arm's length, by being made explicit. Belsey interprets this to imply an advocacy of 'interrogative' texts which will raise an 'internal distance' between them and the ideology which encloses them. The interrogative text

> refuses a single point of view, however complex and comprehensive, but brings points of view into unresolved collision of contradiction (Belsey, p. 92).

By deliberately contradicting itself, the interrogative text renders its ideological framework *visible* and so makes it available to the reader for

[7] Pierre Macherey, *A Theory of Literary Production*, trans. Geoffrey Wall, (London: Routledge & Kegan, 1978).

questioning. He is freed to question, rather than forced to accept, 'the obvious'. Such exemplary works leave the critic with little to do except to draw attention to, and praise, them. The critic is anyway kept busy bringing out the unintentional contradictions in those, usually realistic, works that don't do his job for him; in interrogating non-interrogative texts; or getting them to interrogate themselves by articulating what they pass over in silence (Belsey, p. 138). This new critical practice

> insists on finding the plurality, however 'parsimonious', of the text and refuses the pseudominance constructed as the 'obvious' position of its intelligibility by the forms of classic realism (Belsey, p. 129).

It will commend the deliberate self-contradictions, the intentional plurality, of anti-realistic works that defy consistent interpretation. And it will condemn realism, not because it fails to escape ideology (no intelligible text could) but because it does not attempt to undo its own ideology from within by a cold-blooded self-contradiction that denies the reader a fixed view point from which it makes sense.

This sounds promising until we are given examples of interrogative texts and are shown the 'new critical practice' in action. To illustrate her theories, Belsey analyses a passage from John Berger's *A Fortunate Man* – a rather surprising example; for this, sometimes penetrating and occasionally sentimental, account of the work of a GP in a semi-rural practice, is a piece of fairly straightforward, realistic reportage. The excerpt she discusses concerns a 16-year-old girl who seeks help because she can no longer tolerate the conditions in the laundry where she works. The GP comforts her, promises to do something, and sees her on her way. After she has left, he contemplates the wall outside of his surgery window. Once the wall was made of dry stone; now it is cemented together. Belsey interprets this as a symbol of the 'smoothing over of differences in modern society' and this symbol contradicts the general tendency of the story. The seemingly satisfactory resolution of the girl's distress is thrown into question by the image of the cemented wall which reminds us that she is irremoveably fixed in a society that makes her a drudge; it implies that the encounter with the doctor marks not the end of her enslavement but only of her protest against it. Not only Berger's story, but also Berger's analysis of it, seem well within the conventions of realism. Neither constitutes any kind of break with what, elsewhere, would be scornfully dismissed as the 'obvious'; and, furthermore, the critic does not appear to be embarrassed at having resolved the contradictions of the text by elucidating their (non-contradictory) point[8]. Neither the exemplary interrogative text nor the interrogative critic seems to have broken into a space

---

[8] The paradox of the critic-advocate elucidating texts that are intended to be unintelligible and using referential language to discuss novels that are meant to undermine the referential illusion has been insufficiently noticed. It puts the interrogative critic in a rather difficult position *vis-à-vis* the radical vision he is promoting. We shall discuss this paradox in Part III, especially sections 8.4 and 8.5.

outside of what, in Althusserian theory, is described with breathtaking simplicity as 'the dominant ideology'.

This example supports the objection to Belsey's interpretation of the Machereyan programme, that it aims at something that its own premises imply is impossible: if one defines ideology as widely as Belsey does, there can be nothing intelligible outside of it – or what is intelligible must fall squarely within it. The pious hope that ideology may be eluded by being made *deliberately* explicit – either within an anti-realistic novel or outside of a realistic one by an appropriate critical reading – must inevitably be forlorn if ideology is as all-pervasive as those who use it as a stick to beat realism claim that it is. If ideology goes all the way through human consciousness, like 'Brighton Rock' through Brighton Rock, no writer – or critic – could even *begin* to surface from his social immersion sufficiently to make the terms of his engagement with society explicit in his writings so that he could then make the latter's implicit ideology explicit. Nor could any critic wake up out of the 'obvious' to examine the text from a point of view outside of the all-encompassing dominant ideology. Total self-awareness is not possible: we all have a back view which, even if it is not visible to our contemporaries, will become manifest to posterity. A work that wears its ideology on its sleeve is, under the definition of ideology accepted by critics like Belsey, as impossible as a work entirely free of ideology. And criticism cannot liberate consciousness from ideology if the later is co-terminous with all that is expressed linguistically or mediated through language. As Genette (quoted in Macherey, p. 138) pointed out, literature and criticism are mutually implicated since they use the same medium – writing:

> Unlike the art critic or the musicologist, the literary critic uses the same medium as those he is criticizing, a source of formidable confusion – primarily for the critic himself. Thus criticism is simultaneously outside the space of literature, because it speaks of writing, and inside this space because its speech is writing.

Macherey's own position is less radical and more complex: and it is not in the end hostile to realism – even the 'classic' realism of the nineteenth century. The speech of the book – novel, treatise or whatever – 'comes from a certain silence, a matter which endows it with form, a ground on which it traces a figure' (p. 85). It is the role of the literary critic to articulate that silence, to make of that ground a figure in its own right. The work must not be simply accepted as a finished product but investigated in terms of the laws of literary production that made it possible.

> The [critic's] act of knowing is not like listening to a discourse already constituted. . . . It is rather the elaboration of a new discourse, the articulation of a silence (Macherey, p. 6).

The ideological background, 'which constitutes the real support of all forms of expression' is unconscious and it is the critic's job to make that latent knowledge, 'the unconscious not of the author but of the work', explicit. The critic is not, however, working on his own, operating *against* the text, trying to *dismantle* it, like someone trying to pick holes in an argument. The text, far from colluding in the dominant ideology that the radical critic is trying to question or wake up from, actually undermines it *by either consciously or unconsciously making it and its contradictions visible*:

> We always find, at the edge of the text, the language of ideology, momentarily hidden, but eloquent by its very absence . . . the finished literary work *reveals* the gaps in the ideology. Literature is the mythology of its own myths: it has no need of a soothsayer to uncover its secrets (Macherey, p. 60).

> A work is established against an ideology as much as it is from an ideology. Implicitly the work contributes to the exposure of ideology, or at least to a definition of it; thus the absurdity of all attempts to 'demystify' literary works, which are defined precisely by their enterprise of demystification (Macherey, p. 133).

> The mirror [of Tolstoy's novels] reflects term for term the elements of the peasant outlook. By means of this image these terms appear to be contradictory. . . . If we examine the nature of ideology in general . . . it is soon obvious that there can be no ideological contradiction, except if we put ideology in contradiction with itself (Macherey, p. 130).

> The disorder that permeates the work is related to the disorder of ideology (which cannot be organized as a system). The work derives its form from this incompleteness which enables us to identify the active presence of a conflict at its borders. In the defect of the work is articulated a new truth: for those who seek to know this truth it establishes an original relation to the real, it establishes the revealing form of knowledge (Macherey, pp. 155–6).

The works that Macherey is referring to include the novels of Jules Verne and of Tolstoy – scarcely forerunners of the interrogative texts that Belsey advocates. And it will be seen from these quotations that Macherey mounts a powerful case for realistic fiction as a way of making ideology visible, the realistic epiphany as a means of *exposing* what otherwise would remain silent or invisible and so pass unchallenged. And in the enterprise of contesting the dominant ideology, the relationship between the realistic novelist and the radical critic would seem to be co-operative rather than adversarial. Attempting to represent what is out there does not, even if one acquieces in the dominant ideology, necessarily result in a work that confirms that ideology:

> The interest of Verne's work lies in the fact that, through the unity of its project – a unity borrowed from a certain ideological coherence or incoherence . . . by specifically literary means, it reveals the *limits*, and to some extent the *conditions* of this ideological coherence, which is necessarily built upon a discord in the historical reality, and upon a discord between this reality and its *dominant* representation (Macherey, p. 238).

In short,

> no ideology is sufficiently consistent to survive the test of figuration (Macherey, p. 195).

It is ironical that Macherey, who is cited with such approval in *Critical Practice*, should so decisively undermine Belsey's case against realism. Macherey is a Marxist philosopher operating within the frame of reference of Althusser, his teacher and mentor. Let us recall Althusser's conception of ideology:

> What is represented in ideology is not the system of real relations which govern the existence of individuals, but the imaginary relation of those individuals to the real relations in which they live (IISA, p. 39).

It would seem from this that Althusser himself believes in the existence of a reality outside of ideology – a realm of real relations beyond that of the imaginary relations. This is the realm that gets overlooked, distorted, etc. in, by and through ideology. Is there any reason why in principle that realm of real relations should not be intelligible? Or, if it is available to a political philosopher to refer to and make sense of, why it should not also be available to a novelist? One function of the novel could be to describe that realm of real relations and to draw attention to the differences between 'the real relations which govern the existence of individuals' and 'the imaginary relations of those individuals to those relations'. What type of novel could be better equipped to perform that function than a realistic novel?

Or is it possible, after all, that Althusser's theories imply, in spite of Althusser's own views to the contrary, that there is *no* realm of real relations outside of ideology? For there are yet more radical doubts than Althusser's suggestion that we almost always misconstrue reality. We have already brushed against the idea that there may be no reality outside of the ideology-ridden discourses in which reality is systematically distorted. The generalization of this position is that there is no reality outside of language for discourses to refer to and distort; that reality is intra-linguistic and that language refers only to language. To the investigation of this possibility and the critique of realism arising out of it, I have devoted a separate work.[9]

Appendix to Part II   A Note on Althusser's *Ideology and Ideological State Apparatuses*

I have focused on this essay more because it has been influential in the criticism of realism than because of its intrinsic merits. Although it has the distinction of being clearly written – rare in the Althusserian corpus – it is abominably argued even by Marxist standards. It assumes most of what one might reasonably expect it to try to prove. The central point – that the state

[9] See Aperture.

is (only) repressive – is to be accepted because it conforms with the 'strict' Marxist tradition; and we are required to acquiesce in the thesis that the State *is* (repressive) State apparatus because this is 'the classical [presumably classical Marxist] definition' of the state. For the same reason, we have to believe that 'the State . . . has no meaning except as a function of *State power*'. The key thesis – that 'All ideological State apparatuses, whatever they are, contribute to the same result: the reproduction of the relations of production, i.e. of capitalist relations of exploitation' – is merely asserted without proof.

It might be objected that it is unfair to expect Althusser to re-invent the Marxist wheel in an essay intended to develop Marxist thought in a new direction. Even so, it is not easy to accept the bald school-primer manner of the opening pages in which the 'fundamental principles' are stated with a didactic confidence, as if they had been established by the Master and are now beyond reasonable doubt. In places, IISA reads like a *Daily Telegraph* parody of Marxist writing.

Althusser is never sufficiently embarrassed by his inability to find honest arguments in support of the steps so essential to his thesis. We are asked to take his (absolutely central) assertion that Ideology has a material existence on trust because 'a long series of arguments would be necessary to prove it'. Hence his request that the reader 'be favourably disposed towards the idea in the name of materialism'. (*Credo ut intellegam?*)

The reader who grants this curious request does not know what he is letting himself in for. A few pages on, Althusser states that 'where only a single subject is concerned, the existence of the ideas of his belief is material' but adds that the adjective 'material' has different modalities: 'the material-ities of a displacement for going to mass, of kneeling down . . . of a sentence . . . or an "internal" verbal discourse (consciousness), are not one and the same materiality' (p. 43). Rather! However, 'I shall leave on one side the problem of a theory of differences between the modalities of materiality'. (Perhaps it would be better.) Nevertheless, 'at the risk of being taken for a Neo-Aristotelian . . . I shall say that "matter is discussed in many senses" '.

Lest the faithful should be uneasy, he hastily interpolates: 'NB Marx had a very high regard for Aristotle,' Althusser, too, can therefore 'discuss matter in many senses' because Aristotle did and Aristotle has been endorsed from the top.

Althusser's thesis – that the state is *only* repressive and that it survives by concealing its true nature from the vast majority of its citizens who are oppressed by it – betrays a repugnant paranoia that makes even end-stage Sartre seem benign. It is demonstrably untrue. There are of course many instances of countries where unjust and tyrannical regimes make little attempt to conceal their own nature from the oppressed and in such countries the classes that hold state power appear to have at least as firm a grip on it as those in which, according to the Althusserian vision, an ISA-mediated whitewashing job is carried out. The counter-examples of, say, South Africa, Poland or Chile would not however impress a writer who continues:

> I only need one example and proof of this: Lenin's anguished concern to revolutionize the educational State Apparatus (among others) . . .

(An example is scarcely a proof. We have already commented on the characteristic intellectual vice of Marxist writing – the citation of authorities as a substitute for argument: to demonstrate that a thesis is orthodox is all that is required in order to prove that it is true. We have here another instance of the intellectually derelict practice of citing the beliefs of the Heroes of the Revolution as incontrovertible evidence in favour of an argument and gives an indication of what passes for thought in Marxist circles. If Lenin thought so, then it must be true.)

What makes this kind of argument reprehensible is that it impairs judgement and discrimination. Whatever one may think about the iniquities that take place in the name of the State in say France or England, they are on a smaller scale than those in, say, South Africa or Poland where it is not the minority that is oppressed but the majority. In South Africa, no amount of ideological whitewashing can conceal the true state of affairs from the oppressed (however much it may help the oppressors to deceive themselves).

Althusser's arguments also iniquitously fail to discriminate between western democracies and countries such as the USSR where there is a conscious effort on the part of a state cadre to manipulate the presentation of reality in accordance with a narrow, explicit ideology – where, in other words, ideology is centralized and consciously deployed. Or Poland where the colonizing power controls all means of self-expression. Failure to maintain these distinctions in our thoughts may eventually undermine the difference in fact. So long as we regard democracies as Fascist Totalitarian States, thus long shall we hasten the process by which the former are transformed into the latter. At the very least, the universal paranoia of the New Left thinkers discredited left-wing thought and assisted the cause of the moderately repressive right-wing governments that came to power in the late 70s and early 80s. Recent developments in Britain that lead one to think that right-wing totalitarianism has come a little nearer are at least in part due to a preceding climate of left-wing academic opinion that proclaimed that totalitarianism was already present.

PART III
PRACTICE (1)
Anti-Realism

Introduction

In the first two parts of this book, I have considered arguments that have been advanced to support the belief that realistic fiction is either outmoded (reality is no longer realistic, the cinema has rendered realistic fiction obsolete); impossible (stories and reality are differently constructed); or positively pernicious (realism colludes with the dominant ideology that underwrites repressive social formations). As mentioned in *Aperture*, I have examined other, more radical, arguments against realism in an earlier work, *Not Saussure*[1]. It will be useful to mention these arguments briefly because what follows is addressed to the arguments dealt with in *Not Saussure* as well to those discussed in the first two parts of the present book.

The post-Saussurean case against realism is that discourse cannot refer to a genuinely extra-linguistic reality. 'Criticism', Robert Scholes tells us, 'has taken the very idea of "aboutness" away from us. It has taught us that language is tautological, if it is not nonsense, and to the extent that it is about anything it is about itself'[2]. In *Not Saussure*, I identified two sorts of reasons for believing language to be 'tautological' or self-referring: either (a) reality is more or less intra-linguistic; or (b) language is a closed system, referring only to a second-order reality it creates within itself. I argued that (a) is based upon a misinterpretation of the evidence that had earlier been adduced in support of the Sapir–Whorf hypothesis that 'we dissect nature along lines laid down by our native languages'[3]. I showed that the examples most commonly used to support this version, as well as more extreme post-Saussurean brands, of linguistic relativism, depended for their apparent force upon the assumption that there is an extra-linguistic reality being linguistically divided in different ways. In other words that there *is* a pre- or extra-linguistically differentiated reality. The claim (b) that there is an extra-linguistic reality, but that language cannot gain access to it, was shown to be dependent on several false arguments. The most important of them was that language, being a system, must be closed off from anything outside of itself. The counter-arguments put

[1] Raymond Tallis, *Not Saussure*, (London: Macmillan, 1988).
[2] Robert Scholes, 'The Fictional Criticism of the Future', *TriQuarterly*, 34 (Fall, 1975).
[3] John B. Carroll (ed.) *Language, Thought and Reality: Selected Writings of Benjamin Lee Whorf* (Cambridge, Mass.: MIT Press, 1956), p. 213.

forward in *Not Saussure* included the observation that many systems (including the nervous system) are *not* closed and re-stating the distinction between the behaviour of verbal types (which, indeed, is not determined by particular patterns of reality) and that of verbal tokens (which very often is). I considered the need to re-assert the distinction between type and token (and, at other times, between *langue* and *parole*, sign and signifier, signified and referent and meaning and reference) as symptomatic of an almost incredible carelessness in the use of key terms. It was upon such carelessness that much exciting post-Saussurean theory was founded.

I think I have demonstrated, both in the present work and in *Not Saussure* that the major theoretical arguments against realism do not hold water. Moreover, they are, in many instances, pragmatically self-refuting: to express, prove or defend them is implicitly to demonstrate their falsity. Despite this, they have helped to create a climate of critical opinion in which the more serious and thoughtful practitioners of realistic fiction feel uneasy. By contrast, anti-realists can write secure in the knowledge that their texts will be welcomed, if not by the general reading public, at least by the audience that counts – the professional or university readership. The critique of realism has apparently carried the day in Academe.

My next task, and the business of this third part of the book, is to show that, even if the ideas of the radical critics of realism were actually true, they would still not justify the welcome that is given to most of the existing brands of anti-realism. Indeed, the kinds of texts that would survive the most fundamental criticisms of realism do not, and probably could not, exist. The connexion between victorious 'Theory' and current anti-realistic practice is not as clear, or as happy, as certain critics would have us believe. There is a certain amount of hypocrisy in the relationship between many critics' theoretical beliefs and their evaluation of individual authors.

Since the line of argument is not so clearly defined in these next three chapters, a map may be helpful. A brief discussion of the main types of anti-realism (7.1) is followed by the identification of whimsicality as an almost universal characteristic of anti-realistic fiction (7.2). Whimsy is not as exciting to read as it is to write and our examination of it takes us on to the first source of unhappiness in the relationship between theory and practice: the 'sharp descent' in the level of excitement when we move from advanced critical theory to the corresponding novelistic practice (7.3). This raises the suspicion that fictions able to meet the requirements of radical critics may not exist (7.4).

Settling for less, and special pleading that will enable the theory to be read into the practice (8.1) generate more problems than they solve. One can find any theory illustrated, anticipated, fulfilled or proved in almost any practice and this raises the spectre of 'the demise of evaluation' (8.2): Philippe Sollers may prove to be no more acceptable on theoretical grounds than inferior writers such as Gustave Flaubert and Arthur Hailey. The welcome some critics have given to the demise of evaluation is shown to be hypocritical. The crisis within literary criticism bodes ill for anti-realistic fiction because (unlike realistic fictions that can do their work without critical help) they are dependent upon critics to speak on their behalf, to explain what they are and what they are doing. This critical help however, is often self-defeating: the critic cannot advocate an anti-realistic novel without to some extent explaining it; and the process of mediating between text and reader 'recuperates' the text and so neutralizes its intended radical impact (8.3). Moreover, critical writing, which uses the old 'referential' modes of discourse, implicitly undermines the case against referential realism (8.4). So, too, does the contempt or patronizing concern many advanced critics display for the average (i.e. non-professional) reader (8.5). Certain critical postures and strategic re-definitions of the role of the critic may be traced to a desperate longing to be useful in a world which needs literary criticism even less than it needs literature (8.6).

Not all advanced critics are equally blind to the self-contradictions inherent in radical literary theory and critical practice. Some are able to recognize when a tactical retreat is called for. Under a fog of ambiguity about the scope of reference (9.1) – or rather non-reference – and with some radical re-drawing of the boundaries between realism and anti-realism (9.2), certain untenable positions may be abandoned without loss of face: theory bows out. Part III ends with a brief statement as to why a consistent anti-realistic fiction and an anti-realistic critical theory that genuinely answers to the radical notions mobilized in the attack on realism must be impossible. (9.3).

7

Anti-Realism in Practice

7.1 The Varieties of Anti-Realism

The house of anti-realistic fiction has many windows. There are, as Boyd has pointed out,[1] at least as many varieties of anti-realism as there are of realism. An encyclopaedic survey would, however, be tedious and not especially illuminating. For the present purposes, it will be sufficient to identify the major trends and to see how or whether they are justified by, or justify, the theories of advanced critics. It is not suggested that contemporary fiction is written to critical prescription though some critics feel that it should be.[2] Nor is it implied that the authors of certain anti-realistic novels have always been aware of the ideas that have prepared the way for the favourable reception of their books – though it has to be said that practitioners are increasingly also literary critics or literary theorists. The 'postmodern' novel often seems as if it has been written by academics for academics and is often about academics and even, explicitly as well as implicitly, about literary theory.

It is possible to draw up a rough list of trends in, or types of, anti-realistic fiction, placing them in ascending order of 'radicalness', according to the extent to which they deviate from realism:

(a) Deviant Details
Conventional narrative style and presentation of character but incorporating one or two anti-realistic details such as a protagonist who is 'fey' or an event, of symbolic importance, that is inexplicable in everyday terms. A sword, for example, may appear out of a perfectly ordinary lake.

(b) Deviant Worlds
Narrative style and method of presentation of character differ little from that of nineteenth-century realism, but the 'world' in which the events take place deviates, in important ways, from the world which the writer actually knows

[1] Michael Boyd, *The Reflexive Novel. Fiction as Critique* London and Toronto: Lewisburg Bucknell University Press, 1983, p. 19.
[2] For example: '. . . indeed the major lesson taught by the reflexive novel is the primacy of theory and, indeed, much postmodern fiction needs to catch up with postmodern criticism'. Boyd *op. cit.* p. 8.

and lives in. Animals are able to think like human beings; or the year is 3,000 AD so that men are able to fly without planes; or the universe is populated by six-inchers with gossamer wings. Science fiction (or – as those who recognize it that it has little to do with science like to call it – 'space fiction'),[3] animal fiction, some gothic fiction and 'realistic' fairy stories or magic realism, would fall into this category. Such novels aim to talk plausibly and coherently about an explicitly imaginary world.

(c) Deviant Tone
The manner in which characters speak, the linguistic register of descriptions, the transitions from one theme to another, are all at deliberate odds with the events narrated or the circumstances or nature of the characters or the content of what they are saying. A tramp rotting in the mud will discourse in scholarly pedantic English; a man dying in a hail of gunfire will blandly state the fact in plain English. Camp over-or under-statement, absurd precision amidst chaos, crazy innocence of observation – are different facets of this tonal deviancy.

(d) Unreal World
The events and characters are situated in a space whose laws do not conform to that of the world the writer or reader inhabits. This world – dream-like, discontinuous, dehumanized, etc – is implicitly a reflection of, or an allegory for, the 'unreal reality' (see Chapter 1) that comprises the actual world of the reader/writer. Coherence and plausibility are established only to be undermined.

(e) Unworld
The trends noted in (d) are more pronounced. In so far as there are identifiable events, they have no logical or causal relation to one another; in so far as there are characters they are not coherent individuals with predictable behavior or intelligible emotions. The umbrella gets itself ready to greet the sewing machine on the dissection table and the green horse in the pharmacy prepares to die of an overdose of curtains.

(f) Word Worlds
The novel no longer presents or projects a deviant world but remains resolutely and explicitly intra-linguistic. In the most timid examples, it does so by referring to itself and reminding the reader from time to time that he is reading a novel – that is to say that he is looking at words on a page that cannot gain access to an extra-linguistic reality. In the more daring cases, explicit fiction disintegrates to networks of allusion or word games. Ultimately,

---

[3] So-called 'science fiction' rarely contains science as scientists understand or practise it. Sometimes it is 'technology' fiction; more often it is limp semi-realistic fiction padded out with *Ripley's Believe It or Not* allusions to science.

reflexiveness is taken down from the genre to individual words. These words are intended to mean only their sounds and so do not reach outside of themselves to any referent other than language itself.

(g) Un

No characters, no stories, no temporal ordering of events, no syntactic ordering of sentences, no games, no allusions. The text fragments into sentences that do not apparently relate to one another. In the ultimate anti-realistic novel, the sentence itself falls apart and individual letters drift unmoored on the white spaces of the page. There may be an attempt to by-pass language altogether. This may mean silence (not easily published) or, as in the case of Artaud, screams (which do not easily lend themselves to novelistic presentation).

Clearly, anti-realism encompasses a multitude of fictional styles that do not always serve compatible ends. *A Glastonbury Romance* has very little in common with *How It Is*, *A Severed Head* with *Lois*, or *Tender Buttons* with *Shame*. Nevertheless, the very fact that they are anti-realistic, howsoever differently, means that they are liable to be viewed with advanced critical favour because they 'break with' the metaphysical or narrative conventions of the realistic novel. King Arthur's sword appearing out of the flood at the end of *A Glastonbury Romance* is at odds with the expectations of an ordinary person arriving in the West Country down the M5; and *How It Is* creates a fictional space that bears little or no relation to the world as it is ordered by the commonsense or everyday experience of anyone travelling down any motorway.

It will be evident that anti-realistic fictions corresponding to types (a) and (b) would not stand up to the criticisms advanced against realism. Such fictions still assume that there is an extra-linguistic reality and that language can gain access to it, that it can be expressed in stories. And this is true to a lesser extent of most fictions incorporating the features listed under (c) to (e). Only fictions of types (f) and (g) come anywhere near to possessing the required characteristics. It is doubtful whether any pure fictions of type (g) actually exist or, as we shall discuss, *could* exist. Nevertheless, current hostility to realism has created a climate of indiscriminate hospitality towards any mode of deviation from realistic narrative. Zany content and deviant form are treated with the same respect: the choice of an unborn child as one's narrator and the omission of punctuation are equally lauded as acts of rebellion against the tyranny of realism. Type (a) anti-realism is treated with the respect due to it if it were responding to radical criticisms that, at the very least, demand type (g) fiction. This is due in part to the fact (to be discussed in Chapter 8) that it is possible, if one is so inclined, to find any critical theory exemplified in almost any novelistic practice. The large ideas about language, politics, reality, consciousness and society that are deployed in the attack on realism do not provide a basis for discrimination between different styles of anti-realism or (more pertinently) different qualities of writing.

The discussion of realism and anti-realism is often clouded by the fact that the boundary between realism and anti-realism cannot be drawn sharply: it will depend, among other things, on how reality is experienced or what parts of reality are considered as appropriate to be described, or played with, in the novel. A realistic account of life amongst the 'sexual outlaws' of Greenwich Village may seem unrealistic to someone who has passed his years in rural England or rural Zimbabwe. This kind of argument provides a useful smoke-screen for critics trying to find advanced virtues in fiction they enjoy for shamefully old-fashioned reasons. Nevertheless, lines can be drawn: a talking animal falls on one side of the line, a talking human being on the other.

The classification given above suggests that there are 'degrees' of anti-realism. There are also degrees to which anti-realism is sustained. Many anti-realistic novels are only patchily so, incorporating popular anti-realistic mannerisms and tricks against a realistic or would-be realistic background. Sometimes this may because the writer can manage only anti-realistic arias against a background of realistic recitative, possibly because he feels only a faint commitment to anti-realism. John Fowles's *French Lieutenant's Woman* is a pertinent case here. For the first four-fifths of the novel, we are offered a brilliantly imagined realistic tale. And then there is a pause where the author, presenting himself as watching the sleeping protagonist, reflects on the fact that he is writing a novel and that he is hesitating over two possible endings. Fowles has taken on board the message of the new theoreticians of the novel: he has learned from them that a novel is an artefact, something someone has made up rather than a report on reality; but he can do no more than acknowledge this dutifully. More often, unstable anti-realism is more calculating than this. The novelist knows which side his bread is buttered on.

For the advantages of indulging in a bit of anti-realism are incalculable; at the very least, it enables the author to elude potential adverse critical evaluation. It is easier to see whether something is well written if it aims to be realistic; it can be checked for plausibility, for example. But if it 'subverts' its own narrative purposes, then the novelist is in a no-lose situation. Implausibility is no longer the sad result of incompetence but the outcome of an intention to transcend or eschew the conventional modes of competence. Since it is rarely possible to distinguish with confidence competent anti-realism from incompetent realism, deliberate implausibility from failed plausibility, a thousand varities of talentless vanity can flourish in the shade of the big ideas launched against realism. A vast quantity of second-order, opportunistic, trendy, fellow-travelling trash has been smuggled in under the shadow of those few (*very* few) works that honestly try to respond to the radical scepticism on the basis of which realism has been attacked.

I have not given examples corresponding to the trends in anti-realism for the reason that categorizing an individual work will depend on interpreting its intention. As I have noted already, it is possible to find almost any theory exemplified in almost any practice. This causes the more thoughtful crticis – those who think the radical thoughts rather than merely reciting or writing them – a certain amount of embarrassment. The description of any particular work will be influenced by the explanatory framework of ideas that justifies it. Now it may be unclear how much of the oddness of a particular novel is due to empirical deviation of the fictional world from the world in which the writer sits down to write and how much to purely stylistic innovation. An apparently causeless event, for example, may be the product of a style in which causal links are omitted or suppressed in order to create a certain tone of voice. Likewise, tonal deviation (a tramp rotting in a ditch discoursing with manic pedantry in pure scholarly English upon a lost text of Arnold Geulincx) may be interpreted as the product of an intention to subvert the established order, which associates erudition with social elevation, or to guy Academe, or to mock the metaphysical aspirations of man, or to illustrate the distance between signs and referents. The varieties of anti-realism are in part a reflection of the different ways in which a 'text' can be interpreted and the different ideas it can be credited with embodying or the different rebellions it can be seen to signal.

Nevertheless, it cannot be denied that the flight from realism has produced a wide spectrum of quite distinct literary styles, tones, attitudes and intentions. From the opaque texts of the post-Mallarmean novelists of the *Tel Quel* school (Blanchot, Sollers), to the mocking South Americans with their carnivals of words (Marquez, Asturias), from the cool poker-faced laughter, verbal pyrotechnics and heavy erudition of the American academic novel (Barthelme, Barth, etc.) to the derivative energies of the British anti-realistic scene (D.M. Thomas, B.S. Johnson), the anti-realistic novel seems to be vigorously alive. Whether it is anything else is another matter. Many believe that behind the energy and the laughter, the puckish pedantry and the elephantine erudition, there is anguish, visionary dissent, and/or a profound critique of language, literature and reality. Less gullible critics – armed, perhaps with the very scepticism that some of these admired novelists are credited with – might see only boredom with reality and, behind that boredom, a pathologically diminished imagination that is unable to find other people, the world, the life around it, worthy of investigation. The frantic 'verbal energy' and wild implausibility of many novelists could well be the result of a flight from the world and from a life in which they have no interest: reality bores so surreality lures.

In this investigation of the relationship between radical criticism and novelistic practice, I shall confine myself to a handful of 'paradigm' cases in which the relationship between theory and practice, between critic and author, or between critic and creator within the author, is especially clear-cut. Even these cases – Alain Robbe-Grillet, Raymond Roussel, Donald Barthelme – are touched on only insofar as they relate to my thesis and of these only Barthelme is given anything approaching an extended treatment. The choice of Barthelme is not arbitrary: if he did not exist, I should have had to have invented him. Of all contemporary practitioners, he is the supreme instance of a writer the apparent value of whose works depends almost exclusively on being viewed through the lens of theory. Before focusing on the whimsical Barthelme, however, it might be helpful to make one or two general comments about whimsy in anti-realism.

7.2 Among the Whimlings

The house of anti-realistic fiction has many windows; but beneath the surface variety there is monotony. Again and again, in works that are superficially very diverse, we meet up with the same feature: whimsy. Whimsicality is a thread linking many contrasting modes of anti-realism. It unites such widely differing writers as Raymond Roussel and Richard Brautigan, Flann O'Brien and Boris Vian, Gabriel Garcia Marquez and Samuel Beckett, Louis Aragon and Salman Rushdie – writers whom critics have, by an irony that has escaped some of them, taken very seriously indeed. Many novelists, for example Truman Capote or B.S. Johnson – are patchily whimsical. And others (John Fowles is a striking recent example) suddenly wake up in a cold sweat realizing that they have not kept up with the critical demand to go beyond realism and proceed to pen their own post-realistic fatuities.[4] Even apparently anti-whimsical writers such as Alain Robbe-Grillet like to tease the reader with whimsical self-contradictions (see Section 7.3).

While whimsicality was only one strain of anti-realistic writing in the Modern movement, it is almost the defining characteristic of contemporary anti-realism, in particular of American postmodern writing,[5] Philip Stevick[6] has noted the strong family resemblance between these opening passages of three contemporary American novels:

[4] The case of John Fowles seems especially tragic. He is a realizer of real worlds, a story-teller of immense talent. *The Collector*, a sustained imagining of two utterly different consciousnesses, is a masterpiece of realism. But *The French Lieutenant's Woman*, potentially a great realistic novel, is flawed by the alternative endings (cf. Sarraute, Borges, Pinget) offered to the reader. It appears that Fowles feels obliged to remind his readers that they are reading a novel. The reader is not so dim (though a thousand critics assume he is) and it is doubtful whether Fowles really has such a low opinion of his readers. The spoiling of *The French Lieutenant's Woman* seems more the result of the author's guilt at being insufficiently modern or postmodern than anxiety about the reader's too ready suspension of disbelief. His recent *Mantissa* could have been written only by someone in the grip of the theoreticians. A meditation on the act of literary creation, on the nature of the muse, endlessly whimsical, impeccably self-reflexive, etc., it is utterly tedious.

[5] 'Postmodern' has the ring of the salesman. One is reminded of the soap powder advertisement: 'whiter than white'. 'Modern' means 'pertaining to or originating in the current age or period . . . characteristic of the present and recent times' (Oxford English Dictionary). The attraction of 'postmodern' is presumably that it means *absolutely* the latest'. No surprise, then, that the term first gained wide currency in the land of the salesman where to speak is to sell and to sell is to hype.

[6] Philip Stevick, Scheherezade runs out of plots, goes on talking: the King, puzzled, listens: An Essay on New Fiction *Triquarterly*, 1973.

An aristocrat was riding down the street in his carriage. He ran over my father.

   After the ceremony I walked back to the city. I was trying to think of the reason my father had died. Then I remembered: he was run over by a carriage. (Donald Barthelme, *City Life*)

He was found lying dead near the television set on the front room floor of a small rented house in Los Angeles. My wife had gone to the store to get some ice cream. It was an early-in-the-night-just-a-few-blocks-away store. We were in an ice cream mood. The telephone rang. It was her brother to say that her father had died that afternoon. (Richard Brautigan, *The World War One Los Angeles Airplane*)

Paul stepped off the curb and got hit by a truck. He didn't know what it was that hit him first, but now, here on his back, under the truck, there could be no doubt. Is it me? he wondered. Have I walked the earth and come here? (Robert Coover, *A Pedestrian Accident*)

Thus a trend – or an epidemic. Stevick speaks of these beginnings showing 'an extraordinary innocence, either genuine or feigned'. He then describes them, unbelievably, as 'chilling' in their directness; and so he provides us with a spectacular example of a critic believing himself to have the feelings he would expect to have on theoretical grounds. He speaks also of the 'epistemic dislocation' these passages bring about – clearly reading back into them the theory he has brought to them. But what they actually instantiate, more than anything else, is – whimsy.

Increasingly, whimsicality is affecting, and infecting, the contemporary novel – form and content, tone and structure, the attitude of the writer to his work and the contract between the writer and the reader. For this reason, it would be worthwhile trying to capture the features of the whimsical writer; to construct an 'ideal type' in the Weberian sense. The wretched specimen that swims into view will give us some idea of how Grand Theory relates to practice.

Whimlings[7] refuse to be serious, to be tethered by reason or ball-and-chained by empirical probability or verifiable fact. They prefer caprice, fantasy, fancifulness, to 'stolid' plausibility, coherence and conformity to the probable. A whimling hits upon a tone of voice and allows that voice to pick its way across a world composed of whatever occurs to it as the pen writes and in whatever order it happens to occur. There is a highly advertised abdication of authorial control – chance or the unconscious dictates the work. Or at least there is a pretence of such abdication; for we must not forget that the whimling wants to be published as much as any other writer. He must therefore charm and amuse, as well as kid and possibly annoy, his readers. Nevertheless, he must pretend to innocence – his style, even when complex, adult matters are

---

[7] Whimling: 'A miserable, insignificant creature'. Oxford English Dictionary. The word is obsolete but the referent lives on.

under discussion, has a kind of Daisy Ashford innocence. The whimling is simply unaware of how amusing or astonishing he is. Or he must appear to be so. His naivety is, however, like his claim to pure improvisation, false: the bland statements of the extraordinary ('Yesterday my father died. Oh dear, how I wish I could remember his name'; 'The blue-veined silences of her smiling skies annoyed me a little'; 'Our talk in the ditch was seldom of topography') conceal a knowingness. The whimling likes to tease and his humour is as many-layered as an onion, his consciousness and self-consciousness receding from the reader in infinite regression.

The whimling is not concerned to get us to notice a piece of the world. His behaviour is essentially attention-seeking: having no world he wishes to reveal to us, no story he wishes to tell (no story that we would believe in anyway), he displays himself. The obstrusive brilliance of his thoughts and language is subordinated to no external purpose; the contrived (and sometimes laboured) frivolousness, the unremitting Arielity of his non-referential recits, makes us constantly aware of his work as a *work*, as *his* work, and so of him. He plays with language (an early sense of 'whim' was a play on words) and with ideas but does not really *use* either. He does not, for example, develop or apply or criticize ideas: to allude to them is enough (and for knowing allusion fourth-hand acquaintance is sufficient). For the whimling, a brilliant child dancing in the spotlight of an admiring gaze, wishes only to allude to himself. Thus the Ideal Type.

Why is the whimling tolerated? Why are his works so successful that others are encouraged to follow his example and experimental fiction is becoming increasingly identified with whimsicality? After all, in everyday life whimlings are unpleasant creatures. Being teased or kidded by a self-regarding knowingness is the kind of boring or annoying experience we would hope to have left behind us with our school days. Whimlings, how-ever, have theory on their side. For a start, they are the voice of the uncon-scious, of the repressed id; for both they and the unconscious are fond of puns and operate by random association. For this – and other weighty theoretical reasons – they have the power to 'enchant'.

> We are all familiar with the disconcerting effect of the proximity of extremes, or, quite simply, with the sudden vicinity of things that have no relation to each other; a mere act of enumeration that heaps them altogether has a power of enchantment all of its own . . .[8]

How does whimsicality fit in with the ideas that have been used to attack realism? How does it relate to the beliefs that reality is no longer realistic; that stories cannot be about reality (because they, or the language in which they are cast, are sealed off from extra-linguistic reality); that reality is intra-linguistic, so that all texts are inter-texts and society itself an infinite text; or that all discourse is politically compromised? The connexions are tenuous;

[8] Michel Foucault *The Order of Things* (London: Tavistock, 1970) p. xvi.

but in a world where thoughts are often alluded to but rarely thought through, a tenuous connexion is more than enough to give whimsicality the academic respectability it enjoys.

For example, whimsicality can be seen as 'the only valid response' to a world over which no one has any control, to a reality whose truth must be forever hidden, to a language whose meanings belong to itself rather than to its speakers. The whimling knows that he lacks the power to influence events, to gain access to the truth, even to control the meaning of his utterances. He therefore concludes (Socratic ironist that he is) that all he is left with is (possibly subversive) play. 'Man is only human when he plays', Marcuse informed the whimlings of the 60s and cited the prestigious authority of Schiller's *Letters on the Aesthetic Education of Man*.[9] The artist, who plays and plays all day – playing with ideas, playing upon words, playing with readers, playing on genres – must therefore be totally human. There is of course a difference between playing in the Schillerian sense and mucking about (as there is a difference between playing the piano and mucking about on it); but the idea of 'play' is sufficiently vague for the works of whimlings to be interpreted generously. The whimling is uniquely committed to play in a world of serious people; confronted with modern reality his sensitive mind can only crumble into (publishable and sometimes best-selling) whimsy. What else is there for him to do? He is not going to change the world – his language can hardly make it across to its own signifieds, never mind reaching (and moving) the hearts and minds of the people or blanching the red necks of the hawks in the Pentagon. All he can hope (and this hope lies hidden like the Hamlet sorrow in Coco-plated heart of the clown) is that his play may break the conceptual moulds (both senses) that have made this ghastly world possible. In the meantime, the important thing is not to be stupid enough to be serious in the way that serious people are.

There is genuine, as opposed to merely literary, laughter in the absurd contrast between the Ariclity of whimsical anti-realism and the gravity, profundity and obscurity of the theoretical ideas mobilized to justify it. This discrepancy was evident in one of the earliest and noisiest phases of the higher whimsy – French surrealism – and Barthelme and postmodern fiction may be regarded as the faint glow off the ashes of surrealism. For this reason, a brief glance at French surrealism is warranted.

The French surrealists combined art with 'direct action', writing with scandal. Manifestos connected poetry and novels with anarchic behaviour in the street and salons, in the theatre and the bistro, with the aim of astonishing and terrorizing all who were not surrealists, of awakening them perhaps to surreality. The moral and physical terrorism that marked the surrealist movement was intended (it was claimed) to undermine and possibly abolish bourgeois reality. There was a dream of transforming the world. Certainly it

---

[9] Quoted and discussed in the much quoted and much discussed *Eros and Civilisation* by Herbert Marcuse (London: Sphere, 1970). See chapter 9, 'The Aesthetic Dimension'.

brought to the fore the anger, the jeering, the hatred that may sometimes lie underneath the assumption of a child-like innocence, the mask of whimsicality.

The career of surrealism (curiously summarized by Roger Shattuck in the words 'love and laughter')[10] is interesting as well as, at times, nauseating. The Great Shock of the First World War, the collapse of certain belief systems and the birth of others, in particular the Marxist dream, the increasingly rapid transformation of the world by technology and the discovery by Freud of the genius of the unconscious may all have played their part in the emergence of surrealism. In practice, it seems to have originated out of the bullying and cruelty of the Dadaists and to have been in part inspired by the psychopath Jacques Vache. (His favourite trick was coming into a theatre threatening to fire at the audience – snigger, snigger – and he subsequently distinguished himself by murdering two of his friends.) It was fuelled by a series of self-publicists issuing a succession of hectoring manifestos marked by the most atrocious bragging and self-deflating and self-inflating pomposity:

> Laws, moralities, aesthetics have been created to make you respect fragile things. What is fragile should be broken. . . . Our heroes are the parricides . . . the anonymous criminals of common law, the refined perpetrators of sacrilege.[11]

And it was wound up by hype (ironical hype, but hype nonetheless)

> Buy, buy the damnation of your soul . . . here is the machine for capsizing your mind . . . here is where the kingdom of the instantaneous begins.[12]

The kingdom did not, of course, begin. The hope that chance would do the work of the imagination and that the self-promotion of those who allowed the unconscious to operate through them would transform random clusters of words so that they entrapped the spaces between the disparate meanings of their component parts rather than remaining merely mentally uninhabitable verbals clots was not fulfilled. As Shattuck, a favourable critic, admits, there is little you can do with the products of automatic writing; they 'usually present the same aspect of monotony and irrelevance' (*ibid*, p. 34).

The surrealists had no doctrines, Nadeau tells us, only certain values 'which they brandished like flags: omnipotence of the unconscious and its manifestations: dreams and automatic writing; and consequently the destruction of logic and everything based on it. Destruction also of religion, of morality, of the family, those straitjackets that kept man from living according to his desires' (*ibid*, p. 105). But he adds, 'their great illusion was to suppose that their enemies would collapse at the mere sound of their words or upon reading their writings. They still believed, according to Breton's

[10] Maurice Nadeau *The History of Surrealism* (trans. Richard Howard) Pelican 1973.
[11] Louis Aragon, quoted Nadeau *op. cit.* p. 53.
[12] Aragon, quoted Nadeau *History of Surrealism*, p. 41.

phrase, in the "omnipotence of thought" '. And they were, of course, proved wrong, most notably by the Second World War, where madmen greater than themselves and a collective madness greater than anything they could aspire to, set about destroying religion, morality and family, with a degree of success greater than they had ever imagined.

Surrealism fizzled out; but not before it had tried to take possession of the world of politics whose seriousness it tried both to mock and to share. Aragon (a not atypical and certainly a central figure) became a Stalinist, fellow-travelling with one of the most oppressive and unimaginative political regimes the world has ever seen, believing that he could harness the surrealist abolition of reality to the abolition of inequality and oppression. When the war broke out (real violence, real terror), Aragon showed himself to be an ordinary brave man and wrote patriotic verse. After the war, he resumed his political stupidity and was perhaps the last prominent French literary figure to wake up out of the Stalinst dream. A disrespect for reality does not conduce to political intelligence.[13] After the death of surrealism, its ghost lived on. In the 1960s it manifested itself in the feeble second-order stuff of Pop Culture and Pop Art and, most interestingly, in advertisements. What began in publicity ended as publicity. There is an especially intriguing aspect of this symmetrical trajectory. Breton's Second Surrealist Manifesto informed its readers that 'the simplest surrealistic act consists of going out into the street revolver in hand and firing at random into the crowd as often as possible'.[14]

[13] In the 'spirit of love and laughter' he wrote verses of incomparable banality which (such is the power of theory) are in print even now

> I sing the violent domination of the Proletariat
> over the bourgeoisie
> for the annihilation of this bourgeoisie
> for the total annihilation of this bourgeois . . .
> Death to those who endanger the October conquests
> Death to the saboteurs of the Five-year Plan
> Your turn Communist Youth . . .
> (Red Front, quoted Nadeau, *op. cit.* p. 316.).

The world had to wait for the speeches of Brezhnev's last years before again being offered such a feast for the mind and heart, such a combination of political insight, humane under-standing and historical sense, such immaculate verbal music.

Once one sees through the meta-hypocrisy of those whose constant cry is 'away with hypocrisy', it is difficult to feel anything other than ill-will. It is almost pleasing to recall that the promised 'abolition of reality' by the surrealists has had the expected outcome. Indeed, on the best evidence available – obituary columns – it is apparent that reality has abolished the surrealists. Those who pretended to want to 'destroy literature' – although, unlike 99.99 per cent of the world they lived by literature – have ended up where, perhaps, they secretly hoped to end: in the history of literature. They will not be there long. Soon it may not even be necessary to refer to them except for the sake of completeness.

[14] André Breton, *Second Surrealist Manifesto*, quoted Nadeau, *op. cit.* p. 57. Recently, surrealist techniques have been utilized to a considerable degree by cigarette advertisers charged with obscuring the relationship between cigarette smoking and death without breaking the law by suggesting that smoking promotes cardio-pulmonary health. To manu-facture and sell cigarettes is to create a slowed-down version of Breton's simplest surrealist act. Children are spared but, apart from this grave deficiency, the analogy is complete and the twee surrealism of the cigarette advertisers answers to the surrealist dream.

A few happy accidents – the occasional felicitous phrase or hint of a strik-ing thought – should not distract us from the fundamentally negative, indeed destructive, tendency of surrealism. Behind it was an inveterate dis-honesty and an abhorrent hypocrisy. This is captured in the contrast between their virulent grave-dancing hatred of 'the bourgeoisie', of the political and literary establishment, and their nauseously sentimental attitudes ('Love and Laughter') towards those whom they liked and admired – themselves, their friends, their lovers. Equally hypocritical was the way in which practitioners attributed the source of their 'works' to the anonymous unconscious but publicized and pushed them under the names that belonged to their con-scious selves. They despised literature and the literary establishment but fought hard – with each other as well as against the world – to establish themselves as literary figures. The history of surrealism is not that of an undifferentiated, nameless Id but of certain large posturing Egos.

As the dust settled down, one thing emerged very clearly: the contrast between the excitement of the theoretical manifestos and the unrelieved dullness of the works that resulted. The theory of nonsense is, in the long run, considerably more absorbing than nonsense itself – which must be why Maurice Nadeau's *History of Surrealism* concerns itself mainly with manifes-tos and quarrels rather than actual works. (We shall return to the 'sharp drop' in temperature produced by the move from theory to practice in the next section.)

The surrealists are dead but the central surrealist vice – the cultivation of whimsy – continues to flourish. A cynical explanation of the continuing attraction of whimsy lies readily to hand. To write without the constraints of plausibility is far less difficult – and hence less painful – than to operate within them. It is easier to invent any imaginary world than it is to imagine the actual one, to be fanciful rather than precise. 'When you're dry,' Apollinaire used to advise his friends, 'write anything, any sentence, and forge straight ahead' (André Billy, quoted in Nadeau, p. 94). Surrealism is dead but it won't lie down. Its posthumous life is most evident in postmodern fiction.

The postmodern whimling, however, is spared the task of astonishing or execrating the bourgeoisie and bringing about the revolution of conscious-ness. As a result of changes discussed in Chapter 1 of this book, reality has, we are to understand, already been abolished; or it has been unmasked as a linguistic construct; or it is unknowable so that 'artifice is the only available reality there is'.[15] There is little point any longer in trying to shock anyone. Even the bourgeoisie[16] hold nothing sacred, least of all Great Literature. (To hold something sacred, you have to have heard of it. Homer is unlikely to be over-rated in Twin Oaks, Ohio.) The people experiment with drugs (at least 10 million cocaine addicts in the States) and sex; they watch films rather than

---

15 Perry Meisel, quoted in Graff, *op. cit.* p. 62.
16 The bourgeoisie were once, like the barbarians in Cavafy's poem, 'a kind of solution'. Now, shocking but unshockable, they fail to deliver the outrage the wicked-child-artist needs so badly.

read books; and we now recognize that it is the agencies of oppressive govern-ments, rather than those who would liberate us from oppression, who tend to 'fire at random into the crowd'. At any rate, firing at random into a crowd no longer seems as progressive as it once did. Direct action might lead to irrita-tion but it is scarcely able to awaken. There is nothing left for the whimling to cause outrage with. Moreover, many of the theories have lost their gloss of newness: puns, dreams, the unconscious, etc. have camp rather than magical value. Freud is mainstream old hat; the only way to rehabilitate him is to do what Lacan did and render him incomprehensible.[17] The dream of trans-forming consciousness, or society, or both, allowing the unconscious to invade the daylit realm of the Ego has been replaced by more modest aims. The writer might subvert the genre in which he writes or bunny-hop mischievously around the incongruous *donnés* of ordinary life. Or he might mince about in front of the bemused reader. In any case, all that remains of the surrealist legacy is its central flaw: the dissociation between literary activity and respon-sibility: pure and futile play that may or may not have a message for busy Americans bent on profit, self-betterment and world domination – little drops of moonshine to stay the hurrying man.

The essential fault of surrealism, Wallace Stevens said, is that it invents without discovery. And 'eventually a wholly imaginary world is entirely without interest'. That 'eventually' comes very soon for those who are not taken in by the solemn, large ideas invoked to keep Ariel in flight;[18] or to make his brief hops seem like intercontinental travel. The postmodern successors of surrealism neither invent nor discover. They merely play with other people's inventions and discoveries. Their modes of writing are essentially parasitic. The reliance on whimsy permits their narratives to develop without the friction of reality slowing the unfolding of the text. This is of course exhilarating for a writer who finds it hard to *imagine* what he knows from daily experience, who cannot face the task of realizing on the page the world he is familiar with from his actual life. How much easier to say of a hero-ine – a Miss Lizard – that she has 'a slightly greenish face'[19] and leave it at that than to attempt to describe the appearance of a particular person in a cer-tain attitude in a specific light. How much easier it is to play tennis without the net. Or to play a round of golf on the moon where, as John Updike says, a chip shot will go for miles. Tempting for the writer but intolerable for the reader. The ache to escape from the empty spaces of free-wheeling discourse, from the vacuum of a knowing innocence that does not wish you to take anything seriously, from the endless labyrinth of tease, into the fresh air of 'illusionist' narrative referring to a real world, is overwhelming.

[17] See Raymond Tallis, *The Strange Case of Jacques L.* P.N. Review 14(4) 1987 pp. 23–6.

[18] A pose that is especially suspect in a writer who has achieved enormous fame in the grimly competitive American literary scene. Ariel has to do an awful lot of shouting to get his whispers heard – to sell his stories in a land of salesmen.

[19] 'Miss Lizzie' in *Sixty Stories*. (New York: Putnam, 1981)

The reason that life among the whimlings quickly becomes tedious is obvious. If authorial caprice is the only arbiter of the sequence of written events, if the choice of voice within a text, of sentences within the voice, of words within a sentence, is dictated by random association, then nothing in the text is of the slightest interest. The heroine has seven legs; she might just as well have had fourteen. The hero's death by exposure to the laughter of green eyes was unforeseen but occasioned no surprise because surprise presupposes a framework of expectation and that has long since been dismantled. Where the rules of the game are so lax, the outcome, while quite unpredictable, is scarcely something anyone could be bothered to predict. Once one abandons plausibility – of event, of character, of tone of voice – then everything becomes possible; but, precisely because of that, nothing is of interest. Take away the framework of expectancy and nothing is left but boredom. The tee-total rose that swopped puns with the bibulous door-stop did not amuse us; for the accident of association could have as well served up a flatulent daisy whose emissions flattened an entire town in the neighbourhood of a leopard composing a treatise on particle physics.

7.3 A Sharp Descent

The theory behind the rejection of realism is often very exciting – especially when bolstered by talk of the liberation (of language, of consciousness) from the constraints of plodding, conscientious, literal-minded realism. Alas, the practical consequences are not. The transition from fevered theory to exemplary text is almost invariably accompanied by a sharp drop in excitement. This anti-climax is almost as pervasive a feature of anti-realism as whimsy and for this reason is worthy of treatment in its own right.

The contrast between the richness of the theoretical cases advanced for it and the poverty of the achievements of anti-realism is felt particularly acutely when one is presented with the writings of a novelist who is an eloquent theoretician on his own behalf. Robbe-Grillet is such a writer and he furnishes us with one of the most remarkable examples of the sudden drop in temperature that may be experienced when one moves from theory to practice.

That Robbe-Grillet's practice is as dull as his theories are exciting is especially well demonstrated in the collection *Towards A New Novel*[20] where theory and practice are brought together in the same volume. In the attractively written and combative theoretical sections of this book, the reader is given thrilling promises. The 'real writer' (e.g. A. Robbe-Grillet) has 'nothing to say', only 'a manner of speaking'. He 'has to create a world' (i.e. write a book) 'out of nothing, out of dust' – for the real writer does not utilize the pre-packaged reality of the naive realists. He will not fall victim to the old myths of depth. When, for example, he introduces his hero, he will present

---

[20] Alain Robbe-Grillet, *Snapshot and Towards a New Novel*, trans. Barbara Wright (London: Calder & Boyars, 1965).

him stripped of all those things that are usually attributed to heroes (feelings, thoughts, beliefs) – for they prevent the hero from being truly *present*. Robbe-Grillet will also offer the same service to objects: recognizing (as his predecessors have not) that objects *exist* before they *signify*, he will present them free of anthropomorphic metaphors. The town will not 'nestle' at the foot of the hills: towns *are* before they *nestle* and hills do not have feet.

> The first impact of objects should be that of their *presence* and . . . this presence should continue to dominate, taking precedence over any explanatory theory which would attempt to imprison them in some system of reference whether it be sentimental, sociological, Freudian, metaphysical, or any other.

Objects and subjects will thus be liberated from the sentimentalizing gaze of so-called realists.

This stylistic revolution will, we are assured, have enormous implications: the real writer will even contribute to political revolution by virtue of his being 'fully aware of the current problems of his own language, convinced of their extreme importance and desirous of solving them from within'.

The excited reader turns to the performance: the texts that will show him what can and should be done by a real writer. He is offered three short prose passages: *Snapshots*. The first is a rather dull description of some people walking on a beach; the second is a rather dull description of some tailor's dummies in a shop; the third is a rather dull description of some people on an escalator. The reader's excitement ebbs. His critical sense returns. He begins to wonder whether M. Robbe-Grillet can really believe that a description from which all interest has been drained is objective in the sense of revealing objects in their pure presence. Of course it does not: the objects – tailor's dummies, bodies on an escalator, etc. – are presented to the reader as *examples*. And the prose in which they are presented serves not to disclose them in their pure, dehumanized presence, but to signify the kind of prose that M. Robbe-Grillet thinks might liberate objects from the prison of an anthropomorphic gaze. Moreover, approximately two minutes thought about 'the current problems of his own language' – or any problems of any language – from within or from without, would have shown him that it is not possible to write as if from outside of human consciousness. While it may be possible to write a description that is wholly without interest in the sense of being dull it is not possible to compose one that is wholly without interest in the sense of being utterly without any viewpoint. Language cannot be used to reveal objects in themselves but only objects viewed from within a consciousness that *makes sense* of them. Words do not, cannot, stand proxy for objects that materialize one or more of their senses.[21] 'The view from nowhere' is one of the regulative ideas of science and, if it is instantiated anywhere, it is in the

---

[21] The 'proxy' theory is discussed in chapter 4 of *Not Saussure*.

almost asemic formulae of the particle physicist. Elsewhere, it is a will o' the wisp.

It is disconcerting to discover that one finds something dull when there are such excellent theoretical reason for finding it exciting; it is hard not to believe that 'the music is better than it sounds'. The disappointed reader of the brief *Snapshots* may look further into Robbe-Grillet's work and then suffer the anguish of those who try to read the longer texts. He may attempt *Jealousy* and encounter the following beginning:

> Now the shadow of the column – the column which supports the south-west corner of the roof – divides the corresponding corner of the veranda into two equal parts. This veranda is a wide, covered gallery surrounding the house on three sides. Since its width is the same for the central portion as for the sides, the line of shadow cast by the column extends precisely to the corner of the house; but it stops there, for only the veranda flagstones are reached by the sun, which is still too high in the sky. The wooden walls of the house – that is, front and west gable-end – are still protected from the sun by the roof (common to the house proper and the terrace). So at this moment the shadow of the outer edge of the roof coincides exactly with the right-angle formed by the terrace and the two vertical surfaces of the corner of the house.[22]

Jealousy consists almost entirely of such interminable 'exact' descriptions. And this is the dominant feature of much of Robbe-Grillet's fiction. In some cases – for example *In the Labyrinth* – 'physical pandiculation' is compounded by a repetitiveness that sympathetic critics are always tempted to describe as 'hypnotic'.

Now it might be protested that Robbe-Grillet is a straw man. Far from representing a radical break with realism, he is the worst possible kind of realist – one for whom realism consists of a literal-minded copying of reality. In short, precisely the kind of novelist mocked by advanced critics. His novels are the reduction to absurdity of conscientious or 'secretarial' realism. One might be forgiven for thinking this; especially as Robbe-Grillet provides *In the Labyrinth* with a portentous preface in which he has this to say:

> . . . the reality here in question is strictly physical, that is to say has no allegorical significance. The reader should therefore see in it only the objects, the gestures, the words and events that are told, without seeking to give them either more or less meaning than they would have in his own life, or his own death.[23]

But this is where more theory comes to rescue the novels from the execration of the terminally bored reader. For all is not what it at first appears to be. The

[22] Alain Robbe-Grillet *Jealousy* trans. Richard Howard, (London: Calder 1960), p. 9.

[23] Alain Robbe-Grillet, preface to *In the Labyrinth*, trans. Christine Brooke-Rose (London: Calder & Boyars, 1967). I could have chosen many other examples from Robbe-Grillet. For example, this from *The House of Assignation* 'The door of the apartment is ajar, the apartment door is wide open, despite the late hour, the apartment door is closed' Trans. Richard Howard, p. 151.

surface of manic mimetic fidelity conceals more subtle intentions. Jonathan Culler tells us that in the opening paragraph of *In the Labyrinth*

> descriptions of the weather seem at first to establish a context ('outside it is raining') but when the next sentence introduces a contradiction ('outside the sun is shining') *we are forced to realize* the only reality in question is that of writing itself which . . . uses the concept of the world in order to display its own laws[24] (The italics are mine).

Culler's interpretation (which is shared by many other critics) strikes me as a misreading. For the second paragraph of the novel seems to suggest that the two sentences refer to different weather conditions that may prevail at different times outside as opposed to inside where the I 'is safe and sheltered'. But a critic who cannot get as far as the second paragraph of a novel written by Robbe-Grillet deserves sympathy rather than condemnation. But even if Culler's reading were upheld, it hardly seems plausible that the act of writing down two apparently contradictory statements should *force* the reader 'to realize that the only reality in question is that of writing itself'. Without appropriate critical guidance and support, the reader is more likely to imagine that there has been some mistake or that he is being taken for a ride.

It seems equally implausible that the 'famous' account of a tomato, which is described in the *The Erasers* first as perfect then as flawed, should have such a complex impact on the reader as Culler and other interpreters suggest. Apparently, it

> plays on the fact that this description at first appears to have a purely referential function, which is troubled when the writer introduces uncertainties and thus lifts our attention away from a supposed object to the process of writing itself (Culler, *ibid*, p. 193).

Is *this*, then, what Robbe-Grillet is about? Is this how he will solve, or at least explore 'the current problems of our language' and so, indirectly, make a contribution to the revolution? He takes a tomato (or possibly a turnip) at random and describes it at first as if it were saleable and then teases his readers by telling them that it isn't. Oh that every revolution could be so bloodlessly incited! Or so easily. For once the method has been established, it can presumably be practised by anyone at any time. To tear the mimetic contract to shreds, to subject the referential function of language to a radical critique and to undermine the foundations of bourgeois reality, all I have to do is to write :

THIS PAGE IS NOT ABOUT THE NOVELS OF ROBBE-GRILLET[25]

---

[24] Jonathan Culler, *Structuralist Poetics* (London: Routledge & Kegan Paul, 1975), p. 193.

[25] This is no exaggeration. Consider the long discussions prompted by Magritte's painting of a pipe, entitled *Ceci n'est pas une pipe.* Or the critical interest excited by Beckett's *Molloy* because its second part begins 'It is midnight. The rain is beating on the windows' and ends 'It was not midnight. It was not raining.' (London: Calder, 1973).

The disappointed reader, stupefied by Robbe-Grillet's fiction, despite its many anti-realistic virtues, maybe inclined to question whether a consistent anti-realism is possible. A moment's thought will show that it is only within the framework of a certain critical theory that contradictory statements about tomatoes and/or the weather count as a critique of referential language. In other words, in order to recognize that reference is under attack, the reader will require the aid of referential statements by the author or a sympathetic critic. Without such assistance, he would be more likely to grant such contradictions only 'the meaning that they would have in his own life, or his own death' – that is to say, not much meaning. And he might, not unreasonably, doubt whether it is all that easy to produce novels able to withstand the radical critique of language and literature that has brought realism into such critical disfavour. He might even question whether such novels do or even can exist and suspect that the kind of anti-realistic novel the critic talks about is nothing more than a twinkle in his eye. But this is to anticipate.

7.4 Does Anti-Realism Exist?

Few if any novels applauded for their anti-realism are sufficiently radical in their break with realism to justify the welcome they have received from radical critics. Of course many writers take shelter under the wide umbrella of profound ideas that owe their hospitality to their vagueness and their vagueness to their unimaginability. A post-Saussurean critique of language will not in fact favour explicit fictions larded with fables and myths, or bogged down in jokey self-reference, over even naive realism. The failure of language to reach outside of itself would not rationalize a preference for *Finnegans Wake* over *The Carpetbaggers*. And if meaning is rooted in language rather than experience, the reduction of the world to a pundemonium will not liberate the reader from the opposite belief – that language is usually used to express meanings that are at least in part extra-linguistic in origin. For puns have to use words that make sense and have reference in order to work. To appreciate the pun – and to appreciate that it is a pun – we must recognize the reference of the words – as the scholarly industry of Joycean exegesis makes clear. 'Prit prot paradrattto blunk' would not count as a pun – or as language drawing attention to itself – because it has neither reference nor meaning. Both *The Carpetbaggers* and *Finnegans Wake* are at least partially intelligible and seemingly to some extent 'about' something; and insofar as they are intelligible and referential and their intelligibility depends on their reference, each falls short of the requirement to be about nothing. The contamination of reference – what we might call, modifying Barthes – '*l'effet de référence*', is inescapable.

Short of total unintelligibility, an anti-realistic novel cannot claim even theoretical superiority over its realistic counterparts. Anti-realistic quirks of content (goblins, talking animals, the attribution of implausible feelings, location on some exotic planet) or of style (dead-pan amidst horrors, suppression of causal and temporal connecting links, the use of random words) hardly qualify as an adequate response to the supposed problem of the self-referring nature of language or help to persuade us that the way we talk about reality in everyday life may be of practical use but is quite divorced from reality itself. Moreover, few novelists seem able, or inclined, to sustain anti-realism for more than a page or two at a time, or to take it down to the level of the sentence. Just as the so-called alternative worlds that certain writers are supposed to create in their books are in fact largely made up of the familiar world with a few gratuitous and distracting inaccuracies thrown in, so most anti-realistic novels are conventional realistic novels spoiled by deliberate errors. The fabulists parasitize the contents, the logic and the language of everyday reality; and their invented worlds stand in relation to the real one as morse code stands to English and not as French stands in relation to English. In many cases, anti-realism involves taking over the superficial aspects of realistic description, its stalest and most cliché-ridden features, and subverting (or rather playing around with) them without subjecting them to any genuine critical scrutiny.

Consider what is expected of an anti-realistic text if it is to be above reproach:

(a) It should be free of all the usual trappings of realism: a plausible, coherent narrative with a beginning, a middle and an end; identifiable characters; and a unified narrative voice. The reader should not know who is speaking and should not be offered a position from which the narrated events – and hence reality and hence his own life – can be made intelligible.

(b) It should reflect the unreal nature of contemporary reality. Either by its form or in its content (if it *must* have content) it should show that reality is fantastical, discontinuous and no longer intelligible in terms of the large metaphysical or theological ideas.

(c) It should criticize, not collude in, the prevailing ideology; and since ideology is co-terminous with language and intelligibility, it should remain outside of language and be totally unintelligible.

(d) It should, nonetheless, reflect the dehumanized face of contemporary reality, presenting the decentred alienated subjects of a technologically based civilization. Its world should be primarily composed of objects and only secondarily of meanings.

(e) It should be self-reflexive to the point of infinite regression. It should refer to its own genre, to other texts, to other genres, to the manner in which it is constructed and to the fact that it is constructed.

(f) It should be non-referential. It should not be 'about' anything (except, possibly, itself). If it has an identifiable theme or referent, it should be concerned with the distance between the signifier and the signified, the gap between language and reality, between reference and meaning.

(g) It should be intransitive. It should be 'writable' but not 'readable' – offering the reader no meaning other than that which he himself has put into it. The reader, not the writer, should produce the meaning of the novel.

No fiction could meet all these requirements since they are in conflict. A text could not, for example, both reflect the nature of contemporary reality *and* be non-referential. Likewise, a novel composed of frozen signifiers cannot refer to itself and certainly cannot refer to its genre.

As well as being in conflict with one another, some of these requirements are also inachievable in themselves. A novel that set out to demonstrate the unreality of reality must presuppose a real world, of books, readers and publishers, to make that demonstration possible, and a real world in which unreal reality is mistakenly taken to be real. A novel that imposed no meaning upon the reader, or did not attempt to influence the meaning the reader read into it, would not be distinguishable from a series of squiggles on a page. The text resistant to interpretation, and free of ideology (which is co-terminous with intelligibility) could not be distinguished from a text written in Chinese being perused by a man with no knowledge of the language, or an English text as it presents itself to the bookworm eating it. A truly unintelligible novel could be identified as such only if its unintelligibility were recognized to have a specifically anti-realistic purpose; if, in other words, its unintelligibility were incomplete or rendered incomplete by the 'recuperative' activity of critics.

Is it rather unfair to expect a novel to meet all these requirements, especially as they do not emanate from a single critic? Perhaps it is, although it has to be pointed out that the welcome that certain novels receive is often rationalized by discerning incompatible virtues in them. We have already seen how Robbe-Grillet's novels somehow manage to be committed both to demonstrating that the presence of objects has primacy over their meaning and to overthrowing the assumption that writing is about anything other than the practice of writing. And Barthes praised Brecht's plays for their revolutionary potential and for demonstrating 'a certain distance between signifier and signified'[26] – an immensely difficult task, one would have thought (rather like – to borrow Saussure's metaphor – separating the front and the back of a sheet of paper), and hardly conducive to making 'revolutionary' statements about anything.

It is certainly not unfair to ask whether any novel meets any of the fundamental requirements of anti-realism – for these requirements have provided the sticks by which to beat realism. Or has a metaphysical hammer been used to crack a rather small aesthetic nut?

Gertrude Stein is one of the few writers who have attempted to take anti-realism down to the level of the sentence and to abandon the referential function of language. The result is predictably boring. Nevertheless, many of her works, some of the most radical of which were written nearly seventy years

---

[26] Barthes, quoted in Culler *Structuralist Poetics*, p. 104.

ago, make the 'experimental' anti-realistic fictions of the present day look stylistically reactionary. They are often also rather less economical than Stein was of means: it takes Thomas Pynchon nearly seven hundred pages to induce the coma that the earlier writer could bring about in a paragraph. Despite her commitment to anti-realism, however, Gertrude Stein often betrayed an uncertainty of purpose when she talked about her work. Although she would spend many nights, we are told, meditating on words and trying to expel from her mind the meanings and associations they normally have, she claimed, when asked the meaning of her famous line 'a rose is a rose is a rose', that 'in that line the rose is red for the first time in English poetry in a hundred years'. Leaving aside the fact that the rose could have been a white one (as I had imagined it) the point is that even this writer, dedicated to the non-referential use of the language, has a lingering wish to restore the pristine referentiality of words; or, indeed, may subscribe to a mimetic theory of language reminiscent of the sages of Laputa:

> Can't you see that when the language was new – as it was with Chaucer and Homer – the poet could use the name of a thing and the thing was really there?.[27]

In countless respects, this (though totally misguided) is preferable to the meta-fictional conceit of the American Academic novelists whose flight from realism yields a third-order stale literary self-consciousness. The staleness of such performances is not of course surprising. Those meta-fictions are not exposed to the critique of comparison with extra-linguistic reality; they are merely messages sent from one egocentric, self-congratulatory polymath (the writer) to another (the reader).

Some critics – more brazen or more honest depending whether one views them sympathetically or with hostility – are able to admit that the novels corresponding to the requirements laid down by their advanced ideas do not exist. One such critic was Roland Barthes. For Barthes, 'the ideal text' is 'the writerly text'. Such a text, 'unimpoverished by any constraint of representation' is 'a galaxy of signifiers, not a structure of signifieds'.[28] It does not impose upon the reader; it is utterly plural; its meanings are indefinite, innumerable. The reader can make of it what he likes. He is required to *participate* in the creation of its meaning and the work, giving full rein to the creativity implicit in the act of reading, effaces the author in favour of the reader. In so far as he exists, the author's act of writing is purely intransitive. The writer in the intransitive sense declines to be a producer of meanings for consumption by a less gifted reader. The writerly text has all the virtues and suggestive power of a Rorschach inkblot.

Now, for Foucault, the writerly text, which has been a long time coming, is already here – and in a big way:

---

[27] Gertrude Stein, quoted in the Editor's Foreword to *Look at at Me Now and Here I Am*, Writings and Lectures 1911–45 ed. Patricia Meyerowitz, (London: Penguin, 1971), p. 7.
[28] Roland Barthes, *S/Z*, trans. Richard Miller. (New York: Hill & Wang, 1974), p. 5.

literature becomes progressively more differentiated from the discourse of ideas, and encloses itself within a radical intransitivity . . . it breaks with the whole definition of genres and forms as adapted to an order of representation, and becomes merely a manifestation of a language which has no other law than that of affirming – in opposition to all other forms of discourse – its own precipitous existence; so there is nothing for it to do but to curve back in a perpetual return upon itself, as if its discourses could have no other content than the expression of its own form; it addresses itself to itself as a writing subjectivity or seeks to re-apprehend the essence of all literature in the movement that brought it into being; and thus all its threads converge upon the finest of points – singular, instantaneous, and yet absolutely universal – upon the simple act of writing. At the moment when language, as spoken and scattered words, becomes an object of knowledge, we see it reappearing in a strictly opposite modality: a silent, cautious deposition of words upon the whiteness of a piece of paper, where it can possess neither sound nor interlocutor, where it has nothing to say but itself, nothing to do but shine in the brightness of its being.[29]

The figure of the intransitive writer, of the *écrivain*, who produces intransitive works about nothing, was anticipated half a century ago in the pages of *Punch*:

> About 1928, in one of the three genuinely funny jokes that *Punch* has produced since the Great War, an intolerable youth is pictured informing his aunt that he intends to 'write'. 'And what are you gong to write about, dear?' asks the Aunt. 'My dear aunt' says the youth crushingly 'one doesn't write *about* anything, one just *writes*'.[30]

In point of fact, 'just writing' – 'ceding the initiative to language' 'silently depositing words upon the whiteness of the paper' where language does nothing 'but shine in the brightness of its being' – is not as easy as it sounds. The ideal text – a work that contributes nothing to the meaning that the reader 'extracts' from it – proves very elusive indeed. Barthes, despite his admiration for intransitive writers and writerly (as opposed to readerly) texts, is forced to admit, like the good honest fellow he is, that intransitive writers and writerly texts do not exist:

> There may be nothing to say about writerly texts. First of all, where can we find them? Certainly not in reading . . . : the writerly text is not a thing, we would have a hard time finding it in a book store. . . . The writerly is the novelistic without the novel, poetry without the poem, the essay without the dissertation, writing without style, production without the producer.[31]

---

[29] Michael Foucault, *The Order of Things* (London: Tavistock, 1970), pp. 299–300.
[30] George Orwell *The Collected Essays, Journals and Letters*, ed. Sonia Orwell and Ian Angus. Vol I: *An Age Like This* 1920–1940 (London: Penguin Books, 1970), p. 557.
[31] Barthes *op. cit.* p. 5.

This is a rather serious admission if one considers the importance of the writerly text in Barthes's scheme of things:

> For Barthes there is a great difference between literature which is merely 'readable' in our time (the classics) and that which is 'writable'. That which is writable is indispensable for us because it is our only defence against the old lies, the exhausted codes of our predecessors. That which is readable is then in some sense inimical, since it perpetuates all this nonsense.[32]

The unsympathetic reader may be reminded of the famous, brief piece by Beachcomber:

16 HORSES STUCK UP A CHIMNEY

The story corresponding to this startling headline has not yet been located.[33]

If one is sympathetic to Barthes's views, however, one might be tempted to argue that the 'ideal text' does not have to be written in order to exist: it is enough if it is read. Indeed, if the reader of the ideal text is to be the producer of its meaning – for the ideal text by definition frees him from servitude to the author, from the lowly status of the passive consumer of the readerly or classic text – it is preferable that it should *not* exist before the reader reads it. The reader should bring it into being – either by deliberate misreading of a readerly text (reading a realistic novel, for example, as if it were mere marks on the page; or reading the instructions on an Air-Fix kit as if it were a *chosiste* novel *chez* Robbe-Grillet); or by close attention to an absolutely blank sheet of paper. The ideal reader corresponding to the ideal text would be a *confabulator* – like those tragic patients with Korsakow's psychosis who, presented with an unmarked square of white paper, read it out fluently. At the very least, the *difference* between the readerly text and the writerly one – between *The Carpetbaggers* and *King Lear* at one end of the scale and, at the other, marks allowed to shine in the brightness of their being – should be due to nothing other than the productive activity of the reader.

It is easy to mock Barthes's and Foucault's ideas but that – as someone once said – is insufficient reason for refraining from doing so. For it is unfair to attack realism in the name of an alternative that does not exist; and the writerly text, like other ideal anti-realistic works, does not exist. Anti-realism or consistent anti-realism does not exist because it could not exist. The truly anti-realistic novel would be unintelligible and therefore unrecognizable as a novel: language entirely committed to demonstrating the self-referentiality of language or to highlighting the distance between signifier and signified

---

32 Robert Scholes *Structuralism in Literature. An Introduction* (New Haven: Yale University Press, 1974), pp. 150–1.

33 Alas, I have not been able to locate the story in Beachcomber's *oeuvre*. Beachcomber anticipated much of modern literary theory; and, in the person of Professor Strabismus of Utrecht (Whom God Preserve), several literary theorists.

would simply be unrecognizable as language. A text that ceased to be a communication emanating from a writer and received by reader would simply cease to be a text. The very process of being recognized as a novel, or even as a piece of language, must undermine the radical-anti-realism of the ideal text. Those few texts that do seem to come near to corresponding to the radical critique of realism do so only with the help of the explanations and advocacy of advanced critics; and this help (as we shall discuss in Chapter 8) is inevitably fatal.

There are two ploys open to the advanced critic who finds that the story corresponding to his startling ideas has not yet been located. He can either settle for less and exaggerate the revolutionary nature of the works he admires; or he can make a determined effort to find his theory in the practice of those writers with whom he feels sympathetic or whom he considers he ought to support. Either of these moves increases the importance of the critic in the republic of letters – hence the title of the next chapter: 'Foregrounding the Critic'.

8

Foregrounding the Critic

We live in a golden age of criticism. The dominant mode of literary expression in the late twentieth century is not poetry, fiction, drama, film, but criticism and theory. By 'dominant' I do not mean 'most popular' or 'widely respected', or 'authoritative', but 'advanced', 'emergent'.[1]

Introduction

If, as seems to be the case, a consistently anti-realistic novel – one able, for example, to shed all explicit and implicit reference to the real world – does not exist, how is the rumour of its existence kept alive? Quite simply, by critics indulging their most characteristic vice: exaggeration. 'Anti-realistic' is, on most of the occasions of its use, a term of the grossest exaggeration. This exaggeration, whose aim is to indicate that a 'revolution' has been effected in the republic of letters by anti-realistic writers, depends upon misrepresenting both realistic and anti-realistic fiction.

The first move is to lampoon realistic novels, implying that realism, or the aim of realism, is to present a remorseless accumulation of facts about situations, persons and events. Realism is presented as 'secretarial' (to use Barthes's phrase) or as 'conscientious'. Serious realistic novelists are literal-minded, slaves to the notebook, anachronistically trying to do for the 1980's what Balzac did for the early, or Zola did for the late, nineteenth century, and in hopeless competition with the cinema.

The second move is to exaggerate the extent to which novels classified as anti-realistic deviate from realism. The gratuitous alteration of a few details of the 'real' world is often counted as sufficient to establish an anti-reality. A writer fond of whimsy or word games is credited with having constructed an 'alternative reality' or 'a world all of his own'. The introduction of a wise-cracking goblin into the cast of characters, a fusillade of puns, the elaboration of a fanciful idea, are not infrequently regarded as sufficient to 'subvert' everyday reality or to create another reality to rival it. But 'alternative worlds' are not so easily made – as is obvious to anyone other than a critic desperate

[1] W.J.T. Mitchell, *The Golden Age of Criticism*, London Review of Books 9(12) 25 June, 1987, pp. 15–18.

to believe in the revolutionary impact of a novel that seems to conform, however slightly, to precepts that are connected, however remotely, with his muddled ideas about the relationship between language, contemporary reality and narrative.

Ironically, it is often hard-line anti-realists who are most susceptible to the virtues of old-fashioned realism. They are willing to forgive 'conservatism' if there is manifest falsification at the empirical level. Gothic romances and Space fictions are so attractive on account of their deviant content that critics are willing to overlook a style that is non-experimental to the point of being sub-literary. The more remote the so-called alternative world, the more it apes the metaphysical profundity of *Star Trek*, the more tyrannous nineteenth century narrative assumptions are allowed to be. (This has been expressed more politely by Yuri Lotman: 'The freer the paradigmatic axis, the more rigid the syntagmatic, and vice versa') Alternatively, novels whose overt purpose is to 'subvert' earlier modes by arch or knowing references are permitted to be mediocre in terms of the old-fashioned realistic virtues to a degree that is nothing short of remarkable. The writer may have negligible perceptiveness or the descriptive powers and the linguistic energy of a remedial-class essayist and yet, on account of an aestheticizing camp narcissism, be treated to lavish praise. And how many novels are credited with a 'deadpan' style when in fact they are merely unobservant, insensitive and inertly written? Distracting absurdities provide an invaluable smoke-screen. Moreover, if a fiction is stuffed with outworn myths and/or anachronistic 'symbolic' events – for something, after all has to fill the emptiness when a writer breaks with 'so-called' reality – this is fine, so long as the resultant text is sufficiently advanced to make it clear that its author doesn't believe in any of the myths or symbolic happenings; so long, that is, as it wears its 'fictiveness' on its sleeve. Indeed, the presence of explicit (i.e. not-believed) myth is credited with being a challenge to the myths implicit in the reality so uncritically replicated by conventional realism.

In short, a little bit of anti-realism goes a long way. A man who introduces a goblin into the kitchenette of a semi-detached house is so obviously alert to the fact that realism is *passé* that the right-thinking critic is at once disarmed. He need not fear that *this* writer is a brain-washed servant of the consensus and of the forces that legitimate contemporary political reality. Indeed, if he has established his credentials by writing about goblins, he can even be forgiven for attempting *l'effet de réel* and the critic can flex some of his old pre-post-modern muscles: 'the goblin Sergei is wonderfully realized' etc. For as long as a novel doesn't look as if it were intended to be plausible, then anything, even a bit of realism, is permitted.

8.1 Hope out of Hype: Finding the theory in the practice

It is time to get down to cases. The choice is, of course, overwhelming. Most of the varieties of anti-realism described in Section 7.1 have numerous exemplars, though types (g) (Word Worlds) and (h) (Un) are less popular. There is little point in discussing a large number of writers to whom the same observations apply to varying degrees. Better, instead, to examine in detail a single paradigm case. One writer whose critical reception may be explained almost entirely by the need for critics to find something answering to the radical ideas directed against realism is Donald Barthelme. If Barthelme did not exist, I should have had to have invented him.

Philip Stevick, a leading American critic of fiction, tells us that Barthelme's stories 'stand as touchstones for narrative art of the last two decades'.[2] And Durand and Couturier,[3] (of whom more later) assert that 'for many readers interested in the experiments of modern fiction, Donald Barthelme is the great example of American new fictional enquiry'. Consider these extracts from the collection *Great Days*, described on its publication as 'an important addition to an already impressive body of work'.

> I was sitting in my brand-new Butler building, surrounded by steel of high quality folded at ninety-degree angles. The only thing prettier than ladies is an I-beam painted bright yellow. I told 'em I wanted a big door. A big door in front where a girl could hide her car if she wanted to evade the gaze of her husband the rat-poison salesman. You ever been out with a rat-poison salesman? They are fine fellows with little red eyes.[4]

> Mr White drew forth his pistol and shot Mr Lynch dead with it.
> 'Good Lord! He is dead!' cried Mrs Teach. Dr Balfour knelt over the body. 'Yes he is dead' he said. All assisted the Doctor in placing the carcase on the sofa.
> 'There is but one more card on the vase' said Mrs Teach, peering at the article in question. 'Dare we look at it?'
> Yes, yes' was the answer, in a subdued murmur.[5]

> – What did you do today?
> – Went to the grocery store and Xeroxed a box of English muffins, two

[2] Philip Stevick, quoted on the blurb of Donald Barthelme, *Great Days*, (New York: Farrer Straus & Giroux, 1979).

[3] Maurice Couturier and Regis Durand, *Donald Barthelme*, (London: Methuen, 1981). And who are these readers interested in the experiments of modern fiction? Many of them are professional or (to use Gore Vidal's term) 'involuntary' readers, such as students. The symbiosis between writer and critic is thus a very close one: the writer survives through finding a place on a course, his works counting as key texts though they are ignored by common readers; the critic ensures his own survival by favouring texts that require critical exegesis. It would be only a small exaggeration to say that the syllabus, rather than the open market of the book trade, was the economic space of postmodernism.

[4] The Abduction from the Seraglio in Great Days.

[5] The Question Party in Great Days.

pounds of ground veal and an apple. In flagrant violation of the Copy-
right Act.
– You had your nap, I remember that –
– I had my nap.
– Lunch, I remember that, slept with Susie after lunch, then your nap,
woke up, right?, went Xeroxing, right? read a book, not a whole book but
a part of a book – [6]

etc. etc.

Voices from the grave of surrealism: false naivety ('the only thing prettier
than ladies is an I-beam' etc); absurdity (a card game continued over the dead
body of a participant who has just been shot); impossibility (a box of English
muffins is xeroxed); inconsequentiality (I-beam, ladies, husbands, rat-poison
salesmen); and faint humour (rat-poison salesmen have rats' little red eyes).
Whimsy, whimsy, whimsy; and the faint smile of the reader of the first of
Barthelme's collected *Sixty Stories*[7] will have stiffened into a corpse-like
rictus long before he gets anywhere near the sixtieth.

Barthelme's stories never allow you to forget their author. Like a
precocious child, he is always before us, as he plays with this and subverts
that, echoes here and alludes there – and all in the service of an emptiness
that has only its its impeccable theoretical credentials to distinguish its calcu-
lated 'child-like vision' (the usual term of praise) from dull childishness. The
tone of this warmed-over surrealism is very similar to that of the original stuff:

> We hung a woman on the ceiling of an empty room, and every day
> received visits from anxious men bearing heavy secrets. This was how
> we came to know Georges Bessiere, like a blow of the fist. We were
> working at a task enigmatic to ourselves, in front of a volume of
> Fantomas, fastened to the wall by forks. The visitors, born under remote
> stars or next door, helped elaborate this formidable machine for killing
> what is in order to fulfil what is not. At number 15, Rue de Grenelle, we
> opened a romantic Inn for unclassifiable ideas and continuing revolts.
> All that still remained of hope in this despairing universe would turn its
> last, raving glances towards our pathetic stall. It was a question of
> formulating a new declaration of the rights of man.[8]

It is difficult to believe that Barthelme's work was not conceived in the
romantic Inn for unclassifiable ideas or that it was not composed according to
the following method:

> Have someone bring you writing materials after getting settled in a place
> as favourable as possible to your mind's concentration on itself. Put
> yourself in the most passive, or receptive, state you can. Forget about
> your genius, your talents, and those of everyone else . . . Write quickly

6 The New Music in Great Days.
7 Donald Barthelme, *Sixty Stories* op. cit.
8 Louis Aragon, quoted in Maurice Nadeau, *The History of Surrealism* trans. by Richard
   Howard, (London: Penguin, 1973), p. 99–100.

without a preconceived subject, fast enough not to remember and not to be tempted to read over what you have written. The first sentence will come all by itself . . . It is rather difficult to make a decision about the next . . . But it shouldn't matter to you anyway. Continue as long as you like. If silence threatens to take over, you have made a mistake.[9]

It is obvious why an author should be attracted to automatic writing: it solves the problem of knowing what to say. 'Endings' one of Barthelme's characters tells us 'are elusive, middles are nowhere to be found, but worst of all is to begin, to begin, to begin . . .' It is less obvious what a reader is supposed to do with the results. For some critics, the reader's uncertainty as to the purpose or even the value of the work is an essential part of the postmodern experience. It is questionable, however, whether such uncertainty is intrinsically valuable. Is not knowing whether to read on or to throw a story out of the window important or useful? Is it any different from not knowing whether to switch off, or to continue watching, a quiz programme? If it is no different, the question then arises as to why critics do not turn their attention to these programmes. It may seem absurd to ask this question but the very pointlessness of some of Barthelme's stories is one of his many weaknesses that are interpreted as strengths by sympathetic critics.

The praise Barthelme has received from critics is not entirely underserved. For he has one faculty in abundance: an absolute pitch for linguistic register. For a whimling, this is invaluable; since it permits him to create, rather as Beckett does, dissonances – between tone and content, between character and utterance, or within the discourses of a single character – that are momentarily amusing and even sometimes charming. Nevertheless, it has to be said that he is inferior in this respect to A.A. Milne, whom no one has yet claimed for post-modernism.

What of Barthelme's relationship to the advanced critics and their ideas? Consider this much quoted passage from his widely praised 'novel' *Snow White*:

> 'Try to be a man about whom nothing is known' our father said, when we were young. Our father said several other interesting things, but we have forgotten what they were. . . . Our father was a man about whom nothing was known. Nothing is known about him still. He gave us the recipes. He was not very interesting. A tree is more interesting. A suitcase is more interesting. A canned good is more interesting.[10]

Confronted with this passage, it is easy to see how it might be received by a sympathetic critic. He would look straight past the surface fatuity and

---

[9] Nadeau, *op. cit.*p. 97–8. We are reminded of Winnie the Pooh's thoughts on the same matter: 'Poetry and hums aren't things which you get, they're things which get *you*. And all you can do is to go where they can find you' A.A. Milne, *The House at Pooh Corner* (London: Methuen, 1928), p. 144.

[10] Donald Barthelme, *Snow White* (London: Jonathan Cape, 1968).

inconsequence, past the smirk of a man who is 'kidding along', to an impeccable modernism or postmodernism.

1 Reality is no longer realistic, so this text is laudably unrealistic.
2 All plausible stories are artefacts, so this piece must be praised for wearing its artefactual status on its sleeve. Temporo-causal sequences are also artefacts, so its evident inconsequentiality must be welcomed.
3 The apparent intelligibility of 'reality' is the product of an ideology concerned to create subjects who will co-operate without protest in the process of reproducing the means of production. This passage, which denies the reader a stable viewpoint from which he can understand it – he doesn't know what attitude to take – will undermine the historically derived intelligibility, the reality, of 'the real'.
4 In parodying Henry James's advice to authors – to be someone 'on whom nothing is lost' – the passage reminds the reader that literature is not about the world but about other literature.[11]
5 Finally, it is obvious that the text is about nothing other than language itself. 'A canned good', for example, is a phrase that draws attention to the signs of language by treating a mass noun as if it were a count noun. It is commendably 'post-Saussurean'.

All in all, an exemplary passage.
Is this a grotesque and unfair parody of the modern critical way with favoured texts? By no means. A passing acquaintance with the critical literature on American postmodern fiction will confirm that I have by no means exaggerated the lengths to which critics are willing to go in order to find theoretical justification for the *jeux d'esprit* they admire. That the higher whimsy can occasion the wildest academic hype is well illustrated in the recent book on Barthelme by Maurice Couturier and Regis Durand. Couturier quotes a few lines from *The Piano Player*, one of the sixty stories in Barthelme's *Sixty Stories*:

> 'You're supposed to be curing a ham'.
> 'The ham died', she said. 'I couldn't cure it'.

He comments that such 'acts of linguistic vandalism . . . contribute to changing our representation of reality in a drastic way'.[12] This will come as

---

[11] Gerald Graff devotes nearly three pages to the Jamesian echoes of the passage. 'Barthelme inverts the assumptions about character, psychology and the authority of the artist upon which James, the "father" of the "modernist" recipe for the novel, had depended' he begins and then proceeds to a portentous analysis of the relationship between Barthelme and James and between modernism and postmodernism. (Gerald Graff, The Myth of the Postmodernist Breakthrough, *TriQuarterly*, 1973). Interestingly, Graff does this in the course of an essay that is largely hostile to the claims of postmodernism. Moreover, he notes in passing the contrast between James's 'earnest dedication to his craft' and Barthelme', 'irreverent stance towards his own work'. Presumably Barthelme's flippancy is just something else for the critic to take seriously.
[12] quoted in Couturier and Durand, *op. cit.* p. 12

something of a surprise to anyone who remembers having been at school where 'acts of linguistic vandalism' are commonplace. Little do children know that when they crack such jokes as 'Two girls went for a tramp in the woods. He died', they are dramatically changing 'our' representation of reality. Couturier must have a very labile 'representation of reality' – whatever this may be – for he tells us that this passage:

> The world is sagging, snagging, scaling, spalling, pilling, pinging, pitting, warping, checking, fading, chipping, cracking, yellowing, leaking, staling, shrinking, and in dynamic unbalance[13]

'does not simply portray a changing world' but 'also helps to change it . . . by assaulting it with multiple words and unheard of phrases'. It is, to put it mildly, difficult to believe this claim. Leaving aside that Barthelme's works are praised elsewhere for non-reference to reality (see below) – so that it is difficult to see how they could be 'about' the world, never mind able to change it – one would have thought such a vulnerability to metaphysical upset would scarcely be compatible with life. A more credible interpretation of the passage is that it is a bit of doodling; at any rate, it suggests a writer who has nothing to say but nonetheless continues to write down words at random while that nothing occurs to him. This view, though harsh and cynical, is certainly less harsh and cynical than what Couturier and Durand have to say about society as a whole (*vide infra*) and a sight more plausible than their claimed response to the passage:

> He gives the impression that reality has lost its power to force words upon him and his characters, that language is at last free from it and constitutes a private world where everything is possible at any moment.[14]

'A private world where everything is possible at any moment' sounds like a revival of the kingdom of the instantaneous in the Romantic Inn for unclassifiable ideas. Barthelme's references to nightingales flying by with traffic lights stuck to their legs and to pianos which strike people dead strongly suggest ye olde automatic writing. But we are offered something much more advanced. In Barthelme's hands, the modern novel has become 'a laboratory of discourse'. For he is a 'post-Saussurean writer'; he has spotted something very big that writers have overlooked since the first calloused hand clutched the first reed:

> Until the middle of the twentieth century, western writers generally considered language as an instrument, a vehicle by which to convey their original ideas and stored up images . . . Now this theory has been emphatically rejected.[15]

[13] *op. cit.* p. 22
[14] *op. cit.* p. 54
[15] *op. cit.* p. 35.

What is 'at stake' in Barthelme's prose is 'a radical questioning of the symbolic process itself'. In particular, Barthelme

> loses confidence in signs, having realized what we would call their arbitrary nature and their liability to being manipulated.[16]

Barthelme's 'major discovery', however, is 'that our culture and society are based on illusion and lies'. How clever of him to have noticed that and how fortunate we are to be living in a time when there is someone around to stop us from overlooking it. One would, of course, be interested to know when he made this discovery, whether or not he reported it to the authorities and how he got round the Paradox of the Theban Liar.

In case the unsympathetic reader might be inclined to complain that Barthelme's stories are inconsequential – just bits of prose that peter out – our critics are at pains to point out that this apparent weakness is a strength: 'To read Barthelme is to experience the power and strangeness of fragmentation'. The hidden might of bits, perhaps.

The genuflections of Messieurs Couturier and Durand before the slender talents of Mr Barthelme are grotesque but not exceptional instances of academic hype. Academic hyping is an endemic disease of partisan critics. Their confidence – and others' confidence in their judgements – depends on their failure to reflect on the fact that it is possible to find anything in anything. They are as innocent of the invalidity of *a posteriori coding* as the Fundamentalist who comes round to my door telling me that AIDS was predicted in Revelation Chapter 16, Verse 12 or the schizophrenic patient who sees the number of the bus he must catch written in the patterns of flowers in his hedge.

If we grant Barthelme the status of a great revolutionary novelist and short-story writer, of a 'post-Saussurean' prose artist, then we may be obliged to make room for some unexpected names in the postmodern cannon. A.A. Milne's *Winnie the Pooh*, for example, must count as a pathbreaking work. Milne is a grandmaster when it comes to playing with dissonant linguistic registers. He constantly draws attention to language and plays with words, and his stories are full of jokey self-reference. Moreover, the reader is denied a stable viewpoint from which he can make sense of Winnie and his friends. What, after all, is Pooh? A bear? A toy bear? A projection of Christopher Robin's nursery consciousness? Any of these interpretations is possible but none is consistently supported. Or, if *Winnie the Pooh* is too obvious an exemplar of all the postmodern, indeed post-Saussurean, virtues, consider this excerpt from another (comparatively modern) writer, many of whose techniques anticipate Barthelme's stylistic innovations in 'the laboratory of discourse'. (Mike, Rex and Bert are steam railway engines.)

---

[16] *op. cit.* p. 22.

> The engines were being cleaned and polished for the day. Bert, who was going out first, had a tall chimney in his funnel to draw up his fire.
>
> 'We've got visitors today', said his driver. Rex yawned.
>
> 'We have 'em everyday', grunted Mike.
>
> 'But these are special', said his driver. 'One takes "moving pictures" and the other writes books. So mind you all behave'.
>
> 'I don't want to be a moving picture in a book', protested Bert, 'I want to stay as I am'.[17]

The clean-cut, style is reminiscent of Barthelme but, as in the case of that writer, the surface naivety is belied by underlying sophistication. There is, of course, a total break with realism. Railway engines do not talk; and they certainly do not, like Rex in the above passage, yawn. The attribution of emotions such as boredom to machines is unsettling, denying the reader a stable viewpoint on these 'characters'. Its purpose is to subvert the 'mechanical' attribution of feelings and experiences to selves in classic realism. The metal engines are parodies of the rigidly ordered thing-like inner selves portrayed in those realistic novels Robbe-Grillet rebelled against. The critique of realism, however, goes much deeper than this; for the story is self-reflexive to an almost vertiginous degree. This is worthy of further examination.

The visitors, we are told, were 'clergymen, one fat, the other thin'. The reader familiar with Rev. W. Awdrey's tales will be able to deduce from this and from evidence given elsewhere that 'the thin clergyman' is none other than the 'author', i.e. the Rev. W. Awdrey. If one accepts the notion of the author (or Author) as origin of 'his' works, we may think of Awdrey as the progenitor of the very Rex who yawned at the prospect of meeting him and of Bert who rebels at the thought of becoming 'a moving picture in a book'.[18] We thus have a quasi-Russellian paradox of characters rebelling against the person who has created the fictive space in which they have their verbal being.[19]

Bert's indirect reference to Awdrey, therefore, is more than a piece of sly dramatic irony: it is nothing less than a frontal attack on illusionism. For it draws attention to the essentially self-referring nature of fiction. The story every narrative tells is the drama of its own creation. But the implications of Rex's boredom with his author go deeper still: beneath the surface humour we sense the inescapable contradictions of the written. Yawning Rex (and protesting Bert) *embody* its warring significations. A text is a play of differences,

---

[17] Rev. W. Awdrey, *Small Railway Engines*, Kay & Ward, London, 1967, p. 18.

[18] A further twist of the knife: insofar as Bert *is* a picture in a book, he is a still picture; but he is also a moving picture in the sense of being a picture that engages our attention and hence (though we know he is only signifiers or dots of coloured print on a page) our emotions.

[19] The fact that Mr. Awdrey (the 'Author') is a clergyman opens up a theological dimension, pointing to the analogy between the relationship the author has with his characters and that between God and 'real' individuals in a 'real' world. This interpretation, however, depends upon the existential accident of Awdrey's being both an author and a clergyman and for this reason may be suspect.

that is to say of non-presence[20] and the essence of writing (and so of all discourse) is the *absence* of the producer of the linguistic signs. In *Small Railway Engines*, however, the author is explicitly referred to and, by operation of the referential illusion, he is implicitly in the same space as his characters. This implicit presence becomes explicit when, a few pages on, Mr. Awdrey actually *enters the action*:

> Wherever the [railway] line came near the road . . . there the two clergymen were, squinting into their cameras.
> Bert found this rather upsetting. 'They might wave at an engine' he complained.
> 'They can't wave *and* get good pictures', said his driver; but Bert didn't understand. He thought they were being unfriendly.[21]

Worse is to come. The next time the 'clergymen' pass Bert, their car sends a shower of muddy water all over him. The author, that is to say, splashes one of his characters with mud. An obvious interpretation lies to hand: mud is undifferentiated matter, that inexpressible residue of reality, Lacan's Real, which lies beyond the page and, indeed, beyond discourse. An alternative interpretation may, however, offer itself to the reader who has appreciated the implications of an author's transgressing the boundary, at once grammatical and ontological, separating him from his characters. Under this interpretation, mud stands for the inarticulable silence eroding the smooth surface of the text, for the unconscious of the author who is caught up, as any writer must be, in the unconscious of the viewpoint from which he is writing. The impact of this episode is heightened by the tension between the story-relative existence of the fictional Bert and the 'real' existence of Mr. Awdrey who, except insofar as he lets himself into the fictive space of his story, transcends it. Here, as elsewhere, the reader is denied a viewpoint from which to make coherent sense of the literal mud-slinging episode and the metaphorical (and metaphysical) mud-slinging that follows.

The ironies are multiplied and the tension further heightened by the pictures that accompany the story. The illustrations seem at first merely to serve the text. But it soon becomes clear that they are there primarily to escalate the battle of its warring significations and that ultimately they will be decisive to the text's work of self-destruction. One picture shows Mr. Awdrey, Bert and the splashed mud in the full plenitude of their presence: the reader is brought smack against an aporia; that of the author's presence in a work whose existence as a fictional text is predicated on his absence.

---

[20] See *Not Saussure* chapter 6.

[21] Awdrey, *op. cit*, p. 22. 'They can't wave and get good pictures' neatly encapsulates the impossibility of being at once a participant in, and a recorder of, events. Awdrey may wish to imply that the problem is resolved in the act of creation in which not only the 'representation of reality' but the 'reality' that is represented is constructed. In short, he may be adumbrating a conventionalist critique of illusionism.

The power of pictures to disturb and astonish has been well described by Couturier and Durand discussing Barthelme:

> The reader's embarrassment is even worse, of course, when the fiction he reads includes pictures . . . All these devices stagger our imagination, baffle our intelligence and eventually induce us to evolve our private interpretation, no matter how extravagant it may be, to escape the tension and embarrassment.[22]

There is no such escape for the attentive reader of *Small Railway Engines*. Even before he has been led up the cul de sac of aporia, the project of rendering the story intelligible has been made unachievable by a semi-systematic inconsistency in the manner in which the consciousness of the engines is conceived. Sometimes they are like naughty children, sometimes like naughty adults and sometimes like machines. They grumble amongst themselves as if they were human and yet there are many cases in which they seem to share precisely the limitations of consciousness that one would expect of locomotives in the pre-diesel era. The scope of their freedom is also difficult to determine: they run largely to timetables and require drivers to run them; and yet they sometimes misbehave, get carried away and do something foolish, or rebel. They seem to have freedom only to be naughty.[23] In short, precisely those contradictions which classic realism cannot foreground are here most prominent. The reader, denied a point of view from which all the events presented or implied in the story can be rendered intelligible, is profoundly unsettled. In short, *Small Railway Engines* is an 'interrogative text' which, as Catherine Belsey has remarked

> challenges the realist conception of art and invites the spectators to reflect on fiction as a discursive practice and the ways in which discourse allows them to grasp their relation to the real relations in which they live.[24]

My use of the Rev. W. Awdrey's work must not be construed as placing it on the same plane of worthlessness as that of Donald Barthelme. Awdrey's stories have given enormous pleasure to innumerable small children and their parents. Moreover, I could have found the supposedly distinctive Barthelmean devices in virtually any episode of *Monty Python's Flying Circus* or any issue of the *Beano*. Self-reference, to a degree that a critic who reads his experiences from his theories would describe as 'vertiginous', is to be found everywhere in popular humour. The characters in the *Beano* are constantly threatening to walk out of the cartoon if they don't get their own way and not a few of them have been knocked into the adjacent story or into the middle of next week's issue by the force of a physical blow. But no one

---

[22] Couturier and Durand, pp. 16–17. This is another good example of how literary theorists tend to attribute to themselves the emotions their theories lead to expect.

[23] The theological dimension again?

[24] Catherine Belsey, *Critical Practice*, (London: Methuen, 1980), p. 131

pretends that the *Beano* is a laboratory of discourse. The character who turns away from the events on stage to ask the audience how they are enjoying the show is a cliche. And everyone will be familiar with this tale:

> It was a dark and stormy night and the robbers were in the cave. One of them said: 'Tell us a tale!' and the tale began thus: 'It was a dark and stormy night and the robbers were in the cave. One of them said: 'Tell us a tale!' and the tale began thus: 'It was. . . .'

This year I sent my mother-in-law a postcard showing a couple looking at a particularly ill-favoured cow. The husband says to the wife: 'That reminds me. Have we sent your mother a postcard yet?'

The point of my excursion into children's literature is to show how the large, often obscure, ideas invoked to defend writers such as Barthelme are not very useful for helping one to distinguish between, say, a deliberate refusal to be realistic and a mere failure to be realistic, due to lack of imagination or narrative skill; or between the anti-realism of an advanced novel and the unrealism of a children's story. Critical arguments adduced from the nature of language, for example, are too radical to permit an evaluation of different types of anti-or non-realism; or to discriminate between anti-realisms – to be sensitive to the different intentions behind the anti-realisms of pornography, of True Romance, of children's stories and of certain experimental narratives. They are all types of explicit fiction: no one would think them true to life.

In other words, the more radical the theory, the fewer constraints are there upon the critical conclusions that can be drawn from it. The big ideas may may used to legitimate all forms of currently fashionable anti-realism: the goblins as well as the self-destroying narratives; the allegories and fables as well as the syntactical adventures; the whimsicality as well as the blank pages. But there is no reason why we should be other than sceptical about the linking of large ideas and certain fictions. The suggestion that the writing of 'space fiction' is always a response to doubts about the validity of any attempt to describe contemporary reality is as plausible as the claim that *Noddy in Toyland* (a classic novella in the genre of anti-realistic 'explicit' fiction written in the late 1940s) was Enid Blyton's admission of her inability to come to terms with the enormities of the Cold War. No less implausible is the suggestion that a 'sensitive' mind when faced with 'the horror of contemporary reality' will find his mind breaking down into best-selling whimsy of the kind perpetrated by Richard Brautigan. Since it is a good deal easier to fantasize about invented monstrosities than it is to describe even a small part of the world around one's pen, it seems more likely that, in the majority of instances, the break with realism is the result of imaginative failure than, say, a refusal to endorse the reality constructed by the dominant power groups. Likewise it seems credulous in the extreme to believe that a predilection for word games is a response to the Chandos Letter crisis or to the discovery that language, being a non-representational mode of signification using arbitrary signs with their own rules of combination, cannot reach out to 'reality'. It seems more reasonable to relate it to the spirit of fun or the desire to be seen to be clever that motivates most word-play in everyday life. With a few exceptions, a novelist's retreat into erudition seems less likely to spring from metaphysical doubt than from a preference for what is easier – knowing allusion to what has already been said – over what is difficult – speaking of what has not yet been described. A little of the scepticism that pervades many critics' attitude to the non-literary world seems to be called for in their dealings with writers whom they have decided to admire. Why that scepticism is not apparent is easy to understand. The prudent advanced critic, conscious of the notorious blunders made by art critics when first confronted with non-perspectival paintings, will be inclined to give corresponding works in the literary field the benefit of the doubt. When an author such as Barthelme writes like an exceptionally fluent six-year-old, it is safer to assume that he is choosing not to write realistically rather than he does not feel up to the challenge of doing so.

8.2 Crisis in Criticism: The Demise of Evaluation

One of Borges's fictional essays is an interesting commentary on the theory-based hyping of works of art.[25] He then presents the case of a writer, a producer of consummately mediocre poems, who was able to summon up a whole host of impressive reasons why they were in fact the works of a genius. His true talent lay, Borges comments, in his commentaries on his own works. The image of an artist who put only his (minimal) talent into his work and his genius into promoting it is not entirely fanciful. Nor is the idea of a criticism that is more exciting the work it is discussing.

Anything can be read into anything: an arbitrarily constructed *a posteriori* code can be used to uncover apparently significant relations between quite disparate things. It is hardly surprising then that a few puns or an undistinguished *jeu d'esprit* or two can be sufficient to establish an author as one who is writing at the cutting edge of human consciousness and responding to 'post-Saussurean' or some other criticism of realistic fiction. It is easy to find the theory in the practice; all that is necessary is that the critic should be sympathetic to the author and be himself an uncritical swallower of radical ideas. The trouble is, it is far too easy. As we have seen, the criteria that place Donald Barthelme on the side of the angels will also put A.A. Milne, Rev. W. Awdrey and a host of other writers of children's books in the forefront of the *avant garde*. Once you start reading anti-realist theory into the practice, you can find it everywhere and in children's literature most of all.

Academic hype, then, soon leads to the problem that Borges had foreseen

---

25 An Examination of the Work of Herbert Quain, in J.L. Borges, *Fictions*, trs. A. Kerrigan (London: Weidenfeld & Nicolson, 1962).

in his story: the total demise of discrimination, the end of evaluation. It is only a small exaggeration to say that literary criticism over the last thirty years or so has been conducted to a greater or lesser degree in the shadow of certain large-scale theories whose tendency is to undermine the validity of critical *evaluation*. The well-informed academic critic now has innumerable reasons – political and social as well as philosophical, linguistic and more specifically literary – for declining to say whether the work he is discussing is good or bad. Critics still take sides – but the objects of their most explicit advocacy tends to be critical theories rather than works of literature. Passing judgement on the new and re-evaluating the old are dangerous games which the contemporary critic usually spares himself. At the most, he will *re-read* the old – in the light of a new theory – and if he finds it wanting it will be for ideological rather than aesthetic reasons.

One can sympathize; for it is almost impossible to be both advanced and discriminating. Roland Barthes and other illustrious figures have made it impermissible to judge fiction by the criteria that ordinary readers would use. The classical virtues of good fiction have been re-classified as the vices of 'classic' realism. As Nuttall has said,[26] 'one of the immemorial ways of praising a writer, that is by saying that he or she is true to life, has become obscurely tabu, as if it involved some fundamental misconception of the nature of literature and the world'. Plausibility, coherence, vividness, accuracy, perceptiveness, intensity of evocation, etc are denigrated as mere '*effets de réel*'. They are symptomatic of a writer who is bent on misleading us into thinking that his novel is 'about' the real world. It is implausibility, incoherence, staleness, inaccuracy, imperceptiveness that are to be singled out for praise; for they will draw attention to the novel's status as a piece of *writing*, rather than as a window on, or a moving mirror of, some reality. Unfortunately, implausibility can be deliberate or unwilled, a sign of success or failure, of advanced competence and elementary incompetence.

At first sight, it would seem that distinguishing naive incompetence from the deliberate shunning of the usual forms of competence should be relatively easy. The childish style of Daisy Ashford's *The Young Visiters* and the child-like prose of *The Autobiography of Alice B. Toklas* may be judged differently according to their different intentions. We can, after all, interpret Alice B. Toklas in the light of *Three Lives* and other of Gertrude Stein's works that preceded it. Similarly, we might be expected to read *Small Railway Engines* in a different spirit from that in which we read certain of Donald Barthelme's stories because we know that Barthelme is an American academic whereas the Rev. W. Awdry is an English parson who may be safely presumed to be innocent of literary-critical theory.

Unfortunately, interpreting, and hence evaluating, a text in the light of the author's (or, perhaps, the Author's) probable intentions inferred from what we know of his other writing and of his life, is a move that recent critical

[26] A.D. Nuttall, *A New Mimesis*, (London: Methuen, 1983), p. vii–viii.

theory has rendered inadmissable. For we are now asked to reject the idea that the author is somehow 'behind the work', that his intentions are relevant, that he is the *source* of its meanings and that his biography offers clues to the meaning of his writings.[27] It is the language, not an individual subject, that speaks in a text. One simply cannot intend a work as if one were its source and the guarantor of its meanings.

Advanced critics therefore lack criteria by which they might decide between, say, deliberate anti-realism and talentless unrealism; between the noble refusal of the fraudulent competence of realism and simple incompetence. So we are left with theories applied to literature of such a nature that almost any text can be seen to be justified by almost any one of the theories. For the theories relate to language as a whole and to the relation between language and reality. Some are even about the nature of consciousness itself. From the point of view of a theory which asserts that discourse, insofar as it is intelligible, is infused with ideology, Catherine Cookson and Alain Robbe-Grillet are distinguished only by the greater literary competence of the former. And the radical nominalism of the Lacanian critics makes Arthur Hailey and Maurice Blanchot equally naive in their use of language. Likewise, it would not be difficult to prove that the essential theme of the Poldark novels, as much as of the rather less interesting *contes* of Donald Barthelme, is the nature of fiction itself. In other words, advanced theories can be used to demonstrate the presence or absence of certain properties in almost any text. Since we know that interpretation has no final ground and that texts can be endlessly and differently reinterpreted and that ultimately we have no basis in the writer's supposed intention for settling on one interpretation rather than another, we may maintain that an inconsistency in a novel by Catherine Cookson is an attack on the narrative contract between author and reader while it is simply a mistake in one of Robbe-Grillet's novels with equal plausibility as we may claim the opposite.

There looms the spectre of the complete demise of critical evaluation – the end of criticism in the sense of literary or aesthetic judgement. This has not caused as much alarm as it should have done; indeed some have welcomed the demise of evaluative criticism. Since traditional criticism has been displaced by literary theory, the study of individual texts in order to interpret and evaluate them has given way to the more ambitious aim of mastering the underlying sign-systems which generate them. From the point of view of this intention, all texts are of potentially equal interest: it is up to the critic to make them interesting. And all readings are equally acceptable: a Barthesian textual analysis, for example, which treats the written page as merely a 'galaxy of signifiers' would not attempt to adjudicate between one 'creative' reading and another. Post-Saussurean analysis may be applied equally to *Paradise Lost* and the caption beneath the topless model in the *Sun* newspaper. 'Liter-

---

[27] Terry Eagleton, *Literary Theory* (Oxford: Blackwell, 1983), p. 205.

ary theory' Terry Eagleton assures us 'can handle Bob Dylan just as well as John Milton'.[27]

And there is no reason why the literary critic should confine himself to written texts: car number plates or parties may prove equally amenable to literary criticism:

> If you have nothing better to do at a party, you can always try on a literary critical analysis of it, speak of its styles and genres, discriminate its significant nuances or formalize its sign-system. Such a 'text' can prove quite as rich as one of the canonical works, and critical dissections of it quite as ingenious as those of Shakespeare.[28]

Just as, one supposes, a physicist interested in the structure of matter would not value faces above stones. For a literary critic turned semiologist or 'theorist' all sign-systems are of equal interest and hence of equal value. He does not prefer 'good' works over 'bad', the canon of 'literature' over the rest: literature is merely 'what gets taught' and is therefore defined not in terms of its intrinsic properties but on the basis of the purely extrinsic accident that it serves someone's (ideological) purpose to have it valued and therefore taught. 'Literature as such', outside of the politically interested discourses that establish the canon, simply does not exist.

In the absence of a defined object of study, literary theory becomes a *jeu sans frontières*. It can spread itself across a variety of other disciplines – anthropology, linguistics, sociology, political theory, and so on. Alternatively, it may try to unify itself – in so-called 'theory'. Richard Rorty has written of theory, understood as a general method of approaching texts or discourses, as

> a kind of writing . . . which is neither the evaluation of the relative merits of intellectual productions, nor intellectual history, nor moral philosophy, nor social prophecy, but all of these mingled together in a new genre.[29]

The theorist will tend to see himself as an eternally vigilant mind, the consciousness or even the conscience, of disciplines unconscious until his arrival of their status as 'discursive practices'. In certain quarters 'theory' is seen as the natural successor to literary theory which in turn has displaced literary criticism. 'Theory' is not to everyone's taste; for some, it seems to be composed of theories meta-theorized to the point where you cannot remember where they came from and can no longer see or care whether they are true. Theorists mock readers who, after a few pages of 'theory', thirst for first-order discourse, for facts and reports on experiences, for perceptions and ideas. They are amused by the naivety of those who do not wish merely to situate ideas but also to work with them, to try to understand them, to test

[28] Eagleton, *op. cit.*, p. 202.
[29] Richard Rorty, Professionalised Philosophy and Transcendental Culture, *Georgia Review*, 30 (1976), pp. 763–4.

them, to develop and extend them. For 'theory' is all about knowing all about theories without engaging with them on their own terms; it is about being able to 'place', for example, the General Theory of Relativity without having to know how to derive its fundamental equations. (Which may account for why 'theorists' often look like struggling amateurs eternally playing an away match amongst professionals of other disciplines, taking from each discipline whatever attracts them because it seems new, shiny or fast moving.)

Some critics have not been able to accept the total dissolution of literary studies but they have accepted the implication that *sub specie structuralis* all texts are equal. One such critic is John Carey, who is prominent both as an academic and as a literary journalist. Several years ago he wrote an article in the *Times Literary Supplement* that triggered a good deal of, often acrimonious, discussion.[30] His central claim was that it is no longer part of the critic's business to aim at or to pretend to objective evaluation of the works he studies and discusses. For his own part, he welcomed the 'dislodgement of evaluation' which, he claimed, had been effected 'with remarkably little fuss'. Nowadays, he said, 'almost no one believes in the possibility of objective or "correct" literary judgements'.

Professor Carey admitted that, like any other reader, he had preferences; but he denied that these preferences had any validity. The assertion that *King Lear* is superior to last Wednesday's episode of *Coronation Street* is merely to express a personal opinion that has little or no bearing on the intrinsic merits of the dramatic works in question. So that what an individual has to say in praise, or in condemnation, of a particular book is of interest only in terms of what it can 'tell us about people making the judgements, including ourselves', about 'the individual's motives and assumptions, the determining configurations of personality, imagination and background of the debators.' Critical value judgements then, merely supply data for the social psychologist to analyse.

Although Carey's views are unlikely to have been arrived at outside of current critical *Zeitgeist*, the reasons he gives in support of his critical nihilism have almost nothing to do with modern literary theory. He appeals to science in order to undermine evaluative criticism. Since he is, a Professor of English and not a Professor of Physics, the physics he appeals to is, understandably, the nineteenth-century atomist-materialist variety he learned about as a schoolboy and not the physics of the 1980s where the work of fifty years, culminating in Alain Aspect's famous experiment of 1982, has put the ghost decisively back in the atom.[31] This Victorian physics furnishes Carey with a vision of the universe that situates the literary critic in the larger scheme of things. The universe, he tells us, was brought about by accident and the Second Law of Thermodynamics (which he accepts quite uncritically as an

---

[30] John Carey, Viewpoint, *Times Literary Supplement*, 22 February 1980.
[31] P.C.W. Davies and J.R. Brown (eds), *The Ghost in the Atom* (Cambridge: Cambridge University Press, 1986).

eternal truth) predicts that it will eventually disappear under a similar dispensation. We are, he concludes, temporary occupants of a cooling solar system. Life, therefore, is ultimately senseless and all values are relative and transient: absolute values cannot 'retain their credibility in a Godless universe'. There can therefore be no eternal canon of good literature.

The eventual heat-death of the universe, and the failure of critics to agree on their estimate of the relative worth of different works of literature, taken together undermine the implicit claims of evaluative criticism; indeed, critical disagreements provide empirical evidence for that relativity of all values which Professor Carey sees to follow from man's place in the universe. Since 'human life is an accident of chemistry' ('O' level rather than 'A' level chemistry), Carey believes that literary evaluation, seen aright, 'might seem almost comically irrelevant'.

So much for theory. What of Professor Carey's practice? Does he practise his un-preaching? In both of his roles – as an academic critic and as a literary journalist – Carey behaves as if he did not believe in 'the demise of evaluation'. As may be imagined, Professor Carey did not reach his present position as the holder of the Merton Chair of English at Oxford by paying equal attention to Harold Robbins, Barbara Cartland and William Shakespeare. He has edited the poetry of John Donne and established his reputation as literary critic on the basis of book-length studies of Thackeray, Dickens and Donne. He has, in other words, concentrated on those writers who rank high in the conventional critical cannon. His bibliography does not, for example, include *Harold Robbins: Life, Mind and Art*. Nor has he written much on the rejected manuscripts of a talentless, unknown contemporary writer. His belief in evaluative criticism is therefore implicit in the authors he has chosen to write about and the enormous labour he has expended upon them to the exclusion of others.

There is a cynical interpretation of this. The predicament of the ambitious academic who does not believe in evaluative criticism is well described by Terry Eagleton (a fellow Oxonian):

> Nobody is likely to be dismissed from an academic job for trying on a little semiotic analysis of Edmund Spenser; they are likely to be shown the door, or refused entry through it in the first place, if they question whether the 'tradition' from Spenser to Shakespeare and Milton is the best or only way of carving up discourse into a syllabus. It is at this point that the canon is trundled out to blast offenders out of the literary arena.[32]

And he adds, with even more pertinence to the critic in question:

> Nobody will penalize me heavily if I dislike a particular Donne poem, but if I argue that Donne is not literature at all then in certain circumstances I am at risk of losing my job.

[32] Eagleton, *op. cit.* p. 205.

Thus Mr Eagleton. As a Fellow and Tutor in English at Wadham College Oxford, he is well qualified to tell us how to remain unblasted out of the literary arena.

Should we account for the discrepancy between Professor Carey's theory and his practice on the grounds of vulgar opportunism? That, as an ambitious young man, he read the battle and saw that to preach the baselessness of literary evaluation would not help his career towards the desired goal of an Oxford Chair? This seems highly unlikely; and even more so when we see Professor Carey in his other role – that of a literary journalist. There his commitment to evaluation – freely chosen one assumes because the pressures a literary editor can exert upon a prominent academic critic must be very slight – is quite clear. As an academic, Professor Carey is able to choose the authors to whom he turns his attention and his values may therefore be expressed in his choice of writers. He does not have such control over the books that come his way as a newspaper critic and there his values, no longer implicit in the choice of works to consider, become explicit.

Carey must value his literary journalism, because he has recently republished it in collected form. It is not therefore unfair to examine it with a view to testing the sincerity of his views about the demise of evaluative criticism. Consider his review of a novel by Kingsley Amis.[33] To judge from what Professor Carey says about it, the novel – *Stanley and the Women* – suggests an off-form Amis, with his comic vision, linguistic skill and mimetic genius almost extinguished by his myopic lounge-bar conservatism. Professor Carey disapproves of the novel and his disapproval sounds like evaluation. The main ground of disapproval is Amis's choice of a 'middle-aged chauvinist alchoholic' as the novel's point of view: it is hard, he says, 'to forgive Amis for inventing a character who obliges him to write in these clogged vocables'. As well as evaluating the book as a whole, Carey evaluates parts of the book and compares them with others: 'Steve is undoubtedly the best thing in the book'. The 'undoubtedly' seems to suggest that he regards his evaluations as not being mere material for a social psychologist to study. And he refers to a scene which 'stands out dazzlingly from the rest'. And to a character (Nash) who is 'the only figure capable of the brilliance and range of mind we have come to expect from Amis'. One evaluation leads to another: the character Nash would have been a much better narrator than Stanley. ' "Dr Nash and the women" could have been an outstanding novel'. Carey then, does not appear to hesitate in ranking the novel Amis did write well below the novel he might have written had he first sought the advice of the Merton Professor of English. It is difficult to imagine how Carey's opinions about this novel would look from the standpoint of a universe undergoing heat-death. Are they appropriate for one who is but an accident of chemistry? And are they any better founded than those of the 'middle-aged chauvinist alcoholic' he resents occupying the novel's point of view?

[33] John Carey, Kingsley among the Amazons, *Sunday Times*, 20 May 1984.

An ambivalent attitude towards evaluation marked much of surrealist literary theory. It is very irritating, if, having announced a technique for turning everyone into a genius, you find yourself surrounded by people who think they are geniuses after they have followed your advice. And very awkward if you have demonstrated that all true genius is rooted in the unconscious and everyone's unconscious is as good as everyone else's. 'Surrealism is within the compass of every unconscious . . . We have no talent . . . we who have made ourselves, in our works, the deaf receptacles of so many echoes, the modest *recording devices* that are not hypnotized by the designs they trace' (Nadeau, op. cit., p. 97). Does this mean that all who apply the method will become great poets? This is too much for the great egoists: there must be some discrimination, some evaluation, some quality control even when one is dealing with the products of the unconscious. So Aragon: 'Surrealism is . . . no longer an inexplicable visitation, but a faculty that is exercised. Of a variable scope, depending on individual forces. And whose results are of unequal interest . . . If you write, by a surrealist method, wretched idiocies, they will be wretched idiocies' (Nadeau, op. cit., p. 98). The denial of intrinsic merit seems fine so long it enables one to invert the conventional evaluations and to assert that the sound of a streetwalker vomiting is sweeter than *The Song of Songs*. It is less attractive when it raises the possibility that E.J. Thribb may be regarded as being as good as, or better, or no different from L. Aragon or A. Breton.

An inconsistent attitude to apparently fundamental beliefs is exceedingly common amongst advanced critics. We shall later examine critics who disbelieve in the possibility of reference and yet behave in a way that is quite inconsistent with that belief. Indeed, one could say that the radical critic who practises as if he didn't believe his unbelievable views is one of the commonest species in the contemporary republic of letters. Like Professor Carey, they are often formidably intelligent and in command of an immense range of scholarship. And for this reason, their inconsistencies, and their easy accommodation to them, are difficult to understand.

Not all critics are as comfortable as Professor Carey with the conflict between their theory and their critical practice. Catherine Belsey questions whether we should speak of 'literature' at all:

> If we accept the case for the primacy of the signifier, it becomes clear that the existence of the term gives no particular authority to the assumption that there is a body of texts with their own specific practices, which can be usefully isolated as 'literature'. Quite apart from the value judgements frequently implied in the term . . . it is not at all apparent that it is helpful to isolate other discourses . . . from the discourse we call literature.[34]

But how can you continue to operate as a literary critic when you have demonstrated to your own satisfaction that the evaluation of one text as

[34] Belsey, *op. cit.* p. 144.

'literary' and others as not has no basis other than the ideologically inspired decision that some works should be revered and get 'taught' and others should not? Belsey's answer is disarmingly honest: you continue to use the word but cancel it out once you have used it:

> I have used the word [literature] here, but reluctantly, 'under erasure' as Derrida puts it when of necessity he employs a term belonging to a theoretical and discursive framework which is undermined by his work as a whole.

The '*Sous rature*' move permits you to wriggle out of the difficult position of writing about something whose objective existence you deny. You make your self-contradictions explicit by writing

and so transcending it. In this way the demise or dislodgement of evaluative criticism and of the value judgements implicit in the term literature do not have the unfortunate consequence of the demise or dislodgement of the critic. No wonder it has been effected 'with remarkably little fuss': nobody has been made redundant.[35]

8.3 Mediator Against Message: Radical Critic Versus Radical Text

We rarely approach books innocent of their intention. Much anti-realistic fiction is ushered into our presence by critics and blurb-writers who are anxious to make its purpose clear in advance of our encountering it, so that it shall not be misunderstood and dismissed at dull, incompetent, implausible or simply unintelligible. As Culler has pointed out, 'any work can be made intelligible if one invents appropriate conventions'.[36] This sounds fine: an apparently dull novel can be seen to 'represent' the emptiness of modern life (godless heavens, etc.); a seemingly badly written one to subvert the conventions of the slick popular novel; an implausible one to criticize the '*effet de réel*' so cheaply achieved by authors who have learnt the tricks of the trade; and an unintelligible one to parade as an exemplary 'opaque text' that breaks

[35] John Carey's dismissal of evaluative criticism promoted a brisk correspondence. Some of his correspondents suggested that, by refusing to believe that there was any basis for valuing one bit of writing above another, Carey had removed the rationale for teaching English Literature at all. What would teachers expect students to gain from studying the subject? 'They expect', ran his reply 'students to emerge who feel more fulfilled as human beings from studying the subject of their choice, and who have learnt to understand themselves and other people better. Part of that understanding will be an appreciation of the irreducible differences in literary taste (and in other subjective areas such as politics and religion), between themselves and others'. A last-ditch position. One would think that there would be less roundabout ways of discovering this than reading conflicting and groundless views about works which lack intrinsic merits.

[36] Jonathan Culler, *Structuralist Poetics*, Routledge & Kegan Paul, 1975, p. 107.

with the myth of reference. The midwife-critic ensures the safe delivery of the novel into an often uncaring, usually stupid, and invariably unenlightened world of complacent, frequently bourgeois, readers who, not having noticed the emptiness of the heavens, the constructed (and hence artificial) nature of reality and the manner in which 'language gets overlooked', etc. are liable to misinterpret, and so reject, it.

The relationship between the radical critic and the radical text may not be as happy as this would suggest. Indeed, we may sometimes have a case of midwife turned neonaticide: the very process of ensuring a safe delivery may destroy the baby. In mediating between the *avant garde* work and the *arrière garde* reader he may neutralize the former's radical force. For a critic who explains also *recuperates* and recuperation, even more than rejection and misunderstanding, is the feared enemy of the radically new.

Consider: a work is at first absurd or unintelligible. The reader requires assurance that his initial failure to understand, or indeed, to derive anything from, the work is not due to authorial incompetence, to its being written in a foreign tongue or badly misprinted or to his own poor eyesight. But this very reassurance – 'Reinhart Himmelscheiss's texts are *about* the senselessness of texts, their intention is tear off the mask of meaning' – works *against* its critic-endorsed purpose of undermining 'our usual expectations of textual coherence and significance'. Once, for example, Himmelscheiss's *Nada* is explained as an attempt to represent 'a manic logic operating independently of reality' or a schizophrenic mind, or the failure of language to achieve a purchase on reality, its much-vaunted power to 'disturb' is neutralized. For the common reader is already familiar with the tragi-comic idea of logic operating independently of practical reality or the clinical diagnosis of schizophrenia. The apparent disorder and randomness of Himmelscheiss's *Nichts* may be explained as an attempt to reflect the disorder and senselessness of modern culture. This small parcel of sense makes it possible to get from one end of the novel to the other without howling out against God and creation. But once this explanation is available – showing how the disorder of the work is in fact in an ordered relationship to the disorder of the world – the power of the work to rouse the reader from his bourgeois sleep will disappear along with his philistine irritation. Finally, when critics showed why those eternal, monotonous descriptions in Himmelscheiss's *Le Zero* were necessary (variously: fidelity to reality; a parody of secretarial realism; a demonstration of the inexpressibility of the real), they not only made the work more exciting but also made it rather less radical than it might otherwise have been.

Critical 'recuperation', therefore, may actually work against the intentions the critic claims to lie behind the works recuperated. The very process of extracting the familiar, received ideas – 'reality is unrealistic', 'language expresses nothing', etc. – from the radical works that are supposed to express or 'confront' them, is self-defeating. The history of much modern criticism (and literature) could be re-written as the history of works necessarily deradicalized, or emasculated, by their critical champions. One could multiply the examples, but it would be more useful to focus on a couple of examples.

Consider, for example, Raymond Roussel. He has met with the highest approval for the best possible reasons:

> Roussel's blithe disdain for the representational or referential function of language made him an obvious candidate for praise on the part of those who wanted to privilege the complete self-referentiality of language.[37]

His reward has been to have no less a writer than Michel Foucault devote an entire monograph to him. This was discussed by Jonathan Culler in *Structuralist Poetics* (Culler, *op. cit.*) who tells us that 'To purify his texts, *to give them an order which was not that of communicative intention*' [italics mine] 'Roussel resorted to formal procedures which could serve as generative devices.'

For example, *Locus Solus* is the story of a world created by linguistic machines. Puns give rise to the material of the world and are the dynamo by which the 'story' is propelled through that material. Roussel begins with the phrase *demoiselle à pretendant* ['young girl with suitor'] and turns it into *demoiselle à reitre en dents* ('paviour's beetle with a reiter out of teeth'). This permits him to imagine a paviour's beetle, suspended from a small balloon, slowly creating a mosaic picture of a *reiter*, or German knight, out of human teeth. (The beetle is working in the service of Canterel, the eccentric owner of a private estate near Paris). In order that the teeth shall be placed in the correct position, the weather conditions have to be known in advance. Canterel is able to predict the wind with awesome precision. His meteorological skills are connected with the complex of objects unpacked from the phrase *Napoleon premier empereur*.

Roussel's two 'masterpieces' are generated entirely from such procedures. These, according to Culler, 'make the text a closed system which is a veritable parody of language as a system of differences' (*ibid*, p. 107). It

> displays the infinite play of differences by which a word sends us off to other words instead of linking directly with a world: 'this marvellous quality which makes language rich in its poverty'

Roussel's work

> shows that the response of the imagination to language, when language is freely displayed as the system of difference, permits the production of so many meanings as to undermine the notion of positive and determinate signs

So *that* is what *Locus Solus* is about. Well done, Foucault-Culler for a workmanly exposition of an otherwise opaque text. But, steady on. Isn't there

---

[37] Martin Jay, 'In the Empire of the Gaze', in: *Foucault: A Critical Reader*, ed. David Couzens Hoy (Oxford: Basil Blackwell, 1986), p. 183.

something a bit odd in what is being done here? First of all, the work is reduced to an idea. This may not be altogether good. A work in which there are theories, Proust tells us, is like an article which still has the price tag on it. This is not decisive criticism unless the theories have been better discussed elsewhere or they have been foisted on the work by someone other than the author. Then there is a sense in which the ideas which the work is supposed to advance render it unnecessary. If *Locus Solus* is about 'language as a system of difference', we should be better advised reading Saussure, Jakobson or even the writings of Foucault and Culler who are clearly better at expounding Roussel's ideas than he is himself. But that is not the worst of the difficulties marking the relationship between Foucault-Culler and *Locus Solus*. For the idea to which they reduce the novel is that language is about nothing other than itself. Now if this is simply untrue then the work is scarcely worth discussing. Implicit in the critical exegesis is the belief that language is, indeed, about nothing other than itself. But the very manner in which *Locus Solus* is discussed suggests that reference is possible and that language is not typically about itself at all. So we have the curious situation of a critic championing a book because it seems to confirm the self-referentiality of language in another book that is manifestly *not* self-referential. For the *referential* discourse of *Structural Poetics* is 'about' a novelist called Raymond Roussel and about the rationale of his novel *Locus Solus*. The discussion takes it for granted that language is about the world (and about things in the world, like Raymond Roussel and a book called *Locus Solus* and ideas about the nature of language) while at the same time applauding the novel under discussion for showing how language is not about the world. Another case of the midwife delivering the baby to the grave; or, perhaps, of the chaperone inadvertly raping his charge through an excess of chaperonely attention.

If all language has certain properties (e.g. that of being linked to other language rather than the world), no particular use of language (Raymond Roussell writing *Locus Solus*; or someone telling me that there is a man about to step in front of the car I am driving) could demonstrate it. The fact that Foucault–Culler believes that certain texts *do* have the rare property of demonstrating the non-referentiality of language betrays an uncertainty about the scope of non-reference. Many critics are unable to make up their minds whether self-referentiality is an inescapable feature of language itself or a feature only of certain literary uses of language. This uncertainty is clearly demonstrated in the absurd reference to 'those who want to privilege the complete self-referentiality of language' quoted above. It seems as if certain critics believe that it is possible to demonstrate what is supposed to be an inescapable feature of all language, by a particular, highly atypical, use of language; to show how language normally works by showing it not working. As if one could demonstrate the essence of speech by recording highly abnormal speech acts manifestly designed not to communicate.

The relationship between radical work and radical critic in the case of Roussel is really rather remarkable. It shows us the critical champion destroying the radical impact of the new work by reducing it to an idea which can be comprehended in the usual way, which has been better expressed outside the work (perhaps by the critic), which is actually untrue and whose untruth is demonstrated unwittingly by the critic's own procedures. Surely it must be preferable for a writer to remain neglected, despised and misunderstood. Another, almost as spectacular, instance of the unhappy relationship between the work and its advocates is that of Brecht, a writer, if ever there was one, who has been killed by critical kindness. (As he has often been his own most persuasive critical advocate, he has largely himself to blame.) Even so, he remains one of the most valued prize cows of anti-realism. Different critics like him for different reasons: Marxists admire him as a subverter of bourgeois values and as a satirical scourge; while post-Saussureans admire him as a writer who disrupts the too-smooth relationship between text and reference, spectacle and message, even signifier and signified. His very success with the critics, however, has laid the foundations of his failure. For no one can get near his works without passing through a large ante-room of theory. As a result, Brecht is more admired and enjoyed by some for his theory of the drama than for his actual plays. It is not surprising to learn from Susan Sontag that Barthes cited Brecht's prose writings more than his plays in his seminars and that 'it was not Brecht the maker of didactic spectacles but Brecht the didactic intellectual who finally mattered to Barthes'.[38] Not the playwright but the theoretician of the theatre. Not the works, but the explanation of the works, the proof of how and why they should work.

The aspect of Brecht that has most captivated critics is his theory of alienation and of the *Verfremdungseffekt* and his conviction that the world should not be presented in the theatre in a realistic way, for plausibility itself blunts the impulse to question and forecloses radical political debate. The intention of Brechtian theatre is to present reality in such a way that the audience is aware that what is presented is a *spectacle*, a construct. By seeing the theatrical spectacle as *constructed*, the audience will *see* it rather than merely *swallow* it. The response will be intellectual rather than emotional or empathetic and there will be a chance that it might be generalized to the greater spectacle of reality outside of the theatre. The alienation effect, the non-slick, non-smooth, non-realistic presentation of reality, will defamiliarize it. Once reality has lost its 'taken for granted' familiarity, it is available for radical questioning.

Alas, Brechtian exegesis and Brecht's own self-exegesis have together turned the *Verfremdungseffekt* into a familiar technique of modern theatrical practice. We do watch the explicit spectacle of the theatrical production; but our attention is diverted by the meta-spectacle of the Brechtian production techniques. We observe the stage through the intellectual opera-glasses provided by the programme notes. It is hardly surprising then that the Brechtian

[38] Susan Sontag, 'On Roland Barthes', editor's introduction to *Barthes: Selected Writings* (London: Jonathan Cape, 1982), p. xxix.

dream of an audience, awoken to the contradictions of capitalist society, made to see for the first time, their convictions dismantled and refashioned, their received identities shattered, their very sense of unified self fragmented, has never been realized. Thousands have gone to his plays without waking up out of self, language and identity. (This may have been a source of private shame to many.) Instead, his plays have become, as Catherine Belsey (a supporter) admits, 'classics of the bourgeois theatre'. Their revolutionary impact may be judged by the almost total absence of the proletariat from their audiences in the free world and the Arts Council funding necessary to mount them. The truth is that critical analysis, despite demonstrating beyond reasonable doubt that the plays should have nothing short of a revelatory impact on their audiences, has failed to ensure that they earn anything other than the pro- foundest respect. Indeed, by ensuring that we have the rationale of the plays in the forefront of our minds as we watch them, such analysis ensures that they are deprived of any power they may have to disorientate or disturb. Critics would do well to remember the sad truth that lovers learn: you cannot get someone to fall in love with you by listing those of your qualities that should oblige them to do so.

The most striking symptom of the conflict between the radical texts and their champions is the confident manner the latter assume when they say what the former are about or are 'trying to do'. The longer critics have spent with works that question our ability to understand/communicate/know any- thing, the more fluently they are able to say what these works mean. No one who had read anything by Terry Eagleton would believe he had spent so much time reading writers who have fundamental doubts about the relationship between language, self and the world. Consider what he has to say about Lacan:

> Lacan's . . . notoriously sybilline style, a language of the unconscious all
> in itself, is meant to suggest that any attempt to convey a whole,
> unblemished meaning in speech or script is a pre-Freudian illusion.[39]

What a precise suggestion! And how (pre-Freudianly) confident Mr Eagleton is of the meaning of Lacan's style. And how odd this confidence is in the light of his claim that Lacan's style is intended to deny the possibility of a whole, unblemished meaning and his apparent sympathy with the idea that 'whole meaning' is a 'pre-Freudian illusion'. And isn't it odd, furthermore, that there are readers (such as myself) who require the ordinary, non-sybilline, prose of T. Eagleton to spot the intention of Lacan's sybilline stuff?[40]

There seems to be an inescapable conflict between the demands of critical advocacy and exegesis and the works for which the critic provides this kind of support. This may be inevitable. If, as Catherine Belsey has suggested, the interrogative text is aimed at undermining the dominant ideology, but that

---

[39] Terry Eagleton, *op. cit.*, p. 83.
[40] Eagleton is really describing the effect that he thinks, on theoretical grounds, Lacan's prose style should have.

ideology is co-terminous with intelligibility, then the process of helping to make sense of a work must inevitably return it to the ideology from which it is trying to escape. Helping the reader to understand what the work is about must frustrate its purpose of liberating its readers from ideologically unsound consciousness. (It is of course merest sentimentality to believe that making ideology explicit – so that the work wears its ideology on its sleeve – can help free the work from such ideology. If ideology is co-extensive with intelligibility, there is no way that it can be made completely explicit).

The embrace of the radical critic, then, may be the kiss of death for the radical work. In providing the frame of reference within which the work can be appreciated, even understood, the critic also creates the pigeonhole in which it can be tidied away or the grave in which it can be buried. There is, of course, a critical or meta-critical theory of this process of recuperation. The death of innovative works at the hands of their supporters is an extreme example of that more universal process whereby the unfamiliar is made intelligible and thus naturalized. This, Jonathan Culler informs us, (*op. cit.* p. 138) is one of the basic activities of the human mind. If this is the case, then we could scarcely expect even the most advanced critic to be free from its grip or to operate outside of it.

8.4 The Radical Critic Against Himself

We have already seen how a consistent anti-realistic fiction does not yet appear to exist. And 'we now know' (to expropriate Barthes's favourite phrase) that it is almost impossible for a critic championing an apparently anti-realistic work not implicitly or even explicitly to undermine it. We have also had hints that pragmatic self-refutation (see Chapter 1) affects not only the relation between radical critic and radical work but also the radical critic with himself. This is what I propose to discuss next.

Frank Lentricchia has written a propos of Paul de Man as follows:

> What we are witnessing in all of this is a strange discrepancy between a frightfully sobering literary discourse and the actual practice of a critic whose judgements, authoritative in tone and style, betray the theory.[41]

The inconsistency is sometimes quite grotesque, as I have just discussed in the case of the attitude of literary theorists towards Lacan.[42]

The most striking – and from their own standpoint the most damning – feature of post-Saussurean critics is that they use language, like the rest of us, as if it referred to realities outside of itself. Writers who profess to doubt whether language is 'about' anything express those doubts in a language that is apparently naively referential.

[41] Frank Lentricchia, *After the New Criticism* (London: Methuen, 1980), p. 301.
[42] See also *Not Saussure*, Chapter 5.

According to Robert Scholes

> Once we knew that fiction was about life and criticism was about fiction – and everything was simple. Now we know that fiction is about other fiction, is criticism in fact, or metafiction. And we know that criticism is about the impossibility of anything being about life, reality, or even about fiction, or finally about anything. Criticism has taken the very idea of 'aboutness' away from us. Criticism has taught us that language is tautological if it is not nonsense, and to the extent that it is about anything, it is about itself.[43]

Now, if criticism is really not 'about' anything, who are the 'we' that are so confidently referred to? What of the 'now' that is contrasted with the 'once'? If language is tautological and cannot be about itself, how can it be used to refer to what it is 'now' known to be about, in contrast with what it was 'once' thought to be 'about'. If criticism is not about anything, how can it 'teach' us that language is tautologous or nonsense? How can it reform our old, incorrect ideas 'about' the nature of language, of literature and of criticism? Presumably even post-structuralist criticism is 'about' as well as against realism. Indeed, it has to be *about* in order to be against. And such criticism may be about particular novels. *S/Z*, for example, is, at the very least, more about *Sarrasine* than, say, *Père Goriot* or *The Carpetbaggers*, or the nature of light or the particular pair of scissors on my desk. A reader who accepted Scholes's claims would be in the curious position of believing that language is available to talk realistically, or at least truthfully, about its own limitations, as well as those of fiction and criticism, but about *nothing else in the world*. A conception of language that spares reference only to the extent that language can refer to itself in order, for example, to compare old and new ideas about reference and the means by which 'we' moved from the former to the latter seems, to say the least, implausible.

Such idiocy is rarely so blatant. Nevertheless, it is common for radical doubts about language, reference and reality to be (implicitly) suspended so that language can be used to express those doubts. And a similar dispensation seems to operate with regard to other radical doubts – as was earlier discussed in Chapter 1. Frank Kermode tells us that

> The whole movement towards 'secretarial' realism represents a nostalgia for the . . . anachronistic myth of common understanding and shared universes of meaning.[44]

We are meant to understand that Kermode (and we his readers) have gone beyond or woken up out of this myth of common understanding and of shared universes of meaning. But surely the fact that Kermode has readers who understand him, that he is read and understood, and that he wrote in the

---

[43] Robert Scholes, The Fictional Criticism of the Future, *TriQuarterly*, *34* (Fall, 1975).

[44] Quoted in Gerald Graff, *Literature Against Itself Literary Ideas and Modern Society* (Chicago: University of Chicago Press, 1979), p. 186.

expectation of being read or understood, implies that he is writing for a world of persons bound together by a good deal of common understanding and shared meanings. Without the idea of such a world before him, how could he address his readers – for example, a complete stranger such as myself – with such confidence, and about such abstract and global concepts as 'myths of common understanding' and 'shared universes of meaning'?

Here, as in so many places, critical presupposition is totally at odds with critical pronouncement. Ironically, even the patronized 'secretarial' realists (talentless dupes such as Balzac or Zola) rarely pretended to be able to surmount reality, to gather up the whole of the outside world in a single consciousness, as Kermode appears to be able to do. Zola's position that 'a work of art is a corner of creation seen through a temperament'[45] makes far more modest claims for the vision of the artist than Kermode, by implication, makes for the critic. The novelist does not pretend to be a definitive viewpoint, a tor of consciousness; but curiously the critic, who can see through 'anachronistic myths of common understanding', etc., apparently does. It is the critic, not the novelist, who is the more dependent on an assumed common understanding, mythical or otherwise.

Critics who publish books and articles circulating in the real world and referring to other books also circulating in the real world and yet deny that language can refer to reality are rather like the lady who wrote to Bertrand Russell extolling the virtues of solipsism. She thought it the only philosophy that a sensible person could hold and couldn't understand why everyone didn't subscribe to it.

Those who deny that language can give us access to extra-linguistic reality do not hesitate to make authoritative pronouncements about history, even though history can come to an individual only through language. The scope of these pronouncements is sometimes so wide that they seem to have come from the Sellers and Yeatman parodies of elementary text books. Critics allow themselves to make such pronouncements partly because they believe that, in freeing themselves of ideology (or whatever), they have been able to discover the true nature of history and reality. 'Criticism', we are told, 'is the science which offers a knowledge of [the process of literary production] and so, finally, a knowledge of history'.[46] W.J.T. Mitchell in a recent, extraordinary article advancing the claim that the present is the 'Golden Age of Criticism',[47] asserts that recent criticism has developed 'a scientific method of reading, which involves the testing of new hypotheses on texts'. If the testing of hypotheses were all that science was about then my trying to find someone's house for the first time – Perhaps it's down here. Let's try . . . – would be science, too. Be that as it may, let us look at the quality of the 'knowledge of history' produced by this 'science'. Consider, for example, the implicit

45 Emil Zola, quoted in Damien Grant, *Realism* (London: Methuen, 1970), p. 51.
46 Belsey, *op. cit.*, p. 138.
47 W.T.J. Mitchell, *op. cit.*, p. 15.

historiography in Barthes's *S/Z*. (The 'text' he is referring to is Balzac's *Sarrasine*.)

> In the past (says the text), money 'revealed'; it was an index, it furnished a fact, a cause, it had a nature; today it 'represents' (everything): it is an equivalent, an exchange, a representation: a sign ... Shifting from a monarchy based on land to an industrial monarchy, society changed the Book, it passed from the Letter (of nobility) to the Figure (of fortune), from title deeds to ledgers, but it is always subject to a writing. The difference between feudal society and bourgeois society, index and sign is this: the index has an origin, the sign does not: to shift from index to sign is to abolish the last (or first) limit, the origin, the basis, the prop, to enter into the limitless process of equivalence, representations that nothing will ever stop orient, fix, sanction.[48]

S/ZZZZ ... One has to ask: *how does he know?* Particularly when, as he informs us a few lines on, 'the bourgeois sign is a metonymic confusion'. It is unlikely that the historiographical texts from which he derived the information upon which his spectacular speculations are based were written in anything but bourgeois signs.

And consider this:

> Now the 1850s bring the concurrence of three new and important facts in History: the demographic expansion in Europe, the replacement of textile by heavy industry, that is, the birth of modern capitalism, the scission (completed by the revolution of June 1848) of French Society into three mutually hostile classes bringing the definitive ruin of the liberal illusion ... Henceforth ... the writer falls prey to ambiguity, since his consciousness no longer accounts for the whole of his condition.[49]

The last sentence – presumably aimed at showing how a Marxist sense of false consciousness awoke at least as bad a conscience in 'the writer' – is a Barthes classic. Extracted from his first published book, it shows that Barthes arrived at omniscience, indeed unconscious self-parody, very early. It is curious to find it in the same short text as the following:

> All modes of writing have in common the fact of being 'closed'. Writing is in no way an instrument for communication (*ibid*, p. 25).

It is strange that Barthes is able to use writing to make apparently referential historical remarks of a vast scope (based at least in part on others' referential remarks of a slightly lesser scope) while at the same time denying that writing has a communicative function. Everything that Barthes writes would lead one to believe that he thinks he has been in receipt of a vast amount of information communicated through writing.

The clash between the radical view of the medium (writing, language) and

---

[48] Roland Barthes, *S/Z*, trans. Richard Miller (New York: Hill & Wang, 1970), pp. 39–40.
[49] Roland Barthes, *Writing Degree Zero* trans. Annette Lavers and Colin Smith (London: Jonathan Cape, 1967), p. 66.

the messages put forward in that medium becomes most acute when post-Saussurean writers and their fellow-travellers make explicitly political observations. When it is used for castigating the bourgeoisie or pointing out injustices, language suddenly becomes unproblematically referential. This kind of inconsistency is not confined to literary theorists. The most prominent example is Sartre, who did not allow his radical doubts about language to interfere with his using language to denounce abuses. His disbelief in essences, for example, did not inhibit his production of snap, even journalistic, judgements about the 'bourgeoisie' and other vast groupings of people. His doubts about the possibility of true stories (see Chapter 2) were put into cold storage when he read and transmitted stories of oppression. He wrote and acted as a man who believed that language could refer to things, that persons (especially those whom he hated) had specifiable characteristics and that stories – for example about torture in Algeria – could be true. This is entirely to the credit of Sartre the man but discredits much of what he wrote – or toyed with – as a thinker. Barthes, too, puts away his linguistic radicalism when he is angry. His indignation against 'the bourgeoisie' permits him to draw what he might describe as 'bourgeois essentialist' conclusions from the tendency of the *Guide Bleu* to speak of 'types'. He concludes that there is a disease 'of thinking in essences which is at the bottom of every bourgeois mythology of man'.[50] We may think of Barthes as a man whose essence is to despise those (the bourgeoisie) whose essence (according to him) is to think in essences.

The inconsistency of the originators is found also in their followers. Terry Eagleton's *Literary Theory* gives post-Saussurean linguistic radicals a very sympathetic hearing. He clearly considers their wildest claims to be far from absurd. And yet he permits himself a 'Political Conclusion' in which he uses language as if statements made in it were referential and did not owe their meaning entirely to language itself. Half-way through his book, he writes

> It was impossible any longer to see reality simply as something 'out there' . . . reality was not reflected by language but *produced* by it.[51]

He praises this view for being contrary to common sense, common sense having always got things wrong. On page 194, however, we read this:

> As I write, it is estimated that the world contains over 60,000 nuclear warheads, many with a capacity a thousand times greater than the bomb which destroyed Hiroshima. The possibility that these weapons will be used in our lifetime is steadily growing. The approximate cost of these weapons is $500 billion a year. Five per cent of this sum . . . could drastically, fundamentally alleviate the problem of the poverty-stricken Third World.

These are totally admirable sentiments but they certainly sound as if they come from a man for whom the belief that reality is 'out there' and that

[50] Roland Barthes, *Mythologies*, trans. Annette Lavers (London: Jonathan Cape, 1972), p. 75.
[51] Eagleton, *op. cit.*, p. 108.

language refers to it rather than making it is not regarded as a mere foible of an invariably faulty common sense. A 'stockpile of arms' is not an effect of language. Though such monstrosities could not have come into being without a complex technological society founded upon language, they remain incontestably extra-linguistic.

Eagleton's non-radical use of language is particularly interesting in someone who has written only a few pages earlier of modernist literary forms that 'pulverize order, subvert meaning and explode our self-assurance'. One assumes that he has been exposed to modernist forms, otherwise he would not have written in the first-person plural. So how are we to explain that the highly ordered and very self-assured sentence in which he speaks of pulverized order and exploded self-assurance? For non-literary experiences that pulverize order and explode self-assurance – epileptic fits for example – rarely give birth to such articulate accounts of themselves. Even assuming that the modernist forms did their dirty work yesterday and he has now recovered, it would be difficult to explain how such precise memories could be laid down.

It is hard to believe that Eagleton is simply insincere and lacking in the necessary cunning to conceal the fact. Is he merely forgetful? After all, it cannot always be easy to remember to write in accordance with ideas that are readily recited but impossible to imagine. Nevertheless, it is puzzling to encounter such inadvertent self-exposure in someone apparently so intelligent. The same uncertainty troubles us when we read Barthes. In *Writing Degree Zero*, he identifies 'lucidity' as a merely rhetorical device: *La Clarté*, he tells us, was adopted as a national virtue because the ascendant bourgeoisie had seen it as

> The ideal appendage to a certain type of discourse, that which is given
> over to a permanent intention to persuade.[52]

Lucidity only *seems* to be the result of *any* proper or perfect use of language; in practice, it is a particular way of using language to dazzle and so to blind, with the effect of light. Lucidity is thus a curse, a temptation to be avoided. One would consequently expect Barthes himself to avoid lucidity like the plague. In practice, he writes lucidly for quite long stretches – for example in *Mythologiques* (with the exception of the pretentious theoretical essay at the end); in *The Elements of Semiology*; and in his autobiography. And it is equally interesting to see those who clearly sympathize with Barthes's suspicion of lucidity doing their best to elucidate in conventional prose the works even of a writer such as Lacan for whom opacity was the supreme virtue, and giving lucid, if self-defeating, explanations of Lacan's style. We have already referred to Eagleton's defence of 'Lacan's . . . notoriously sybilline style', which is sufficiently lucid for its pragmatic self-refutation to be visible.

According to Barthes, lucidity is a rhetorical device that passes itself off as

---

[52] *Writing Degree Zero*, p. 13.

a natural use of language; it attempts to get the reader to overlook language, pretending that language when it functions properly is transparent, effacing itself before a reality it is merely uncovering. This does not prevent him from writing lucidly about lucidity, from writing as if language were transparent, as if it were about something other than itself. One can only presume that the unmasking of the true nature of lucidity is a matter of such urgency that one cannot afford to write other than lucidly about it.

To be fair, it has to be conceded that many commentators in or on the post-Saussurean scene can escape the charge of lucidity. Even Jonathan Culler's excellent commentaries – which move fluently between opaque concepts and unthinkable ideas – are often not so much elucidations as creations of an '*effet de lucidité*'.

Occasional writers will admit that there is a conflict between the uses to which they put language and the theories they have about language, between the presuppositions necessary to advance their views and the views they are advancing. The attempt to wriggle out of the conflict produces some strikingly feeble apologias. Boyd, for example, writes:

> If I seem to impersonate, in the familiar new-critical fashion, the sovereign command of one who seeks artificial closure, or if I too abruptly and arbitrarily cut the chains of signifiers, it is simply because I wish to escape the labyrinth which is the text of the reflexive novel and return to tell, in a language we understand without believing, what I found there.[53]

Of course, if there were no escape from 'the endless chain of signifiers', if the critic, in Robert Scholes's words *had* 'taken the very idea of "aboutness" away from us', then there would be nothing to say. But you cannot publish silence; and you cannot get tenure if you don't publish. The critic, who must keep talking if he is to survive, must therefore learn to live with a constant contradiction between the views he has and the fact that he is stating them. Those who believe in the existence of extra-linguistic reality might be tempted to think that this state of affairs is the result of that reality. It is easy to be cynical about why a critic might not be inclined to stop talking, though his radical views dictate silence. But it is difficult to be cynical enough. After all, it is a safe bet that Cratylus did not get tenure in the Academy.

8.5 Critics Reading Readers

One central idea remains vigorously alive through all the radical doubts exhibited about the nature and status of language, literature, the author and reality. It is that the ordinary unpaid (usually 'bourgeois') reader, unlike the

---

[53] Michael Boyd, *The Reflexive Novel. Fiction as Critique*, (London and Toronto: Lewisburg Bucknell University Press, 1983), p. 8. Of course there is nothing unique about Boyd's book in this respect. Christopher Norris's excellent *Deconstruction* (London: Methuen, 1982) offers many comparable instances.

professional critic, is a fool. And it is this that makes the realistic novel so dangerous: he is liable to *believe* what he reads. The critics' almost touching concern for the welfare of this impressionable creature (a concern that is founded upon contempt and liable to turn quite suddenly and unexpectedly into anger) is reminiscent of the Victorian patriarch's concern about the danger that the reading of romantic novels presented to the moral economy of inexperienced young maidens. The bourgeois reader is a child and the realistic novel exploits his gullibility.

We have already discussed Catherine Belsey's anxious concern for Conan Doyle's readers:

> The success with which the Sherlock Holmes stories achieve an illusion of reality is repeatedly demonstrated . . . According to *The Times* in December 1967, letters to Sherlock Holmes were still commonly addressed to 221B Baker Street, many of them asking for the Detective's help.[54]

This is, of course, very worrying. For, as we shall see shortly, terrible things happen when readers have their heads turned by realistic novels. Leaving these catastrophes aside for the present, we have to consider the dreadful possibility that readers might be *reassured* to an unacceptable degree:

> The experience of reading a realistic text is ultimately reassuring, however harrowing the events of the story, because the world evoked in the fiction, its pattern of cause and effect, of social relationships and moral values, largely confirm the pattern of the world we seem to know.[55]

> Classic narrative of the realist kind is on the whole a conservative form which slides our anxiety at absence under the comforting sign of presence.[56]

So the reader (who happens to be having an amputation of his leg tomorrow, or who has been left by her husband, or who has an ill child, or who is facing redundancy or who is the victim of some injustice in what he or she has the nerve to call real life) will go about the world stupefied by the reassurance emanating from novels whose potent verisimilitude wipes out all else. He will abandon the critical faculty and submit to the collective sleep of state-organized life:

> The interpellation of the reader in the [realistic] literary text could be argued to have a role in reinforcing the concept of the world and of subjectivity which ensure that people 'work by themselves' in the social formation.[57]

Realism presents even greater dangers to its consumers, however, – more specific than losing one's soul to the state, more terrible than writing redundant letters to 221B Baker Street. These are discussed by Michael Boyd who

---

[54] Belsey, *op. cit.* p. 112.
[55] Belsey, *op. cit.* p. 51.
[56] Eagleton, *op. cit.* p. 186.
[57] Belsey, *op. cit.*, p. 57.

cites a story by Robert Coover about a writer's wife who mistakenly takes the manuscript of her husband's latest fiction for a grocery list and almost poisons the family. One interpretation of Coover's story is that it is a rather heavy-handed joke. Boyd, however, tells us that it is 'a cautionary tale', showing 'among other things, the danger of devouring and digesting pieces of printed matter'.[58] I should have thought it showed, rather, the danger of entrusting the cooking and shopping to a somnambulistic moron or how writing 'a cautionary tale' enables one to publish something that is at once moralistic and implausible. The realistic novel not only endangers readers in the real world but puts them at the mercy of fictional characters. Boyd quotes another sobering story – of a reader

> who projects himself so thoroughly into the novel he is reading that he literally enters its world to become the murderer's victim. Again the tone is cautionary: beware of confusing real and fictional realms.[59]

An alternative moral could be drawn from the story: one should not *buy* books but only borrow them, preferably from a public library. The recall (supported with the threat of a fine) might recall the reader to the real world and disentangle him from the clutches of potentially murderous fictional characters.

What is the origin of the belief that the reader is so stupid and therefore so vulnerable? Observation of actual readers shows that they rarely confuse events in novels with those in their own lives, though the former may be a critique of the latter. (And, it must not be forgotten, vice versa: the reader criticizes the novel from the standpoint of his own life.) 'What child' Sir Philip Sidney asks, 'is there that coming to a play and seeing Thebes written in great letters upon an old door doth believe that it is in Thebes?'.[60] Few under-age children, anyway. Certain over-age children, however, are obliged to claim that they are believers themselves in the fictional world of the novel. For it is part of the duty of the critic, and central to the routines of critical rhetoric, to exaggerate the extent to which works of art displace the real world. For reasons that we shall discuss presently, it is the critics' daily experience to be 'spell-bound' and to experience fictional characters as being more real than the ones he meets in his own life. This is quite unlike the experience of the average (unpaid) reader.

Let us imagine the common reader. For such a person, reading books is one thing she does among many. She may value highly the experience of reading fiction, but this still remains an experience, a series of episodes, amongst many others. Since she is not paid for exaggerating the value or impact (pernicious or otherwise) of books in her life, she will recognize that a book – fiction or non-fiction, realistic or anti-realistic – is a book and not

[58] Boyd, *op. cit.* p. 173.
[59] Boyd, *op. cit.* p. 174.
[60] Quoted in Graff, *op. cit.*, p. 152.

some irresistable force operating upon her. She may be reading several books at the same time and will quite likely read any given book in snatches. Unlike the critic, who has devoted his life to the author's works, she may occasionally confuse characters and get a little muddled over some aspects of the plot. However, her reading will often take place in the shadow of the events happening in her own life; she is not, therefore, at liberty to give herself up in total abandonment to the novel.

Thus the common reader. The critic's image of the reader, however, is likely to be based on his reading of other critics – past or present. The stupidity of the all-too-easily manipulated average reader is a distortion derived from other critics' claims about their reading experiences. It is the professional reader not the common reader who 'lives inside books', is 'transformed' by the encounter with a certain fiction, or suffers, as Mr Eagleton claims to suffer in a passage quoted earlier, from 'pulverized order', 'subverted meaning' and 'exploded self-assurance'. What ordinary reader ever thought that writers had their own unique vision of the world? That 'classic realist' authors wrote from a position of total disinterest and absolute lucidity? That novelists create the language they use? What ordinary reader ever believed that a text was totally coherent and had organic unity? And although a few unpaid readers concern themselves with the author behind the text, it is usually professional readers who believe in 'the author's vision', the organic unity of the work, the divine origin of the authorial message. Many, possibly most, unpaid readers are unable to remember the names of the authors of some of the books they read. The *oeuvre* (rather like the canon) exists only for the salaried reader. And it is the latter, not the common reader, who consumes novels with the submissive and fascinated attention he attributes to the casual reader.

The things the reader is supposed to believe in are in fact discredited opinions put forward, and presumably held, largely by critics and those of their students who feel obliged to parrot their meanings in examinations. As we have already discussed (see Chapter 1) many fashionable implausible critical views (that, for example, books are not written by authors) are over-reactions to opposite implausible ideas held by earlier critics (that, for example, authors not only write their books but create worlds and that every sentence in those books is the result of a totally conscious choice). The opposite of nonsense, however, may not be sense; it may merely be the opposite nonsense. The dangerous gullibility of the common reader helps to justify the existence of the vigilant, sceptical, unintoxicated professional reader.

Discussing the 'gains of structuralism', Eagleton points to 'a remorseless demystification of literature'. It is, he says, 'less easy after Greimas and Genette to hear the cut and thrust of rapiers in line 3, or to feel that you know just what it feels like to be a scarecrow after reading *The Hollow Men*.[61] 'Less easy' implies that it was easy before. Demystification is necessary, and possible, only for

[61] Eagleton, *op. cit.* p. 118.

those who have been mystified in the first place. The ability 'to hear the cut and thrust of rapiers in line 3' is an acquired skill; or rather an illusory skill induced by reading a certain sort of criticism founded on the once-popular belief that the power of poetry was dependent on a mimetic relationship between the description and the object described. The structuralist 'discovery' that literature is about itself rather than an extra-literary world (manifestly untrue) is helpful only as a corrective to the belief that literature is not only about reality but actually succeeds in being about it by replicating it.

It was critics, not ordinary readers, who imagined they could 'hear the cut and thrust of rapiers in line 3', their hearing in this case, as their intelligence in so many others, being bewitched by some *theory* of reading or of literature. Readers, being without theories, are less vulnerable. The common reader, not subscribing to the belief that she is always more awake, more alert, more sensitive than other readers, is for that reason saved from joining the long tradition of almost moronic simplification that continues from one critical generation to the next. It is Jacques Derrida, not the ordinary reader, who speaks of 'Western culture' as if it were one thing or one mindful; it is Pierre Macherey, not the average reader, who talks about 'history' as if he had been present at or had access to all of it; it is Roland Barthes, not the man in the street, who talks about 'the text' and 'the author' as if there were only one of each. In short, it is grand theorists, not common readers, who are *terribles simplificateurs*. And they then attribute their vices to readers. We have already seen the spectacular example of Barthes who felt able to summarize 'the bourgoisie' by their habit of 'thinking in essences'. Only a terminal essentialist could believe that he had penetrated to 'the bottom of every bourgeois mythology of man'. Only an essentialist could write (as Barthes writes) that 'the bourgeois sign is a metonymic confusion' that has replaced 'the feudal index'.[62] Only an almost lunatic essentialism could give one the confidence to speak of the *whole* of classical language and refer to it as 'a bringer of euphoria' because it is 'immediately social'[63] or to summarize 'the petit bourgeois' as 'a man unable to imagine the Other'.[64]

We might, catching Barthes's style, define a certain sort of critic as someone unable to imagine the reader as other than the self he has just woken up out of. This is well illustrated by critical views of the 'reading experience' and what that experience amounts to or culminates in. A critic's public – and published – response to a book is an artefact. In the case of the literary journalist, this has to be big enough to make an article of a certain, predetermined length. What shall this response consist of? After all there is an unlimited number of things one can write in response to a novel: the story can be retold; the author's background and previous works can be described; the book can be related to similar works by other writers or contrasted with quite

[62] Barthes, *S/Z* p. 40.
[63] Barthes *Writing Degree Zero*, p. 55.
[64] Barthes, *Mythologies*, p. 141.

different works by yet other writers; stylistic features can be singled out for criticism or praise; and so on. In the kangaroo court of the weekly reviewer summary judgement must also be passed. What shall be the basis of this judgement?

For a long time it was conveniently thought, imagined or asserted that the essence of an appropriate response to a work of literature was a feeling. One read and one was moved. Whether or not this feeling had first been experienced by the author and then extracted from it by the reader was not always clear. It didn't matter: feelings were far too useful as critical devices. The notion that such a complex, protracted and often interrupted experience as reading a novel could culminate in, or be reduced to, a feeling is intrinsically implausible but it has the virtue of being (a) convenient and (b) fitting with the romantic conception of the soul. This conception is a flattering one; for it permits the critic to think of himself as both more unified and more completely given over to feelings than is in fact the case. The romantic critic does not know of those interruptions and intercurrent preoccupations that dilute the usual reading experience, he knows nothing of all those things that make daily indeed, hourly, experience much more chopped up than it is flattering to recall. He knows only the 'disgust' the 'delight', the 'satisfaction', the 'disturbing unease', the 'shock' that blurb writers can carry away from the final paragraphs of his review. A critic is someone who feels sad not because, like you or me, he has missed the bus to work, but because of the sentence structures of a certain piece of fiction. A critic is someone, in short, who is blessed with feelings that have the habit of appearing on cue to give point to his fabricated response to books. Self-taught or university-trained, it scarcely matters; for it is not necessary to go to an institute of higher education to learn how to deceive oneself through 'literary appreciation'. 'Lying about feelings' would be too strong an expression here; few people have the capacity or inclination to notice or remember themselves with such precision as to know whether they are lying about their feelings or not.

Some of the welcome given to both anti-realistic fiction and post-Saussurean criticism may therefore originate from the self-disgust of critics. Anti-realism frees the critic from the burden of claiming to have been 'moved' by a book. It permits the critic to acknowledge that the emotions induced by books are different from those produced by situations in our lives – so different in fact as scarcely to warrant being called feelings at all. We do not participate in the anger of the fictional character in the way in which we participate in the anger of a friend or experience our own anger. (Nor would many realistic novelists wish us to do so.) It must be of considerable relief to critics – especially to regular reviewers who may not feel up to having reportable intense feelings three or four times a week – to learn that language is self-referring and that Little Nell's death and the birth of Levin's son are mere sign clusters not, in the well-trained heart, occasions for overwhelming emotional excitement. Anti-realistic novels, many of which manifestly do *not* aim to move the reader, provide the critic with a perspective from which to criticize not only the realistic novel but also the common reader's (i.e. the common critic's) myths about it.

The language of feelings is a very difficult one, however, for the professional critic to manage without. Feeling-names are useful portmanteau terms for summarizing the imagined or claimed 'impact' of books, as well as for giving the trade what it wants – blurb-fodder. Recidivism is therefore almost inevitable and it is not unusual even for the most advanced critic to describe his 'response' to an anti-realistic novel in terms of feelings he should have got beyond. He forgets the lauded implausibility of explicit fiction and 'remembers' the work as if he had believed in it in the way one is supposed to believe in realistic fiction. Implausibly claiming to be frightened of goblins or to be moved by non-referential sentiments, he makes wild assertions about his emotions, as we saw in the case of critics writing about Donald Barthelme (Section 8.2).

Barthes, as usual, provides us with the best examples of inconsistency and self-contradiction. His position is, as we have seen, that the 'ideal' work is only 'a galaxy of signifiers, not a structure of signifieds'. Nevertheless such a work must be evaluated if the critic is to remain in employment. The way to evaluate 'the work of our modernity' is, surprisingly, to test the feelings they induce in us. Now we are no longer permitted to enjoy or claim to enjoy the mental and moral feelings of the self-deceiving bourgeois reader. Instead, we are allowed the somatic, quasi-sexual feelings of the post-Puritan, liberated reader of the writerly text. The approved feeling triggered by the approved text is not mere 'pleasure' but *bliss* – an orgasmic, swooning experience of disorientation and collapse induced by texts that constitute 'a ribbon of infra-language' in which ideological structures, intellectual solidarity, idiomatic propriety and 'even the sacred armature of syntax' are destroyed in the collision of incompatible languages.[65] The modern critic must seek out texts that 'bring to a crisis his relations with language' and train himself to swoon with the facility of a Victorian maiden reading a dangerous novel. The effect of the approved text is like that of hearing the materiality of the voice when

> The whole presence of the human muzzle . . . succeeds in signifying the
> signified from a great distance and throwing, so to speak, the anonymous
> body of the actor into my ear, it granulates, it crackles, it caresses, it
> grates, it cuts, it comes: that is bliss.[66]

The wheel has come full circle. But the bliss-possessed critic, arrested in status-orgasmicus, is even more implausible than those discredited old-timers who claimed to finish novels tingling with moral consciousness, exquisite sensitivity, heated with higher emotions and lit by eternal verities. The Kleenex-tissue school of literary appreciation has returned – except that now the tissue has to be applied to a different organ. What remains unchanged is

---

[65] Roland Barthes, *The Pleasure of the Text*, trans. Richard Miller, (New York: Hill & Wang, 1975), pp. 7–8.

[66] Barthes, *op. cit.*, p. 67.

hype (and hyperventilation) and, by implication, self-hype. We may confidently look forward to the time when Barthes's views are repudiated and they are attributed to an absorbed reader on the 11.20 from Paddington. Prior to that, however, we may expect the regulations covering the consumption of literature on trains to forbid reading when the train is standing in the station.

One of the many reasons why the ordinary reader may be taken in by the realistic novel is that it addresses itself to the reader 'as a transcendental and non-contradictory subject by positioning him or her as the "unified and unifying subject of its vision" '.[67] Even where a realistic novel explicitly deals with conflicts between the viewpoints of its characters, it cannot let that contradiction rest but must give the reader a standpoint from which the warring viewpoints of the characters can be viewed and situated. This standpoint is established, it will be recalled from Chapter 6, through the hierarchy of discourses which Belsey sees as a characteristic, even inescapable, feature of realistic fiction. In her analysis, the naive reader is set up as a position from which 'the text is most obviously intelligible'. This sounds convincing until we ask ourselves: how does Ms Belsey *know*? Only in virtue of being quite different from the ordinary reader. She is, almost uniquely, in a position to see through novels that might deceive readers postulated to be far less intelligent or perceptive than herself. Only the critic is able to add a further tier to 'the hierarchy of discourses'. In this tier, the intention of the other discourses is made plain and we are given a confident monosemic reading of the novel – and, more significantly, of its rather dim readers.

8.6 Kritikerschuld

In the Introduction to his extraordinary *Guide to Modern World Literature*, Martin Seymour-Smith defines a term that he will use in speaking of certain writers (for example Rilke, Mann, Broch): *Künstlerschuld* or artist-guilt.

> Increasingly in this century poets and writers . . . have been beset by the fear that literature fulfils no useful, but only a selfish function. The writers who feel this particular kind of anguish have been or are almost invariably dedicated to literature to the exclusion of everything else.[68]

Some artists try to mitigate *Künstlerschuld* by a more ferocious dedication to their art (Mann's work as 'active hope'); others by making claims for the importance of art in the world at large (as for example Rilke's *Letter to a Young Workman*). In many instances, however the anguish remains unresolved – a spur to greater art and the source of a deepening unhappiness.[69]

[67] Belsey, *op. cit.* p. 77.
[68] Martin Seymour-Smith, *Guide to Modern World Literature* (London: Hodder & Stoughton, 1975), p. xviii.
[69] Many philosophers, too, suffered from it. Wittgenstein is a notable example. In common with many artists, he frequently toyed with the idea of being a doctor. The traffic, of course, is two-way: many doctors have dreamed of being artists and not a few have defected from medicine to earn their living by writing.

If the creative artist suffers from guilt at the superfluity of his activities in a world dominated by suffering, some of it avoidable and much of it remediable by practical non-artistic action, how much more intensely must the sensitive critic suffer from the anguish of uselessness. The critic is doubly guilty: like the artist, parasitic upon the productive process; but, unlike him, parasitic upon the work of art. *Kritikerschuld*, analogous to *Künstlerschuld* is therefore almost inevitable. Its aetiology has been well described by Terry Eagleton:

> Those who work in the field of cultural practices are unlikely to mistake their activity as utterly central. Men and women do not live by culture alone, the vast majority throughout history have been deprived of any chance of living by it at all, and those few who are fortunate to live by it now are able to do so because of the labour of those who do not. Any cultural or critical theory which does not begin from this single most important fact, and hold it steadily in mind in its activities is in my view unlikely to be worth very much. There is no document of culture which is not also a record of Barbarism.[70]

After Auschwitz, where a nation of *dichter und denker* consented to mass murder and hideous cruelty on a scale to which few parallels can be found in history, no one believes that poets are the secret legislators of the world or that even committed artists can save (or redeem) the people.

Worse still, it could be argued that the work of literary critics adds to, rather than merely failing to substract from, the sum total of oppression in the world. Many developed countries have witnessed an exponential growth of the literary critical industry: expenditure on literary criticism in the United States seems to be exceeded only by that on defence. The result is increasing numbers of reinterpretations of the classics, all equally plausible or implausible and many unhelpful, and collectively impeding the reader's access to the works they deal with. In such a situation, one has to be almost pathologically self-confident to believe that one's own contribution to, say, the vast corpus of studies on Jane Austen is an essential or even useful mediator between the artist and her potential readership. Far from alleviating the suffering of the masses, the self-questioning critic may feel he has only added to the great mass of secondary literature oppressing school children and students.

Doubly superfluous, the critic is in desperate need of salvation. One way out would be to combine literary criticism with some other activity liable to make a more direct contribution to the common good. The critic could anticipate the condition of man in the communist Utopia envisaged by Marx:

> For as soon as the distribution of labour comes into being, each man has a particular, exclusive, sphere of activity, which is forced upon him and from which he cannot escape. He is a hunter, a fisherman, a herdsman or a critical critic, and must remain so if he does not want to lose the means

---

[70] Eagleton, *op. cit.* p. 118.

of his livelihood; while in communist society, where nobody has one exclusive sphere of activity but each can become accomplished in any branch he wishes, society regulates the general production and thus makes it possible for me to do one thing today and another tomorrow, to hunt in the morning, fish in the afternoon, rear cattle in the evening, criticize after dinner . . .[71]

This is a solution that has not, so far as I know, been adopted by any of those critics who anguish over the futility of criticism. Libraries are, after all, very comfortable places – certainly more so than fish farms – and running a seminar for admiring students is undoubtedly a good deal more pleasant than hoeing a turnip field. There is an alternative escape. 'When a priest loses his faith' Ernest Gellner wrote, 'he becomes unfrocked. When a philosopher loses his, he re-defines his subject'.[72] This is the path that many literary critics have chosen. Literary criticism has given way to literary theory or critical theory; and this in turn has given place to textual theory or 'a domain as yet unnamed but often called "theory" for short'.[73] The rise of theory has apparently solved many of the critic's problems. Instead of being twice removed from useful activity, the critic finds himself in the front line in the battle for the world's soul. 'Every contemporary critic'. W.J.T. Mitchell, the editor of *Critical Inquiry*, tells us 'longs to be what Gramsci called an "organic" intellectual, connected by elective affinities with a cause, a social movement, a collective programme'.[74] 'Theory' answers to that longing. As a theorist, the meta-critic is no longer a servant to literature; and what he says may have direct importance in the real world. That at least is the moral attraction of theory. 'New' New Criticism, is not, like the old stuff, addressed to content: it is, to use Barthes's terms, 'a science of the *conditions* of content . . . a science of forms'.[75] Its subject is not the particular work of art but the linguistic and historical conditions that made the work possible. The work is reduced to the status of an instance, a case. This is a new approach, which clearly downgrades the work of art; but this is a cheap price to pay; for 'The most important feature of this process is that it offers a new role and status to the critic'.[76]

For the guilty critic whose ambitions force him to toil uselessly in The Groves of Hackademe, the liberation from service, and hence servitude, to the creative writer is exhilarating. Geoffrey Hartman, a leading 'theorist' of the Yale school, opens his essay *The Interpreter: A Self-Analysis*, with an

---

[71] K. Marx and F. Engels, *The German Ideology*, ed. and introduced by C.J. Arthur, (London: Lawrence & Wishart, 1974), p. 54.

[72] Ernest Gellner, *Words and Things*, (Harmondsworth: Penguin).

[73] Jonathan Culler, *On Deconstruction: Theory and Criticism after Structuralism* (London: Routledge & Kegan Paul, 1983), p. 8.

[74] Mitchell, *op. cit.* p. 17. This longing to be an 'organic' intellectual is amply confirmed in Imre Salusinsky's interviews with leading theorists (*Criticism in Society*, London: Methuen, 1987).

[75] Barthes quoted in Hawkes, *op. cit.* p. 157.

[76] Terence Hawkes, *Structuralism and Semiology* (London: Methuen, 1977), p. 156–7.

admission even more frank than Terence Hawkes's quoted above: 'I have a superiority complex *vis-à-vis* other critics and an inferiority complex *vis-à-vis* art.'[77] How fortunate for him, then, that 'we have entered an era that can challenge even the priority of literature to literary-critical texts'. For this will leave him only with his superiority complex – a much nicer thing to have to live with than an inferiority one. The 'merely' critical does not have to endure a galling secondary role compared with the 'creative'; for, in the eyes of theorists, to criticize is to create and, anyway, the creator may not be as creative as he believes he is. This blurring of the roles of critic and creator is a constant theme in Harold Bloom. 'All poetry', he informs us 'necessarily becomes verse criticism, just as all criticism becomes prose-poetry'.[78] As Lentricchia says, with appropriate vulgarity, Bloom 'would grab a piece of the creative action'. For Bloom, 'the critical event is as poetically compelling as the poetic event'.[79] Other critics would take this further. We have already noted how, according to Mitchell, 'the dominant mode of literary expression' in the current 'golden age of criticism' is not poetry, fiction, drama or film but 'criticism and theory'. Boyd also thinks that we may 'have entered an era' in which creation is *less* creative than criticism. For him,

> the major lesson taught by the reflexive novel is the primacy of theory, and, indeed, much postmodern fiction needs to catch up with postmodern criticism.[80]

There are two strategies open to the critic who wishes to reverse the relationship between works of art and works of criticism in order to hasten the arrival of that future era in which, for example, fiction will be produced only in order that the critic may have the opportunity to develop his theories. The first is to downgrade the work of art or the creative process; and the second is to upgrade the work of criticism and the significance of the critic. We shall look at each of these strategies in turn.

The connexion between the transformation of literary criticism into 'theory' and a change of attitude towards the literary work is particularly clearly expressed by Mitchell:

> Wayne Booth argues that the 'understanding' of the author's intention may be an insufficient goal for interpretation, and posits a process of 'overstanding' as the goal of a more ambitious criticism. This ambition

---

[77] Geoffrey Hartman, *The Fate of Reading and Other Essays,* (Chicago and London: University of Chicago Press, 1975), p. 3.

[78] Harold Bloom, *A Map of Misreading* (New York: Oxford University Press, 1975), p. 3.

[79] Frank Lentricchia, *After the New Criticism* (London: Methuen, 1981), p. 336. In Salusinsky's book *Criticism in Society* (London: Methuen, 1987), Bloom asserts that 'literature cannot authentically touch us unless we begin by being very greatly gifted'. And he adds, rather tetchily, 'I don't know what people are talking about when they think that imaginative fiction . . . is one thing, and a critical essay is something startlingly different . . . someone who cannot see this cannot be taught anything.'

[80] Boyd, *op. cit.*, p. 8.

is at its most scandalous when it claims to free criticism from its traditional subordination to 'primary literature' and asserts that criticism is
itself a mode of creative writing. Most interesting recent criticism is not
just 'commentary' or 'interpretation' of primary texts, but an attempt to
clarify fundamental questions about the nature of literature, its relations
to other arts, its place in the whole fabric of cultural, social and political
reality – what one recently founded critical journal calls (by its own
name) the 'Social Text'.[81]

With this approach, the critic should have no difficulty surpassing the
work of art by 'situating' it, i.e. putting it in its place. If the work, ultimately,
is a piece of Social Text, it clearly has no author (something we shall discuss
presently) and precious little in the way of autonomous meaning. For meaning 'is always constructed by the reader, the result of a "circulation" between
social formation, reader and text'.[82] This is very exciting for the critic:

> It makes him a participant in the work he reads. The critic *creates* the
> finished work by his reading of it, and does not simply remain the inert
> *consumer* of a 'ready-made' product. Thus the critic need not humbly
> efface himself before the work and submit to its demands: on the con-
> trary, he actively constructs its meaning: he *makes* the work exist.[83]

Hawkes cites Barthes's *S/Z* as 'the exhilarating monument to this "total"
rejection of the critic's passive role'.

Neither the work of art nor the artist is more 'original' than either the work
of criticism or the critic. The novel or poem tells us nothing new, only what is
'already known'. It is reasonable then to shift attention from what is apparently said in the text to the conditions of its production and meaning and the
ways in which it might contradict itself due to contradictions inherent in
those conditions. Texts, of course, tend to conceal the means by which they
are produced, passing themselves off as transparent accounts of a world they
refer to ('the world of the author') or as expressions of their authors' consciousnesses. The text naturalizes itself. That is why critics are still needed.
The critic's job is no longer to help the ordinary reader to understand what
the author meant but to unmask what appears natural in the work as artificial,
to show the text as constructed. The most potent way of doing this will be to
point out where the construction fails and demonstrate the text in conflict
with itself – to deconstruct it; in Barbara Johnson's words, to tease out its
'warring significations'.

Clearly the aim of the critic is not to submit to the text but to dominate it;
not to try to extract what can be got out of it but to go beyond it – to see it for
what it is, to put it in its place, to reduce it to an example, an illustration of a
principle, grist to the theoretic mill. A paradigm case here is Poe's *The*

---

[81] Mitchell, *op. cit.*, p. 15. Northrop Frye was, of course, the first great contemporary 'over-
stander', reducing literature to instances of types, situating, rather than evaluating, works.
[82] Belsey, *op. cit.*, p. 60.
[83] Hawkes, *op. cit.*, p. 157.

Purloined Letter. Lacan makes it into a French letter to be filled with his semes. Derrida then takes Lacan's piece and uses it for his purposes. Next, Barbara Johnson grinds her own theoretical axe on Derrida's theories. Then Culler uses it as an example of a deconstructive reading. Finally, I have used it here to show how critics expropriate works of art rather than explicate them. *The Purloined Letter* becomes a purloined text: the author and his intentions are displaced from the work; or, at least, the work is no longer centred upon or regarded as emanating from the author. The origins of the text must be sought in the general conditions of its production and in the language in which it is written. The holder of the pen is no longer using language to express reality, but is rather used by language to reduplicate a reality that is in part a linguistic contract.

The project of putting the author in his place and of demystifying – or downgrading – the work of art is especially associated with Roland Barthes. In The Death of the Author he tells us

> We now know that a text is not a line of words releasing a single 'theological' meaning (the 'message' of the Author – God) but a multi-dimensional space in which a variey of writings, none of them original, blend and clash.[84]

The text in fact is a tissue of quotations drawn from 'the innumerable centres of culture'. These emerge from 'a field without origin' or one that has 'no other origin than language itself, language which ceaselessly calls into question all origins'. The true origin of the work is the interaction between language and reader. 'The reader is the space in which all the quotations that make up a writing are inscribed without any of them being lost; a text's unity lies not in its origin but in its destination. . .'. Thus the reader displaces the author from the centre of the stage: the birth of the reader, Barthes asserts, must be at the cost of the death of the Author.

The comfort that Barthes offers to the critics, however, may be double-edged. The good news is that the reader capable of being a space 'in which *all* the quotations that make up a writing are inscribed without *any* of them being lost' will not be the average, unpaid skimmer galloping through a novel in order to find what happens next. Barthes's reader – upon whom nothing is lost – is clearly a professional critic for whom the text provides the occasion of his or her own productivity. But the bad news is that as soon as the critic becomes a writer rather than a mere reader, he must himself leave the space where the meanings of texts are produced. He will suffer the same fate as the Author, become the mere absence behind the text whose unity resides only in the reader. So the superiority of the reader-critic over the creator vanishes as soon as the critic puts pen to paper and becomes, in his own modest way, a creator. The birth of the reader bumps off the critic as well as the creator;

[84] Barthes, 'The Death of the Author' in *Image = Music = Text*, Essays selected and trans. Stephen Heath (London: Fontana/Glasgow: Collins, 1977), p. 146.

indeed, the amateur reader proves to be a bit of a cuckoo in the nest.

Of course there are ways of getting rid of the ordinary, non-productive reader as well. The arguments I examined in Part II showed how the non-critic could be dismissed as an artefact produced by the text – usually a realistic text that colludes with other manifestations of the Ideological State Apparatus 'to interpellate him as a subject in order that he freely accepts his subjectivity'.[85] Under this interpretation, the reader ceases to be a privileged space in which the text uniquely achieves unity. On the contrary, it is the text that constitutes or creates the unity of the reader:

> the text interpellates the reader as a transcendant and non-contradictory subject by positioning him or her as 'the unified and unifying subject of its vision'.[86]

So the critic's victory over the artist proves to be a Pyrrhic one. By a ghastly domino-effect the death of the author turns into a massacre, with critics and ordinary readers being wiped out along with the Author. All that remains standing is a rather lonely text – that seemingly came from nowhere and is going nowhere, falling from the air into the air – to weave them all together again. And even the text looks rather vulnerable; for according to some theorists, texts owe their meanings to the activity of readers. There are no such things as texts, only interpretations. So all we may be left with are meaningless squiggles unaccountably applied to thin slices of fallen trees.

The tactic of downgrading the artist and the work of art, therefore, leads to a rather short-lived triumph for the critic. It does in the end, however, leave critic and artist on an equal footing and Geoffrey Hartman's inferiority complex remains in remission. He can still claim that 'there is no clear division for post-structuralism between "criticism" and "creation": both modes are subsumed into "writing" as such'.[87] But the critic is still left bearing the creative artist's burden of *Künstlerschuld*. A work of theory may not be precisely what a starving world on the brink of destruction needs most urgently. It must try to establish its importance in the real world rather than staking out its *Lebensraum* in the palace of cultural varieties. It must compete successfully in the list of the world's priorities along with politics, medicine, engineering, etc. For a critic, as much as the artist, dislikes the feeling of being a useless mouth or a ship in a bottle.

Künstlerschuld has provoked many modern artists to magic thinking. Shelley's assertion that 'poets are the unacknowledged legislators of the world' – the touchstone since Auden mocked it of lunatic sentimentality – seems like hard-bitten realism compared with Artaud's claims or hopes for a 'true theatre':

---

[85] Belsey, *op. cit.*, p. 69.
[86] Belsey, *op. cit.*, p. 78.
[87] Eagleton, *op. cit.*, p. 139.

> the plague
> a cholera,
> the black pocks
> only exist because the dance
> and consequently the theatre
> have not begun to exist.[88]

One presumes that if such a theatre did exist there would be a choice of treatment for the diarrhoea which currently kills five million children a year: oral rehydration or (better) a decent theatre.

Theorists entertain similar wild dreams, though they do not state them so vulnerably. For behind 'theory' is a dream of unmasking literature and society at large and in this way contributing to the revolution that will lead to the better future. Exactly how this is going to come about is a little unclear. The blurb to Hawkes's book speaks of 'a new level of general awareness of the ways in which we communicate with one another' and speaks darkly of 'the implications these contain for a society swiftly moving beyond its commitment to the printed page'. Barbara Johnson sees her central role as that of 'deconstructing the rhetoric of authority'.[89] Mitchell confesses that 'theory' 'rarely confronts "real" political issues in any direct political way, trusting to the mysterious power of ideas and symbols to work transformations in the larger culture'. (One way of feeling more comfortable about not confronting real political issues is to put 'real' in inverted commas.)

The dream of being useful – and its fading – is seen most clearly in Barthes's career. An analysis of the conditions of the production of meaning seemed to offer the hope of unmasking the process by which humanly produced meaning is passed off as 'the obvious', the artificial as the natural and the historical as eternal. The essentialism at the heart of the bourgeois mythologies would be dismantled and the domination of the world by iniquitous bourgeois formations – discourses, institutions, practices, power groups – would be made visible and so rendered susceptible to challenge. 'Analysing myths' Barthes argued in 1953, 'is the only effective way for an intellectual to take action'.[90] Twenty years later, having passed through another dream – the 'euphoric' dream of scientificity – he had succumbed to a third dream – that of a permanent state of bliss made possible through experiencing the gaps between sign systems. The semioclastic role of the critic continued to buoy up the theorist: undermining the symbolic order

---

[88] Antonin Artaud, *Le Theatre de la Cruauté*, quoted in Martin Esslin, Artaud (London: Fontana, 1976), p. 89.

[89] In Salusinsky *op. cit.* Hillis Miller advances an even more direct claim in his interview with Salusinsky.

> At the moment, the most appalling fact in our historical situation is to live under the threat of nuclear annihilation. Pushing the button that starts the bombs off cannot occur except through language. Talking about it, studying it, trying in some way to demystify it, might be what the study of literature could do to prevent that from happening. (Salusinsky p. 222).

[90] Barthes, quoted in Jonathan Culler, *Barthes*, Fontana Modern Masters, London, 1983, p. 40.

would inevitably lead to a change in the order of society – a change of course for the better. But it had severely narrowed its ambitions. 'The text', the later Barthes tells us 'is (should be) that uninhibited person who shows his behind to the Political Father'.[91] Not the kind of thing that brings down governments – outside the realms of magic thought.

Nevertheless, the impression remains that 'Man everywhere in chains' is enchained by languages, codes, mythologies, and sign systems that perpetuate the status quo. In pursuit of the goal of liberating him, Terry Eagleton tells us, radical critics will use any method or theory 'which will contribute to the strategic goal of human emancipation, the production of "better people" through the socialist transformation of society'.[92] Structuralism, semiotics, psychoanalysis, deconstruction, reception theory and so on: 'all of these approaches, and others, have their valuable insights which may be put to use' in serving the aim of criticism, which is 'not to interpret literary works, but to master in some disinterested spirit the underlying sign-systems which generate them'.[93] Theory does not by itself produce solutions to specific medical, political or engineering problems but it will contribute to their solution by reforming human consciousness from within or from beneath through its semioclastic activity. The study of English, transformed into the 'disinterested mastery of sign systems', will rise again to serve its ancient triple functions: 'to delight and instruct us, but also, and above all, to save our souls and heal the State'.[94]

This last piece of rhetoric is not Eagleton but quoted by him in the opening chapter of his book, where he subjects the claims made nearly a century ago, on behalf of the rising new subject of English studies, to a masterly and sarcastic analysis. It takes one to know one: the hopes of George Gordon, early Professor of English Literature at Oxford, invested in his subject are not, after all, so different from those of Eagleton (Fellow and Tutor in the same university). Eagleton's hope of producing 'better people' and of bringing about 'the social transformation of society' are ambitions with a similar scope and perhaps even a similar content to those of 'saving the souls of the people' and 'healing the state'.

What both views share is of course an almost child-like magic thinking. Eagleton's belief that investigating the sign-systems of the politically dominant groups will help to avert the nuclear threat or to change the world in the direction of a state of distributive justice is somewhat optimistic. Sign-systems are a function of the rest of the world; language is not a closed system nor itself an *origin* of evil. Eagleton himself is far too intelligent to believe in his own rhetoric – especially when that rhetoric is echoed in the views of others. In the same book he discusses Julia Kristeva's belief that a new language of the semiotic – 'the pattern or play of forces which we can detect

91 Roland Barthes, *The Pleasure of the Text*, p. 53.
92 Eagleton, *op. cit.*, p. 211.
93 Eagleton, *op. cit.*, p. 214.
94 Eagleton, *op. cit.*, p. 23.

inside language' – a residue of the pre-oedipal, pre-linguistic bodily pulsions and drives of the speechless infant – would undermine the symbolic order. This kind of language is implicit, Kristeva believes, in the linguistic experiments of the late Symbolists – especially Mallarmé. The political implication of this feminine discourse is that it might 'disrupt all stable meaning' and so the stable institutions that maintain and embody the social status quo. Kristeva's position, Eagleton points out, is 'easily caricaturable: will reading Mallarmé bring down the bourgeois state?'[95] But his own views are no less easily caricaturable.

If, in the end, the advanced critic ends up by disbelieving his own wild claims on behalf of literary theory and its supposed influence on the affairs of the world, what can he do? He is obliged to retreat to literary criticism and to do what literary critics have always done – which is to practice discrimination, to evaluate works of literature either implicitly or explicitly and promote those which seem potentially to be of benefit to human kind. *How* they practice that discrimination provides the clearest testament to the continuing 'agenbite of inwit' that, despite almost daily redefinitions of their subject, they continue to suffer from. Only intolerable *Kritikerschuld* can explain how even the most radical critic regresses from time to time and praises a realistic novel for all sorts of old-fashioned reasons – humour, merciless accuracy, atmosphere, etc. This regression is most likely to occur when the critic is faced with a novel known to be written by someone stuck in one of the more unpleasant corners of contemporary reality – a South African jail for example. The critic is, after all, a good fellow and despite his doubts about the ability of language to have external reference, he still subscribes to the conventional belief that you should be careful what you say to or about a man who has suffered appallingly at the hands of others. He has a dim fear, perhaps, that as a fairly well-off citizen engaged in non-productive but well-salaried labour, he could, in a world that sees things aright, be regarded as a member of an oppressing class. He would not wish this view to be reinforced by his attacking a novel in terms that its oppressed author would not even understand. To criticize a realistic autobiographical novel written on toilet paper by a black South African in a torture cell on the grounds that it overlooks the non-referential nature of language would be in the worst taste and would portray a heartlessness comparable to that of a man complaining that the tears of a woman in labour spoilt her make-up.

There are other, subtler, reasons for the radical critic's abdication from his radical literary position in the face of a work originating from an author in what might be described as a 'radical' situation. Radical stylistic innovation, which is incorrectly thought of as being *necessarily* anti-realistic, is also connected with or seen as equivalent to the radical stance of a political revolutionary. So an author who is 'existentially' radical, is excused having to be stylistically so. He is permitted to write realistically. An unreformed, naive

95 Eagleton, *op. cit.*, p. 190.

realism is forgiven if you have been beaten up by the Police or persecuted by the KGB. Your credentials are too good for your realistic novel to be considered as an act of collusion with the bourgeois individualistic world picture or as a demonstration of solidarity with that dominant oppressive group who determine what counts as reality. So even advanced theorists, who have been at best tortured only by their consciences, go easy when it comes to criticizing those who have been tortured by the authorities. A feeling of moral inferiority encourages an equating of literary and stylistic breaks with 'bourgeois' realism with life-endangering opposition to the political status quo. The critic is therefore morally, and the writer stylistically, let off the hook.[96]

Guilt, then, can be a potent force in the Academy. This guilt can, finally, be assuaged only by a repudiation of all those advances that transformed literary criticism into literary theory and literary theory into theory. To remind us of the gravity of the situation in which he is writing his book, Eagleton reports: 'as I write, it is estimated that the world contains over 60,000 nuclear warheads'[97]. If this is the case, then it is of course the sheerest irresponsibility to doubt whether language can be used to refer to the world, whether the referent of the phrase '60,000 nuclear warheads' has an extra-linguistic existence; or to maintain, along with Lacan whose views he presents sympathetically, that it is the world of words that creates the world of things. It is obvious that the world of things (e.g. warheads) is not *differentiated*, created, etc. by the world of words (except insofar as sophisticated linguistic communication has been necessary to bring such technological monsters to birth); for warheads speak louder than words. And the I who writes is not, insofar as he is writing about himself, a creation of language, an illusory subject manufactured by the ideological state apparatus, when he is an individual human being who feels a sense of responsibility to other human beings. The critic's guilt tells him that the 'I' who is in recipt of his pay packet is not 'a plurality of texts' but one who can be judged morally for his part in the world's affairs. It also tells him that a realistic novel of protest, written in blood and smuggled out of prison, is not a 'mere galaxy of signifiers' but an attempt to present the truth about a reality that is other than that of marks on a piece of paper. Alas, it also tells him that the hope of unpicking so-called reality by attacking the 'bourgeois use of the sign', the promise of a revelation of consciousness that will free the world from bourgeois domination (and hence from most of its evils), is more magic thinking reminiscent of Count Korzybinski's dream of the healing power of General Semantics.[98] The hope

---

[96] There is, of course, little connexion between being a stylistic and a political revolutionary. See Appendix to this part for further discussion.

[97] Eagleton, *op. cit.*, p. 194.

[98] 'Korzybinski held that widespread and systematic distortion in human reactions to sign systems, and especially that involving the use of language, had produced an endemic "un-sanity" for whose cure he recommended some complex therapies', Max Black, *The Labyrinth of Language* (Harmondsworth: Pelican, 1972), p. 161.

that a semioclastic awakening of human consciousness will halt the sledge-hammer descending on the heads of innocent children or will reverse the exploitation of the world by multi-nationals is unlikely to be fulfilled. For a start, most conflict begins outside of language – it is even sometimes based in old-fashioned moralistic anger ('it is eternally wrong to smash open a baby's head with a sledgehammer') – and it will seek its resolution outside of language. This has been well put by Frank Lentricchia:

> To what end do deconstructors wish to analyse the rhetoric of authority? To show its internal fissures, its slippages, the quicksand on which it stands. What deconstruction does there is what it's been doing with Dickens and whatever. I'm not impressed with that. All it says is: 'We can do with this what we do to literary texts'. The end of this stuff is the analytical moment when it shows the fissured foundation, and the awe at its own capacity to demonstrate it. The showing of that strikes me as irrelevant from the point of view of praxis and social life. You have to say: 'It may be very true that authority stands on an abyss, but in the mean-time the woman at the A&P is making two dollars an hour and has six kids to feed, and her boss doesn't know that the authority of his rhetoric stands on an abyss and probably wouldn't give a shit if one of us told him so.[99]

All that remains to the theorist, then, is to retreat back into literary criticism, to evaluation and to plain referential uses of language – as in the sentence 'As I write, it is estimated that the world contains over 60,000 nuclear warheads',[100] or to lose his guilt in his sense of self-importance somewhere on the flight path of the gravy jet between those international conferences where the men of signifiers meet one another.[101]

---

[99] Salusinsky, *op. cit.*, p. 206.

[100] We all want to be important. What is puzzling is the need critics have felt to be important in a certain way: to be politically important, to be of revolutionary significance. This is perhaps part of the heritage of the 1960s when the millenium seemed round the corner and anyone who was not part of the process of bringing it about was morally derelict. In that decade disinterested scholarship, the pursuit of knowledge and of understanding for its own sake, was brutally devalued by those for whom 'relevance' was everything. The 60s confused the Kingdom of Ends and the Kingdom of Means: practical work (surgery, engineering, food production, being a waiter) had to be 'creative'; aesthetic activities (such as the writing of verse or composing music) had to be of practical benefit through being politically committed. Of course, practical work at its best is creative; and art that is totally free of a higher anger at the remediable woes of the world is shallow morally and probably in other ways. In other words, the two Kingdoms overlap but, ultimately, they are separate. Not to believe this is to betray a serious loss of faith in art.

[101] The rewards for some theorists are enormous. Speaking of Edward Said, Mitchell *(op. cit.)* says that 'he combines the traditional role of "man of letters" with the new figure of the academic superstar'. Such is the 'man of signifiers'.

9

Theory Bows Out

9.1 The Return of Reference

Some advanced critics are aware that the anti-realistic novel, like the story answering to the headline SIXTEEN HORSES STUCK UP A CHIMNEY, has not yet been located. But few critics are as bold as Barthes in admitting that the works that *really* interest them, and the only ones worthy of their attention, have not yet been written. They have to pretend to find the fully-fledged anti-realistic novel, rather than admit that they have invented it, by reading all sorts of theories into different practices. But this creates, as we have seen, more problems than it solves. The excellent reasons for regarding Barthelme's works as a profound critique of realism would also apply to the Rev. W. Awdrey's railway stories. The big ideas can be mobilized and used to defend, to applaud, to license *any* deviation from 'classic realism'.

One response to this impasse is to deny the validity of the distinction between 'good' and 'bad' fiction, between literature and the rest. The canon will then expand to include Awdry as well as Barthelme, Enid Blyton as well as Philippe Sollers. But even those literary critics who pretend to welcome 'the demise of evaluation' will find it difficult to be entirely comfortable with this ploy. For their published works will testify to their preferences. Just as their less advanced colleagues prefer Donne to Harold Robbins, so they find Sollers more interesting than Blyton and some may even find Robbe-Grillet of more interest than Richard Scarry.

There are two other options. One is to hedge on the fundamental ideas and, in particular, to vacillate on the question of non-referentiality. We shall discuss this here. Another is to back out of the claims that there is a sharp distinction between realism and anti-realism and to suggest that even classic realistic novels may be re-read as anti-realistic ones. We shall discuss this in the next section.

The observer of the contemporary literary scene may be forgiven for believing that advanced theory is at least in part founded upon the premise that language is non-referential or that it refers only to itself. Terence Hawkes tells us 'that language does not construct its formations of words by reference to pattern of "reality" but on the basis of its own self-sufficient laws'.[1] This is

[1] Terence Hawkes, *Structuralism and Semiotics* (London: Methuen, 1977), pp. 16–17.

presented as a fundamental insight of post-Saussurean criticism and central to its entire critical proceedings. The reasons for believing this are invalid[2] but they are founded on the assumption that, since language is structured and has internal laws that maintain its structures (i.e. grammar), it is inevitably 'sealed off' from reference to other systems – including extra-linguistic reality. If language does seem to refer to reality, this is because the 'reality' it refers to is intralingusitic:

> the claim that a literary form reflects the world is simply tautological . . .
> realism is plausible not because it reflects the world, but because it is
> constructed out of what is discursively familiar . . . realism reflects the
> world constructed in language.[3]

(This is still a difficult position to defend. For it leads to the conclusion that 'what is intelligible as realism is the conventional and therefore familiar'. From this it should follow that all intelligible writing should seem equally realistic, which is hardly the case in practice: realism, far from being inescapable, is very difficult to achieve, irrespective of whether or not it is merely a fraudulent '*effet de réel*'.) There are even bolder statements of the non-referential position; for example Robert Scholes's already quoted assertion that 'Criticism has taken the very idea of "aboutness" away from us. It has taught us that language is tautological, if it is not nonsense, and to the extent that it is about anything it is about itself'.[4]

These are awkward views to keep faith with. A few years later, we find the same author writing about realism as follows:

> [Realism] is a mode of fiction that is not specifically factual but presents
> a world recognizably bound by the same laws as the world of the author.[5]

> Realism is a matter of perception. The realist presents his impressions of
> the world of experience. A part of his vocabulary and other technical
> instruments he shares with social scientists. The realist writer seeks
> always to give the reader a sense of the way things are . . . The realist's
> truth is a bit more general and typical than the reporter's fact. It may also
> be more vivid and memorable.[6]

There are many ingenious ways of wriggling out of radical ideas, so that the drift from Scholes Type 1 ideas to Scholes Type 2 can take place unobserved.

The first step is to claim that only *literary* language is non-referential. This may at first look like a serious retraction, narrowing the scope of a rather arresting claim. Barthes (sometimes) takes this rather difficult path but comes to his own aid with strategic re-definition:

[2] See *Not Saussure*, Chapter 3.
[3] Catherine Belsey, *Critical Practice* (London: Methuen, 1981), pp. 46–7.
[4] Robert Scholes, The Fictional Criticism of the Future *TriQuarterly*, 34 (Fall 1975).
[5] Robert Scholes, *The Elements of Fiction: An Anthology* (Oxford: Oxford University Press, 1981) p. 928.
[6] *ibid.*, p. 7.

As soon as a fact is narrated no longer with a view to acting directly on reality but intransitively, that is to say, finally outside of any other function than that of the practice of the symbol itself . . . writing begins . . . *Writing* does not designate an operation of recording, notation, representation, depiction . . .; rather it designates a performative . . . in which the enunciation has no other content . . . than the act by which it is uttered.[7]

So self-reference is not a generalized property of language but of certain rather special literary uses of language; otherwise it is business as usual.

This is rather too serious a retreat for some – after all it amounts only to the assertion that, when you are writing to no purpose whatsoever, you are merely writing. Others would prefer a less drastic limitation of the scope of non-referentiality. Paul de Man considers non-referentiality to be a characteristic of *all* language but to be an *explicit* feature only of literary language:

For the statement about language that sign and meaning never coincide, is what is precisely taken for granted in the kinds of language we call literary. Literature, unlike everyday language, begins on the far side of this knowledge; it is the only form of language free from the fallacy of unmediated expression.[8]

The trouble is, nobody seems to know precisely what literature is. Terry Eagleton's conclusion, after a long and futile search for literature, is that it is not an 'objective' category. It is an unstable concept. 'Literature' he says quoting Barthes 'is what gets taught'[9] – not in medical school, one presumes, but in Departments of English. It seems unlikely that the accident of getting taught should be sufficient to determine which parts of language are on the far side and which are on the near side of the knowledge that sign and meaning do not coincide. Change the syllabus and so change the scope of the referentiality of language? It seem unlikely. Nevertheless, Hawkes believes that 'the notion that literary works are ultimately *about* language, that their medium is their message is one of the most fruitful of structuralist ideas.'[10] (The competition is clearly not very fierce). This notion is associated especially with Roman Jakobson, for whom the distinctive feature of poetry is that its language drew attention to itself. Unfortunately, Jakobson also believed in the essential 'literariness' or 'poeticalness' of *all* language 'the "poetic function" forms part of the way all language works, and is not just a special set of "tricks" that poets perform.'[11]

The retreat from 'all language is about itself' to 'only literary language is

---

[7] Roland Barthes, The Death of the Author, available in *Image–Music–Text*, selected and trans. Stephen Heath (London: Fontana, 1977), pp. 145–6.

[8] Quoted in Gerald Graff, *Literature Against Itself* (Chicago: University of Chicago Press, 1979), p. 173.

[9] Terry Eagleton, *Literary Theory* (Oxford: Blackwell, 1983), p. 197.

[10] Hawkes, *op. cit.*, p. 80.

[11] Hawkes, *ibid.*, p. 81.

about itself' seems to be blocked by an extension of the concept of literature to include the whole of language. The way out of this impasses is ingenious but not convincing: literature occurs only when the literary function of language is 'raised to a higher degree' than other competing functions. Literature in other worlds, is differentiated from other language by the amount of 'literariness' in it. (Just as sleeping tablets are distinguished from sand only by the *intensity* of their dormitive virtues.) Literariness, 'by promoting the palpability of signs, deepens the fundamental dichotomy of signs and objects'.[12] The reader may find it difficult to see how a 'fundamental dichotomy' could be 'deepened' – presumably made more fundamental or dichotomous – but it does seem to offer a sufficiently obscure midway position to cover the retreat from the structuralist claim that literature is language talking about itself; or that the 'foregrounding' of the self-referential 'use' of language is the essential characteristic of literature. Not everyone is uncomfortable with structuralist claims, however. Jonathan Culler informs us that:

> Poetry offers the best example of a series of signifiers that is an empty
> but circumscribed space that can be filled in various ways.'[13]

And he adds to his difficulties by also saying that 'the same is true of ordinary language', but warning us that 'this may be obscured by the fact that the sign itself serves as a name for *signifie*'

For those who would prefer to retreat further, the next step is to say that not *all* literature is about language or about language being about itself. For Jakobson, it is *poetic* literature that is characterized by non-referentiality and that poeticalness is less apparent in other forms of literature. Some literature – 'so-called realistic literature' for example – has a lower degree of poeticalness; it is hetero rather than auto-referential and as such (annoyingly) 'still defies interpretation'; though, we are assured, 'the same linguistic methodology . . . is entirely applicable to the metonymical terms of realistic prose'.[14]

Another line of retreat is to see the difference between referential and non-referential uses of language in literature as prescriptive rather than merely descriptive. Literature *should* be non-referential; the 'ideal text' is 'a galaxy of signifiers, not a structure of signifieds.'[15] The ideal text is the writerly text which is opposed to 'its counter value, its negative, reactive value' – the readerly text. And 'we call any readerly text' – Harold Robbins, Balzac, Barbara Cartland, Thomas Mann – 'a classic text'. And we can keep mum for a minute or two about the fact that the writerly text does not yet exist.[16] Since it does not exist, the whole of literature at present consists of readerly texts that at least *seem* to be referential. Reference seems to have

---

[12] Roman Jakobson quoted Hawkes, *ibid.*, p. 81.
[13] Jonathan Culler, *Structuralist Poetics* (London: Routledge & Kegan Paul, 1975), p. 19.
[14] Roman Jakobson, quoted Hawkes, *op. cit.*, p. 82.
[15] Roland Barthes, *S/Z*, trans. by Richard Miller, (New York: Hill & Wang, 1974), p. 5.
[16] The non-existence of the writerly text is discussed in section 7.4.

returned everywhere in literature except in those ideal texts that, being non-existent, hardly constitute exceptions.

Barthes, however, is perhaps undecided on this. 'Does not literature' he says elsewhere (in an essay published in the same year as *S/Z*) 'particularly today make a language of the very conditions of language?'[17] Perhaps literature is language that is self-referential on the side, as it were. If it is, then so, too, is all other writing (or indeed all other speech): 'language never ceases to accompany discourse, holding up to it the mirror of its structure'. So we are back with the idea that all language enjoys, at least as a hobby, being self-referential. Nevertheless it is difficult to let go of the idea that literature has a special meta-linguistic power or status. Language is like literature but literature is in a particularly favourable position to show the essential nature of language; it is at once a sub-category of language and a means of demonstrating its essence:

> at every level, be it that of the argument, the discourse, or the words, the literary work offers structuralism the picture of a structure perfectly homologous with language itself.[18]

Or, as he put it elsewhere,

> structuralism, itself developed from a linguistic model, finds in literature, which is the work of language, an object that has much more than an affinity with it: the two are homogeneous.[19]

Literature is language doing structuralism. This is even more difficult than it sounds; for if language is essentially literary and if literature is composed of language, how can one particular type of literary discourse, one type of use of language, show us what language in general is? Could we use a stick made of air to point out the air and demonstrate what the air essentially is – especially if we assert that air is essentially non-referential, that its essence is *not* to be a pointer. As we noted when we discussed Raymond Roussel, it is difficult to accept that one, highly abnormal, use of language can reveal language *per se*; or that literature *ought* to be what language – all language – cannot help being.

This objection proves awkward for the anti-realist cause; and at this point the radical critic retreats even from his bottom line that only certain exemplary modern texts are non-referential. Culler, a fellow-traveller of advanced critical thought, concedes that

> For all its opposition to models of intelligence and coherence, the radical novel relies on the line between text and ordinary experience just as traditional novels did.[20]

[17] Barthes, *Image–Music–Text* p. 85.
[18] Barthes, quoted by Culler, *Structuralist Poetics*, p. 96.
[19] Roland Barthes, Science v Literature, *Times Literary Supplement*, 28 September 1967.
[20] Culler *Structuralist Poetics* p. 191.

And Terence Hawkes, who approvingly misreads Viktor Shklovsky's *Zoo: or Letters Not About Love* as a demonstration, as well as a discussion, of 'the necessarily reflective or self-reflexive character of art',[21] and who elsewhere in his book variously holds that all literature and all language are non-referential, sometimes advances an entirely different notion of the possibilities of literature and language:

> Like myth, art represents, not the mere embroidery of reality, but a way of *knowing* it, of coping with it, and of changing it.[22]

Hawkes, moreover, reports that, for Shklovsky,

> the essential function of poetic art is to counteract the process of hab-
> ituation encouraged by routine day-to-day modes of perception . . . to
> inculcate a new childlike, non-jaded vision in us . . . to disrupt 'stock
> responses', and to generate a heightened awareness: to restructure our
> ordinary perception of 'reality', so that we end by *seeing* the world
> instead of numbly recognizing it.[23]

Even though the flag is kept limply flying by putting 'reality' in inverted commas or '*sous rature*', the implication is obvious. Literature unpeels our consciousness so that we *notice* a world that we would otherwise overlook. That is the conventional hope (and hype) of referential literature, of literature that is 'about' extra-literary, extra-linguistic reality, about the world outside of the text. As Boyd, a critic generally contemptuous of realism, concludes from his discussion of the formalists, 'defamiliarization is a property of all great art, realist as well as its alternative.'[24]

The retreat from non-referentiality is complete. Literature is no longer language which wears its non-referential essence on its sleeve. This is so obvious one may be left wondering why anyone should have thought otherwise – why even intelligent, creative writers, whose practice indicates quite otherwise, echo the idea that self-reference is the distinctive character of literature, that literature is predominantly about language. It is under-standable that a critic may react to, say, poetry in which the poet whinges about his feelings, tries feebly to change the world and generally obtrudes his puny self, by advocating an alternative poetry in which the poem is an autarkic object and the poet effaced. A poem that does not mean cannot originate in narcissism or terminate in interpreters' PhD theses. Another source of this error is well shown in Anthony Burgess's T.S. Eliot Memorial Lecture, given at Kent University.[25]

---

[21] Hawkes *op. cit.*, p. 143.
[22] Hawkes *ibid.*
[23] Hawkes *ibid.*
[24] Michael Boyd *The Reflexive Novel: Fiction as Critique* (Toronto: Lewisburg Bucknell University Press, 1983), p. 25.
[25] Anthony Burgess *Music and the Novel* T.S. Eliot Memorial Lectures delivered at the University of Kent.

The lecture was concerned about the relationship between music and the novel and the central theme was the aspiration of the novel to the non-referential condition of music. Burgess illustrated his point about the quasi-musical nature of great literature by comparing the opening passage of *Ulysses* with a piece of strikingly undistinguished writing by Wilbur Smith. After having, by ostension, demonstrated the difference between a description that follows the contour of its objects with unsleeping accuracy with one so totally in the grip of clichés as to be somnambulistic, he drew the extraordinary conclusion that the two passages illustrated respectively the opaque and transparent uses of language. Joyce was opaque and Wilbur Smith transparent. Careful use of language in the service of precision became, in Burgess's mind, evidence of a desire to *explore* rather than to *use* language. The basis of this fallacy is easily located: if I pay careful attention to my choice of words, I must be conscious of language and this consciousness must eclipse my consciousness of the world. Language used or generated by such a consciousness must be self-referring. This is of course absurd. Admittedly, there is a sense in which by searching for daring metaphors to capture the precise feel, the precise sense of the real, I am exploring the possibilities of language; but this exploration is always preliminary to employing it to report, or make sense of, extra-linguistic reality. Language used in this way is *not* opaque but (if one must use crude visual analogies) quartz clear. Since, however, visual or pictorial analogies are actively misleading, it would be best not to use this distinction at all.

Hawkes makes precisely the same error in his book. Deliberate attention to language, the disruption or questioning of cliches, makes, he believes, literature a self-reflexive activity. That at least is what he thinks on page 143 where he overlooks the obvious fact that scrupulous use of language is always in the service of a more adequate account of reality. On page 81 of the same book he does not overlook this and he recognizes that, while new perception in a literary work is reflected in the revolutionary use of language, those revolutions refer not to language but to the freshly perceived world. In acknowledging this, he completes his retreat from his earlier radical position. Reference is back.[26]

---

[26] The following passage from Anthony Nuttall's *A New Mimesis* (London: Methuen, 1983) makes several of the points discussed in this section exceptionally clearly:

> A general metaphysical theory cannot be corroborated by special, outstanding examples; if you have *really* dissolved the author, the dissolution applies equally to *Middlemarch* and *Glas*. If, on the other hand *Glas* provides a brilliant example of 'the dissolved author', then other books provide less good examples, and so the author as such has not after all been dissolved. Thus Derrida has perhaps repeated the naive error of the Russian formalists who affirmed that all literature was about itself and offered *Tristram Shandy* as a *typical* novel, or Sartre's error of supposing that he could demonstrate the universally histrionic nature of man by pointing to an obviously and unusually histrionic waiter (p. 37).

9.2 Realism Equals Anti-Realism After All

Consider the dilemma confronting the editor of the *Swinton and Pendlebury Evening News*. He has had the promise of a story that subsequently does not materialize. Unfortunately he has already decided to give it the front page treatment and the headline SIXTEEN HORSES STUCK UP A CHIMNEY has been set up and a space left under it – on the front page – for the details of the story 'corresponding to this startling headline'. It is 4.00 p.m. and the relevant reporter has mysteriously disappeared. The front page cannot be left blank; on the other hand the editor cannot risk his reputation by confabulating a tale that is so striking as to be certain of attracting a good deal of attention. What can he do? One solution, when facts are in short supply, is to resort to comment. The potentially empty space on the front page of the *Swinton and Pendlebury Evening News* is therefore given over to an unusually long editorial speculating about the possibility that there may be more horses up chimneys than most people have hitherto believed. It may well be the condition of the average chimney to host up to sixteen stuck horses. Of course, early reports are not yet confirmed and further investigation may prove that the rumour is unfounded. Nevertheless, it remains possible that, in a Pickwickian sense, ordinary chimneys may be absolutely teeming with displaced equines.

The editor's dilemma is rather similar to the one confronting many critics who have hailed the anti-realist novel only to find that it does not really or fully exist. And there is a comparable solution: to assert that apparently realistic novels are anti-realistic in essence. The view that anti-realism is not the unachieved asymptote of *avante-garde* fiction but the inescapable condition of all of narration can be stated with different degrees of plausibility or foolishness. In the previous section we quoted Boyd, who drew attention to an important feature he considered to be common to all great fiction, whether realistic or otherwise – defamiliarization. This perfectly sound view rather undermines the thesis of his book – which is that the realistic novel is unacceptable and inferior because realism fails 'to be concerned about the nature of reality' and is (quoting J.P. Stern) 'philosophically incurious and epistemologically naive.'[27] This factually untrue statement assists Boyd to a fruitful muddle and enables him to state and not to state the equivalence of realism and anti-realism:

> All writers reacting against realism are essentially concerned with the questioning of the nature of reality. Therefore there is some justice in their claim to the title of neo-realists.[28]

Another critic who takes the same path of retreat is Robert Scholes, who has already provided us with the extremest and crudest version of non-referentialism and the most spectacular retreat from this. Like Hawkes, he uses Shklovsky to dig himself into a deep pit of inconsistency:

[27] Boyd *op. cit.*, p. 7.
[28] Boyd *op. cit.*, p. 18.

Art (Shklovsky tells us) exists to help us recover the sensation of life; it exists to make us feel things, to make the stone *stony*. The end of art is to give a sensation of the object as seen, not as recognized. The technique of art is to make things 'unfamiliar', to make forms obscure, so as to increase the difficulty and duration of perception.[29]

Scholes comments

Shklovsky goes on to illustrate the technique of defamiliarization extensively from the work of Tolstoy, showing us how Tolstoy, by using the point of view of a peasant, or even animal, can make the familiar seem strange, so that we see it again. Defamiliarization is not only a fundamental technique of mimetic art, it is its principal justification as well.[30]

So Boyd tells us that anti-realism is really realism (or neorealism) while Scholes, whom we have earlier seen denying a reference to language, seems to agree with Shklovsky's choice of Tolstoy (yes, Tolstoy) as a writer who has supremely achieved anti-realistic aims. The position that anti-realism, far from being impossible, is actually an inescapable feature even of the realistic novel is taken by Julia Kristeva who, Culler tells us, has observed that

from its very beginnings the novel has contained the seeds of the anti-novel and has been constructed in opposition to various norms . . . it is certainly striking that when structuralists write about classical texts they end by discovering gaps, uncertainties, instances of subversion and other features which it is rather too easy to consider as specifically modern.[31]

Don Quixote, Gargantua and Pantagruel and *Tristram Shandy* are often cited as demonstrating how, even in its infancy, the developing novel was accompanied by developments in the anti-novel. This valid observation is magnified by Barthes, to encompass the totality of Western art:

in the West at least, there is no art which does not point to its own mask . . . the whole of Literature can declare '*Larvatus prodeo*' [As I walk forward, I point out my mask].[32]

(This claim is of course entirely at odds with Barthes's more general complaints about a predominantly bourgeois literature that overlooks itself – its status as language and literature – and pretends to be about the world. For Todorov, too, realism is anti-realistic in as much as it points to itself rather than exclusively to the world. Indeed, he seems to think that the scope of the genre 'reflexive story' is co-terminous with all fiction:

[29] Robert Scholes, *Structuralism in Literature. An Introduction* (New Haven: Yale University Press, 1974), pp. 83–4.
[30] Scholes *ibid.*
[31] Culler, *Structuralist Poetics* p. 191.
[32] Roland Barthes *Writing Degree Zero*, translated by Annette Lavers and Colin Smith (London: Jonathan Cape, 1967), p. 41.

> Every work, every novel, tells through its fabric of events the story of its own creation, its own history . . . the meaning of a work lies in its telling itself, its speaking of its own existence.[33]

The reflexive novel is not, therefore, a dazzlingly modern form.

It is not difficult, of course, to demonstrate that a novel has 'reflexive features' and then to recruit it to the anti-realist camp. Boyd, in his book *The Reflexive Novel*, discusses not only writers such as Barthelme but also Conrad, Virginia Woolf and William Faulkner. His tactic (paralleled by many other post-structuralist critics) is to fasten on certain points in the novel where writing, or fiction is referred to and to argue from these instances that the essential story of the novel is the story of its own creation, that its primary theme is the fictive nature of fiction. One would have thought that, in the case of a novel such as *Chance*, this would prove rather tricky. But there is no difficulty for a critic unashamed to resort to tendentious interpretations.

> In *Chance* Conrad successfully dramatized the deceptive nature of language in his chronicle of de Barral's financial exploits, which were made possible on the strength of a mere word – *thrift*. While denigrating the capacity of words to convey truth, Conrad also works to show the *power* of language.[34]

Even less plausible is Boyd's over-interpretation of a conventional response to one of the characters to the story that Marlow is telling:

> Although the 'I' narrator is 'struck by the absolute verisimilitude' of Marlow's conjecture, his comment to Marlow reveals that he is completely aware of the fictive nature of the story he is listening to: 'You have a ghastly imagination'.[35]

Most absurd of all:

> Lest we become too absorbed in the sense of reality of Marlow's picture, however, we should remember that Conrad works equally hard to undermine this sense of reality. The man and the girl are 'figures from Dickens – pregnant with pathos'.[36]

At any time other than the present 'Golden Age of Criticism', it would hardly seem necessary to point out that it does not follow from the fact that one character compares another character to a literary archetype that he is undermining their realities. If, for example, I refer to my uncle as a 'Falstaffian' figure, I am not suggesting that he exists only in my imagination or as a literary figure. I am not undermining his reality so much as hoping to define it. A novel that refers to other novels, that compares its characters with those from other novels, or makes passing reference to other fiction, does not thereby become sealed off in its self-reflexion.

[33] Todorov, quoted in Hawkes, *op. cit.*, p. 100.
[34] Boyd *op. cit.*, p. 61.
[35] Boyd *op. cit.*, p. 53.
[36] Boyd *ibid.*, p. 54.

Supposing someone were to write as follows:

> Dear Fred,
> Sorry about this dreadful scrawl but time is rather short. I don't think I am going to be able to see you tomorrow because my aunt died rather suddenly and I have to go to the funeral.
> Once again, apologies for the ghastly handwriting but I am in a great hurry.
>
> Your sincerely,
Charles.

This perfectly commonplace letter begins and ends with reference to itself; indeed it also refers to the signifiers of which it is composed. Does it follow from this that the essential theme of the letter is the genre of letter-writing, or the relationship between writing and reality, or between the signifier and the signified? Of course not; and neither does it follow that if Conrad refers to novels, or to the imagination, in the course of his novel that his novel is really about novel-writing and the operation of the imagination in converting reality into fiction.

Boyd seems in fact to accept this elsewhere in his book. He ends his implausible chapter on *Chance* by contradicting all that has gone before:

> Marlow's reply to [the charge of seeking amusement through gossip] may be read as an eloquent apology for art, a justification that derives its force from its attempt to show that the practice of art can enhance our response to life: 'From gossip there springs in us compassion, charity, indignation, the sense of solidarity; and in minds of any largeness an inclination to that indulgence which is next to affection.'[37]

Boyd quotes this with implicit approval although it sounds old-fashioned almost to the point of being Leavisite, connecting the art of fiction with the heightening of moral consciousness.

We have seen how it is possible to find almost any theory exemplified in almost any practice. Wild interpretation of selected passages of realistic novels can make the novels seem to be anti-realistic ones or (in Julia Kristeva's phrase) to contain the seeds of the anti-novel. Just as even apparently unblocked chimneys can be reported as containing 'the seed' or the 'possibility' of sixteen or more horses, so with the help of a criticism that treats literature as 'less an object to which criticism confirms than a free space in which it can sport',[38] hidden anti-realistic intentions can be found in the most apparently realistic of novels. The scope for imaginative re-classification is limitless.

Sarrasine, for example, begins as an at least partly 'realistic work' upon which Barthes intends to perform a hatchet job, showing the contradictions inherent in realistic fiction; however

---

[37] Boyd *ibid.*, p. 54.
[38] Eagleton *op. cit.*, p. 139. The passage refers to Barthes's 'post-scientific' phase.

In a *coup de grâce*, Barthes is able to claim that the very 'contents' of the novella are related to his own method of analysis. . . . Balzac's narrative can be read as peering beyond its own historial moment . . . to Barthes's own modernist period.[39]

The novel, apparently an example of bourgeois realistic fiction, becomes a fore-runner of post-Saussurean criticism. For, 'ultimately [the realist narrative] 'has no *object*: the narrative concerns only itself.'[40] In short

The story *represents* (we are in a readerly art) a generalized collapse of economies: the economy of language, usually protected by the separation of opposites, the economy of genders . . . the economy of the body . . . the economy of money.'[41]

Unrestrained metonymy

Abolishes the power of *legal substitution* on which meaning is based: it is then no longer possible regularly to contrast opposites, sexes, possessions . . .; in a word it is no longer possible to *represent*, to make things *representative*, individuated, separate, assigned; *Sarrasine* represents the very confusion of representation, the unbridled (pandemic) circulation of signs, of sexes, of fortunes.[42]

Well, if you believe that, you'll believe anything. How *Sarrasine* could represent representation or the pathology of representation when representation is no longer possible, only a disciple of Barthes could understand. Barthes himself seems concerned only to find Barthes within Balzac and so to turn the latter's realistic narrative into an anti-realistic discourse and his own argument on its head.[43]

The most startling formulation of the position that realism is really anti-realism (and vice versa) has been offered by Jonathan Culler. With critical tools honed to a razor sharpness by years of meditation on literary theory, Culler is able to divide 'works' into only two types: parables and allegories on the one hand; and the rest.

The second type occurs when external authorities are weak or when we do not know which should apply. If the work makes sense it will be an allegory, but we cannot discover a level at which interpretation may rest and thus are left with a work which, like *Finnegans Wake, Locus Solus* or even Flaubert's *Salammbo*, flaunts the difference between signifier and

---

[39] Eagleton *ibid*.
[40] Eagleton *ibid*.
[41] Barthes, *S/Z* p. 213.
[42] Barthes *ibid.*, p. 215.
[43] One could imagine a critic who would argue that *S/Z* is the 'figure' of Barthes's attempt to wring *B*arthes out of *B*alzac – a metonymous alchemy that can ultimately represent only its own impossibility. If this seems a preposterous parody of post-Structuralist proceedings, the reader should consult Derrida's *Signeponge* where it is argued that the poet Francis Ponge's ultimate aim was to inscribe his own name (literally) upon the world.

signified and seems to take as its implicit theme the difficulties or facti-
tiousness of interpretation.[44]

A work like *Locus Solus* or *Finnegans Wake* or *Salammbo*! The juxtapositions
speak for themselves, but it is a worth pausing to reflect on the plausibility of
the idea that all Flaubert's historical research, his agonizing struggle to
achieve verisimilitude, was devoted to achieving a work whose intention was
fundamentally the same as that of Joyce's philological delirium or Raymond
Roussel's pundemonium. Like the other two, he is condemned to using
words (signifier–signified combinations) simply to flaunt the difference
between two constituents of words that, according to Saussure's own ideas,
are actually indissoluble. The realistic novel is apparently dedicated to the
same unachievable end as the anti-realistic one; and so anti-realism not only
exists now but has always done so; and never more than when its writers think
they are being realistic.

When the world of the book is seen aright, it will be plain that every
chimney is choc-a-bloc with horses.

Postscript to Part III

The burden of the last three chapters has been that, even if the radical ideas
discussed earlier in this book and in *Not Saussure* were true, the creative and
critical consequences that have been claimed to flow from them do not in fact
follow. If language, for example, were essentially non-referential, then all
fiction – not merely realistic fiction – would be impossible; and so too would
all literary criticism. Likewise, if all intelligible writing falls within the scope
of a dominant, and oppressive, ideology, there can be no recognizable literature or literary criticism that does not collude with that ideology. It is not
surprising then, to discover that consistent anti-realistic fiction and consistent
critical advocacy of anti-realism has proved impossible.

Perhaps the most disturbing aspect of recent literary theory is not that it is
untrue but that it undermines, indeed mocks, the fundamental responsibility
of the critic – that of evaluating, discriminating, judging. Since no novel can
answer to the kind of critique that has been launched against realism, we have
no basis for discriminating between one novel and another. The mediocre
and the second-order can flourish in the shade provided by large and confusing critical ideas. The critique of realism which dismisses plausibility opens
the doors not only to sincere attempts to break with superficial verisimilitude
but also fictions, penned by the idle, the untalented and the opportunistic,
that are merely unrealistic rather than anti-realistic.

Deriving a preference for anti-realism over realism from ideas as fundamental as that 'language refers only to itself' or 'the world of words creates the
world of things' indicates a serious mixing of levels. From ideas as fundamental as these, no specific conclusions can ever follow. To suggest that Donald

[44] Culler, *Structuralist Poetics*, p. 230.

Barthelme, for example, represents an advance upon a 'naive' or 'classic' realistic writer such as George Eliot, because the former is more in tune with the big ideas, is as absurd as deriving a preference for cricket over football from a consideration of the fact that the world is a construct out of sense data rather than being composed of mind-independent matter.

All of this is so obvious, the reader may wonder why critics have managed to manoeuvre themselves into such absurd positions. The explanation may lie in the training of literary critics. The typical critic has relatively little experience of continuous, logical or critical thought; his expertise lies rather in producing stories of reading. He will have had relatively little experience of advocating ideas that are put to the test of logic or of experience. A degree course in literature does not fit one for discriminating between one abstract, theoretical idea and another. (This may change, of course, if 'theory' comes to dominate literary studies. But therein may lie the seeds of its own destruction.) The untrained mind will tend, therefore, to choose ideas on the basis of the excitement that they arouse. If Derrida, Lacan, Barthes and other founding fathers of post-Structuralism have had such a good run on the basis of such unpromising material, it is because the uncritical critical mind chooses ideas according to their power to excite and a big falsehood is always more exciting than a small truth.

Appendix to Part III
Realism and the Revolution: Stylistic and Political Conservatism

We saw, in Part II, how realism is regarded by some as inevitably politically reactionary on the grounds that, whatever the surface appearances, it is in complicity with the dominant ideology.[45] This would be true, and realism inevitably part of the Great Ideological Sleep that prevents the revolution (or our seeing the need for it), only if it were also true that realistic writing were incapable of adopting a critical attitude to whatever reality it attempts to express. But there is no reason why realism should not be 'interrogative' at many levels – politically, morally, epistemologically. It is also often assumed that realism must always be stylistically conservative and that realists are opposed to experimentation. This will be discussed in Part IV; suffice it to say here that it is a belief that depends on confusing realism as an *aim* with certain *techniques* used by, for example, great nineteenth-century realists.

A corollary of the belief that realism is (a) politically conservative and (b) non-experimental is the notion that experimental non-realism is associated with progressive, even revolutionary, politics while (inevitably) non-experimental realism is associated with reactionary postures. One might be forgiven for holding this view in the 1930s but there is little reason for

---

[45] Of course, radical left-wing politics, and in particular Marxism, have only relatively recently been associated with hostility to realism. See, for example, Terry Lovell, *Pictures of Reality* (London: British Film Institute) 1980 for a Marxist defence of realism.

believing this now. Nevertheless, the idea that progressive arts and progressive politics go together is so attractive that it will survive any number of contrary instances. So what is the basis of this potent belief?

One form of the argument goes as follows Contemporary reality is horrible, society is in a state of moral disintegration. This is at least in part the result of evil political systems. Great artists are sensitive men; they will be aware more than most of these things; and their works will reflect the degraded state of the world in which they live. These works will consequently be stylistically revolutionary just as their creators' hearts will be politically revolutionary. Stylistic innovation will therefore go hand in hand with political radicalism. Or, if innovation is regarded as being opposed to realism, anti-realism will go with progressive politics while realism will side with conservatism.

The strength of such feeble reasoning lies in its being largely hidden from view as part of a nexus of ideas that are presupposed rather than explicitly advanced. Some of the threads in the argument are worth looking at a little further. The first is the belief that if an artist feels that society is disintegrating, he will produce fragmented works. The notion of such isomorphism between the world at large and literature belongs to a crudity of understanding that has no place outside of the Sixth Form. Sensed disorder is not automatically mirrored in the order or disorder of a work. If that were the case, one would expect an artist who had lost a much loved wife to write works in which every sentence was broken off in the middle. Art is no more a simple mirror of reality, or of an individual's experience of it, than is language itself.

Further, the convenient idea that experimental art and progressive politics go together has some fairly spectacular counter-instances. The great innovative poets of the first half of the century were for the most part politically indifferent, right-wing conservatives or out and out Fascists. And Francis Haskell, in a brilliant historical analysis,[46] has shown how the practice of applying political and social metaphors to art is a relatively recent phenomenon, becoming widespread only in the second quarter of the nineteenth century. But the manner in which style and politics were related soon became somewhat confused. The assumption that revolutionary artists would espouse revolutionary politics led to surprise that Corot was not a supporter of the 1848 revolution and the totally unfounded, but frequently repeated, description of the Impressionists as 'Communards'. The attempt to relate technique more closely to politics was even more unsatisfactory. Paul Signac claimed that he and his friend and fellow-artist Seurat were revolutionary in their political, as well as their aesthetic, attitudes because they painted in a way which was totally unacceptable to conventional bourgeois opinion. The new painting of the 1820s in which, contrary to neo-classical

[46] Francis Haskell, *Art and the Language of Politics* in: *Past and Present in Art and Taste: Selected Essays* (New Haven: Yale University Press, 1987).

practice, colour was emphasized at the expense of line, created an association of colour with freedom and line with tyranny. Those, however, who defended the Davidian standards of classicism maintained that Delacroix and the Romantics were actually promoting a 'counter-revolution' by returning to the colouristic, painterly, 'unfinished' style of the eighteenth century. To quote Haskell:

> Throughout most of the nineteenth century the overwhelming majority of innovating painters were . . . moving away from the doctrines of neo-classicism to a whole variety of less 'finished', less 'idealized' styles. From the artistic point of view, Gericault, Constable, Turner, Delacroix, Courbet, Manet, Cezanne, Gaugin and so on were *metaphorically* on the left – i.e. were artistically 'progressive'. But in actual historical fact, it was the real, and not the metaphorical, Left which was associated in many people's minds with a highly 'finished' neo-classical painting.

It seems unlikely, therefore, that progressive art has any privileged relation to revolutionary politics. And the truth is that most radically innovatory art is politically useless or irrelevant. The direct political influence of works of art is probably in inverse proportion to their degree of stylistic innovation. For example, no one would maintain that canonical anti-realist fiction of the twentieth century – *Finnegans Wake, Locus Solus*, Gertrude Stein's experimental pieces – even aimed at altering, for political reasons, the everyday reality they appear to disdain to describe. *Tender Buttons* does not work synergistically with *Das Kapital* in awakening the sleeping, brainwashed millions to their oppressed state. Despite Colin MacCabe's claim that Joyce is the English-language writer who most strikingly exemplifies Julia Kristeva's theories, Joyce's subversion of the symbolic by the semiotic is unlikely to emancipate the enchained masses.

Although the facts do not oblige by confirming it, the belief that there is an association between progressive politics and 'progressive' art, or between reactionary politics and 'reactionary' art, is intuitively so appealing it is almost impossible to dislodge. The metaphor embedded in the word 'revolutionary' has an extraordinarily tenacious hold on the post-1789 critic. Nevertheless, if one were to lay bets as to which mode of experimental writing were most likely to be associated with a desire to improve the world or at least to do something about its avoidable ills, it would seem reasonable to put one's money on realism. For, at the very least, the realistic writer has to notice the actual world, he has to be well informed about it. He believes in the extra-linguistic pains, as well as the joys, of the world. This was, of course, the position of the early socialists (though it was eventually dogmatized into the official approval of a narrow, tendentious, orthodox, 'tractor realism'); and, more recently, of some feminist critics who, quite rightly, see that post-modernism and 'post-Saussurean' fiction and criticism offer them very little.

PART IV
PRACTICE (2)

Some Theses on Realism

1. Introduction

The arguments of this book have been essentially negative – that certain ideas are untrue and even if they were true, they would not have the aesthetic and critical implications they are believed to have. I should like to end on a positive note by sketching some ideas about realistic fiction and indicating some of its difficulties, its challenges, and its possibilities.

Ultimately a preference for one form or mode of fiction over another boils down to taste and this will be rooted in our personalities. My own preference for realistic fiction reaches back to early childhood. There is, of course, no God-given reason why fiction, or, indeed, any other form of art, should attempt to be realistic. But this can be acknowledged only after it has been made clear that there is equally no sound reason for rejecting realism – in favour of the various forms of anti-realism. Anti-realism does not have the arguments on its side.

This final part of the book does not pretend to be a systematic treatment of its themes; rather, a 'doctrine of scattered occasions'. If in these few pages I clear up some misunderstandings, indicate a few problems and communicate some of my excitement about realistic fiction, then I shall have achieved my aim. My fundamental thesis is, as I have stated elsewhere, that realistic fiction remains the great unfinished aesthetic adventure.

2. Defining Realism

2.1 The Problem of Positive Definition

It seems almost impossible to formulate a definition of realism that will steer clear of epistemological, social and political controversy about the nature of 'reality' and 'the real world'. Robert Scholes, in one of his more useful moments, defines realism as 'a mode of fiction that presents a world recognizably bound by the same laws as the world of the author'.[1] This at first

---

[1] Robert Scholes, *The Elements of Fiction: An Anthology* (Oxford: Oxford University Press, 1981), p. 7.

seems to settle the matter. But the longer we look at it, the more questionable this definition comes to seem. Which, what sort of, laws? Physical laws, social laws? How many novelists are aware of the laws that are supposed to govern the behaviour of material objects? And by whom is it recognized that the world of the author and that of his book are bound by the same laws? The author himself? Or the reader, who, hailing from another country, or another century, can *see* the assumptions the author had about reality and which were invisible to him? And what if reality is a construct – or has to be constructed in order to be captured inside the indubitable construct of a novel? Ideological, epistemological and even ontological questions loom behind the relativistic ones.

2.2 'Unreality' the 'Trouser' Word.

Defining realism positively gets one into all sorts of messes, most centrally that of defining reality. And this leads us to see what is most useful about Scholes's definition. Realism, he tells us, presents a world recognizably *bound* by the same laws as that of the author. Realism is bounded by external, non-literary, constraints. We may not be able to say what lies at the heart of realism, but we can say what, in general, determines its edges. This will seem a less damaging admission once we recognize that 'realism' is a term which, like 'real' itself, owes most of its meaning to its opposition to other terms. (In this respect, it is one of the few words in the language that approximates the structuralist condition of originating out of formal opposition to other terms.)

'The function of real', Austin wrote, 'is not to contribute positively to the characterization of anything but to exclude possible ways of being *not* real . . . It is the negative use that wears the trousers'.[2] And the same may be said of 'realism'. Realism has meant different things in the course of its history because it has been opposed to different movements in literature; it has been printed on different banners.

2.3 Towards a Negative Definition of Realism

Even though realism may be defined positively – Harry Levin's 'willed tendency of art to approximate reality'[3] – it would seem, therefore, preferable to indicate its boundaries rather than to try to characterize its content. And this seems right for other reasons; for realism is an open form, a genre without sharp or continuous edges. Damien Grant's book on the subject[4] lists twenty-seven types of realism and even then his inventory is by no means exhaustive – for example, it omits Magic Realism. At the present time, the two most important boundaries of realism are those which divide it off from (a) fantasy

---

[2] J.L. Austin, *Sense and Sensibilia* (Oxford: Oxford University Press, 1962), p. 70.
[3] Quoted in Damien Grant, *Realism* (London: Methuen 1970).
[4] Grant *op. cit.* pp. 2–3.

and (b) word games. A minimal negative definition of realism, therefore, would include a commitment on the part of the novelist to spending little time on the far side of these boundaries. (This should not prevent him, of course, from depicting a world in which there are characters in the grip of fantasy or addicted to word games.)

2.3.1 *Against Fantasy*

Realism has passed much of its history in a state of opposition to fantasy of all kinds. Many nineteenth-century realists, for example, were consciously anti-romantic. Flaubert's obsessive fidelity to reality was in part a reaction to the romanticism rampant within and around him. Fairies, princes, horses ridden to death, immortal souls untethered to physiological bodies, human zeppelins filled to bursting with noble emotions, were cast aside in favour of ordinary lives, ordinary people. The corollary of the rejection of the exotic and the improbable was a willingness to take notice of the actual world, to describe how a cabbage field by moonlight actually looked.

If realism is defined by its opposition to fantasy, it runs the risk of seeming outdated if, in addition, it is supposed that it is always opposed to the same things. Until fairly recently, to tell many ordinary truths about daily life was to risk prosecution and the realist novelist often saw himself as the scourge of hypocrisy. Now that particular battle is won: men are allowed to ejaculate and women to menstruate, children can hate their parents and spiritual leaders can be corrupt, within as well as outside novels. The sentimentality at the heart of romanticism is exposed and the cruelty, ignorance and heartlessness at the heart of sentimentality is now a commonplace. Readers are no longer accustomed to certain sorts of systematic discrepancies between what they know of the world and what they see referred to in print. Those who are ignorant about much that takes place outside, or even inside, their own lives can no longer legislate, from a moral or aesthetic standpoint, over the contents of a novel. No one has to be fearless now to be frank. Today, the once hypocritically shocked public, though no less hypocritical, demands to be shocked. 'Disturbing' has become the term of critical approval and 'shocking' promotes discussion and sales rather the threat of suppression. Without such plaudits, few novels will make it to the best-seller list.

So one once-revolutionary aspect of realism has degenerated into mere convention. And it is because the battle for frankness has been won – and because of the prevalence of a certain sort of low-grade naturalism – that it is mistakenly thought that realism is old hat. No one will get prosecuted nowadays for describing a happy adulteress, so 'telling the truth' is *passé*. Indeed, fantasy has become *avant garde* again. The revolution seems to be in the hands of those who talk of goblins and horses ridden to death or, in mock-gothic style, play with the idea of them.

This source of reaction against realism is based upon a narrow conception of the truth. Truth may be understood as 'confessional' truth when the battle lines are drawn in a certain place. But there is much more to truth than that which hypocrisy would wish to hide or sentimentality would overlook or romanticism would disdain to notice. The truth has to be imagined as well as betrayed or confessed and therein lies the fundamental challenge of realism. 'Confessional' truth – in which the sins of the world are confessed in a realistic novel – is but one aspect of truth, which came to prominence in only one phase of its history.

There are other sorts of fantasy than those prompted by wishful thinking or hypocrisy. At present, we are faced with a proliferation of novels in which human beings have wholly different properties from those of our acquaintances. Why not? What does it matter if the main character has seven legs instead of two, or can fly, or can communicate by ESP; or goblins take centre stage; or England has been translocated to the planet K9P? To see what is wrong, let us consider a novel whose main character is a goblin. Everyday life provides us with no experience of goblins. We are therefore in no position to evaluate what we are told about Sergei. We cannot say whether the descriptions of his motives or states of minds or his actions are true or false, just or unjust, perceptive or dim. For the goblin exists only insofar as he is described by the author and we are not licensed to imagine beyond, or even into, what is described. In suspending our disbelief in goblins, we have also to suspend our knowledge of the world.

The point is this: we cannot read fantasy critically, in the light of our lives or our knowledge of the world. Fantasy cannot, therefore, illuminate our own lives. The author is in charge and we are therefore denied that interaction between reader and author, between memory and text, between experience and writing, that lies at the heart of a reading that is more than mere day-dreaming or time-killing. Fantasy imposes a passivity on the reader: he either swallows what he is told or he is excluded from the story altogether.

Why can't a novel be a thought experiment? After all, thought experiments have been remarkably productive in science and in philosophy. This is a common argument in favour of fantastical fiction. The answer is very simple: the thought experiment in science and in philosophy only *begins* with a story – 'Suppose I could travel on a beam of light'; 'Suppose there were a mad surgeon who could transplant the two halves of my brain into different bodies' – and then it proceeds to an analysis of the implications of the possibility that is being entertained. The unfolding of the thought experiment, that is to say, is in accordance with generally agreed principles – mathematics, logic, appeal to established facts, etc. And it is in this second phase of the thought experiment that the real science, the real philosophy, gets done. And it is here that the reader is in a position to use his critical faculties, to assess whether the conclusions drawn are valid. In a fantastical story, however, anything goes. You can say what you like about the goblin Sergei. The thought experiment is set up but it is not developed, tested, validated.

Of course, some of the most powerful works of fiction have been fantastical: *Gulliver's Travels* is the obvious example. But such works are few and far between. Successful fantasies have, over the last two centuries, been sports in Western literature. The greatest modern fantasy novels – *1984*, for example – have been scrupulously realistic in their realization and, even though their settings are imaginary, they are wholly imaginable and do not require the reader to suspend his imaginative faculty or his ability bring his own experience to his reading. The point of consciousness of both *Gulliver* and *1984* is a human being with whom we can identify to some extent. Moreover, Swift's first readers (correctly) understood *Gulliver's Travels* as an allegory full of references to contemporary English politics. The novel, in other words, was seen as being about the real world and was, of course, intended as such. And so I would not wish my strictures on fantasy so to narrow the scope of 'serious' literature as to discount pastoral and allegorical fiction, *contes philosophiques*, etc. My point, however, is that a total disregard for the probable will present a serious obstacle to the free operation of the reader's intelligence and imagination. And the effectiveness of fantasy may well depend, as it does in *Gulliver*, on the precision of the realistic details with which it is fleshed out.

The boundary between realism and fantasy will vary from age to age. In a truly religious age, there is room for divine intervention in a realistic work. But fantasy cannot be defended either on relativistic grounds or on the basis that 'there are more things in Heaven and Earth', etc. For to defend realism against fantasy does not mean that one has a quarrel with those who sincerely believe in goblins; but rather with those who play with the idea of goblins or who fake-believe in goblins because they do not believe in anything else. The quarrel, in other words, is with those who invent (or, more usually, crib) mysteries because they are insensitive to the mystery of daily life.

2.3.2 *Against Word Games*

It is natural to think that, if deviation from realism in one direction leads eventually to fantasy, deviation in another terminates in mere word games. But word games and fantasy are more closely connected than this would imply. Just as inflated language becomes mere words, so, fantasy, as it deviates from empiricial reality and its terms lack referents, becomes more explicitly a verbal construct. With the use of the word 'goblin' – which has sense but no reference – we have taken the first step towards a fiction of word games.

En route to the extreme or terminal instances – the Roussellian pundemonium, for example – there are varying degrees of self-reflexiveness – 'Fine writing that, wasn't it?'; 'I'd better leave the stage before the script runs out', etc. I have dealt with the extravagant claims made for word games by theory-drunk critics who seem to have forgotten how boring it was to be a school-child. So I shall here simply note what is lost when fiction becomes obsessively self-reflexive or explicitly verbal, when the genre, the author, or the 'text' is put into the foreground.

If we think of fiction not as a mirror or a window but as a light playing on things, picking out this and that, then the realistic novel directs light on the world while the reflexive novel directs it upon a tiny part of the world – itself or its author. A possible widening of consciousness is sacrificed in favour of a self-regarding narrowing of it; the too-familiar figure of 'the author' occludes the unknown depths of an insufficiently explored world. And the resultant text engages only that part of one's consciousness which is deployed in solving crossword puzzles. (Is crossword puzzle-solving man the highest form of human consciousness?) And that is not the worst of it: most authors of self-reflexive (self-regarding) novels are not very good at compiling crosswords. Or perhaps it is that novels aren't really suited to be crossword puzzles, just as violins make poor scalpels. Of course self-consciousness, including self-consciousness about writing, is a part of reality and it should not be denied its placed in fiction. But it is only a small part of reality and therefore warrants a proportionately small place.

A cynic might interpret the motivation behind certain forms of experimental word-game fiction as follows: 'It seems to be the thing to think about, and be uneasy about, the novel (and of course language). I'm not too keen on competing with linguists or narratologists or cognitive psychologists – though I shall allude knowingly to their work which I have read about in book reviews. I have not come to any earth-shaking conclusions about the novel (or language). What I shall do is write novels that show that I have thought about, and am uneasy about, the novel (and language)'.

Word-game fiction is rather too obviously 'experimental' art. It may prompt the same cynic to reflect rather uncharitably on the contrasting uses of 'experiment' in science and the arts. An experiment in science is a set of procedures undertaken 'in order to discover something unknown, to test a hypothesis, or establish or illustrate some known truth'. Thus the Oxford English Dictionary. In practice, most experiments go wrong: they fail technically or they fail to demonstrate or to support the hypothesis that was being tested. A scientist may do many thousands of experiments before he arrives at results that he can publish. How different is the experience of the experimental novelist, or poet, or playwright. He expects to publish *all* his experiments; he does not have to state what hypothesis they are testing; he does not have to separate the results of the experiment from the experiments themselves; and, finally, he does not have to subject his results to a fairly savage peer review process before they are accepted. For an artist, it is enough that he is 'experimentally inclined'; for the scientist, being 'experimentally inclined' is only the beginning, not the end, of the heartbreak. Of course, the word 'experiment' does have a less strict or demanding sense than the scientific one: it can mean 'having a go'. But the concept of 'experimental' art parasitizes the more taxing sense. Have we not heard talk of Barthelme's works as being a 'laboratory of discourse'?

3. Misconceptions About Realism

Many of the arguments in favour of anti-realism simply rationalize a hostility that is the result of misconceptions about realism. It will be useful to identify and dispel some of the more popular misconceptions.

3.1 Realists Try to Copy Reality

It is often implied that the ultimate aim of realism is to copy reality, or at least a part of it – as if the asymptote of realistic fiction were a total reconstruction of the relevant portions of reality within the pages of the book. This, if true, would make the realistic enterprise at once impossible and futile. Impossible because of the discrepancy in the size and composition of the novel and the world in which its events are set – between (to quote Edmond Gosse[5]) 'the small flat surface of a book and the wide arch of the heavens'. Futile because there would be little point in replicating reality: who wants two identical Tuesdays in the same week?

The source of this misconception lies in the loose use of words, so that the aim of referring to, reporting on, doing justice to, celebrating, analysing, and being constrained by, reality shifts to that of replicating, mirroring, repro-ducing or copying it. Certain intermediate terms – 'mimesis', for example – thicken the confusion. At the heart of the muddle is a tendency to assimilate the iconic truth of a representational mode of signification to the referential truth of an expressive mode of signification – so that accurate or successful descriptions are thought of as if they were pictures.

3.2 Realism is a Method Rather than an Aim

The case against realism is enormously strengthened by confusing the aims of fiction with the methods, the techniques used to achieve those aims. One result of this confusion is a tendency to identify realism with one of its historical phases – usually nineteenth-century realism as exemplified by George Eliot, Tolstoy or Flaubert. Flaubert was a realist; Flaubert used certain techniques to achieve fidelity to the reality he wished to express; these techniques are now used by every Tom, Dick and Harriette who fancies writing a novel and are therefore outworn; realism is therefore *passé*. (A similar argument applied, as we saw earlier, at the level of content: Flaubert's battles – the right to describe ordinary lives with total realism – have long been won; realism is therefore outdated.) Certainly much hostility to realism derives from a boredom with the unthinking, facile use of techniques pio-neered by the nineteenth-century realists and developed by those whose conception of the scope of realism was determined by the frame of reference Flaubert *et al.* had created. As the use of these techniques over the subsequent

[5] Edmond Gosse quoted in Grant *op. cit.* p 70.

century or so has become less critical, less skilled, and less conscious, so a particular type of realism has become degenerate. Naturalism, which is often incorrectly taken to be the terminus of realism, in which the notebook (or tape recorder) is cultivated at the expense of *le mot juste*, has surely fathered many of the blockbusters that occupy today's best-selling lists. The justified contempt inspired by these works has been unjustly extended to the entire aim of realism. But if a monkey plays a violin badly it is hardly fair to condemn all violin music or the instrument itself.

3.3 Realism is Anti-Experimental

Anyone who confuses realism as an aim with certain nineteenth-century techniques used to achieve that aim is going to assume that realistic novelists must be stylistically conservative; that, as Brecht claimed (in attacking Lukacs's theory of realism), they are concerned primarily 'to bring Balzac up to date'. The modern novelist must choose between realism and experimentation. This view is more often implied than stated but here, as elsewhere, it is unstated assumptions that carry the most force because they can go unchallenged.

Virginia Woolf's *Mr Bennett and Mrs Brown* is a classic statement of one modernist reaction against post-Victorian realism. It has sometimes been construed as an attack by an experimentally-inclined anti-realist upon a non-experimental realist. The nub of the disagreement between Bennett and Woolf, however, is not about whether one should write realistically but about what constitutes reality, in this case the reality of a person. For Virginia Woolf, the essence of Mrs Brown was more likely to be captured in an account of her stray memories than through a statement about her source of income, her precise social location or her rent. Bennett apparently thought otherwise.

The interpretation of *Mr Bennett and Mrs Brown* has been clouded by the fact that, although both wrote realistic and non-realistic novels and both were at different times and in different ways experimental, Bennett is best known for his classic realist novels and Woolf for her experimental ones. But if we look at Virginia Woolf's *oeuvre*, we see that the most successful and boldly experimental ones are those which are most faithful to everyday reality – for example *To the Lighthouse* and *Mrs Dalloway* and certain of the stories in *The Haunted House*; whereas fantastical works such as *Flush* and *Orlando* are stylistically less adventurous.

One does not have to be eccentric to see that most of seminal experimental novels of the twentieth century have been realistic. The writing of *The Magic Mountain*, *The Man Without Qualities*, von Doderer's *The Demons*, *Remembrance of Things Past* was at least in part motivated by tenacious determination to give precise expression to, and to try to make sense of, experienced reality. That the reality in question is often 'psychological' or 'inner' does not affect my case. The recognition that reality has an inside as well as an outside, that people daydream and nightdream as well as talk and walk, that there is madness as well as sanity, does not constitute a break with realism. Molly Bloom's soliloquy is a culminating moment in psychological realism. It is even arguable that certain passages in *Finnegans Wake* are realistic; indeed that they attempt to be mimetic to a degree hitherto not attempted in prose. This is occasionally successful, as in the unforgettable ending of *Anna Livia Plurabelle* 'beside the rivering waters of, hitherandthithering waters of. Night!' It is such passages that make *Finnegans Wake* readable.

In summary, to defend realism does not necessarily imply membership of the *arrière garde* so notably represented in Britain by the late C.P. Snow. Nor does it mean that one sees the job of the late twentieth-century novelist to be to re-write the nineteenth-century novel; to write in the 1980s as if one were Fontane or Zola or George Eliot or Galdos; to revive the Flaubertian or the Dickensian world picture. It is entirely possibly that modern realism may lead to the abandonment of the narrative modes, characters and themes that nineteenth-century novelists regarded as central. The task of letting reality into fiction will always demand a questioning attitude to the language and assumptions of one's own life and of the world one knows and will require the author to be as experimental as any of the more obtrusively experimental anti-realists.

3.4 Realism Requires an Uncritical Attitude Towards What is Taken for 'Reality'

Some critics think of realism as philosophically incurious and naive.[6] This is factually untrue (though commonly believed). The profound, slow-burning curiosity that actuates the great novels I mentioned just now testifies to a philosophical astonishment at least as great as that of the more flamboyant anti-realists. A realistic novel can be 'an adventure of ideas' as much as an anti-realist one. Its doubts can go as deep. The fact that many realists do not choose to use fiction to express or explore such doubts is no more to be wondered at than that most realistic fiction is pretty mediocre. Of course, no novel is able to deal with certain philosophical ideas: the natural standpoint, the belief that there is a real world out there, cannot be suspended; there are no realistic novels on the far side of the *epoche*. But there are no anti-realistic novels there, either.

Stern also claims that realism denies that 'in this world there is more than one reality'. I have already dealt with this in Chapter 6, but it is perhaps worth reiterating that there is no reason why contemporary realists should subscribe to the idea of a monocentric reality or a single viewpoint from which reality can be described, summarized and made intelligible. Indeed, one could argue that the polycentric nature of reality and the non-existence of

---

[6] e.g. J.P. Stern. *On Realism* (London: Routledge & Kegan Paul, 1973).

a point of view from which all warring economic interests and warring world pictures could be reconciled is almost a cliché of modern realism. Tolstoy, Sartre and Pirandello provide examples of how a polycentric reality can be presented realistically without the author adjudicating between conflicting subjectivities.

A third claim made against realism is that it takes too much of reality for granted and accepts the deliverances of common sense. Again, this is not a necessary feature of realism. Great realists have to notice the world; and in order to notice it, one has to be astonished by it. Defamiliarization may sometimes be an effect of realism; it is certainly a condition of it.

4. The Challenge of Realism

The possibilities of realism are almost infinite but the difficulties, which anti-realists are spared, are only slightly less. I shall choose a handful. Facing them, being prepared to travel alone with the anguish they cause, is essential if artifice is to be transmuted into art.

4.1 Describing Anything

The terms we use are general, the objects that surround us are particular. Objects and terms meet in the generality of meaning. 'Cat' can be used to refer to a particular cat because 'cat' and actual cats share the same general meaning. Insofar as there is a point-to-point projection between language and world (and it isn't very far), the meaning of words means the (general) meaning of objects. In the flow of ordinary discourse, when events are narrated with a view to conveying information, we don't mind that the objects we talk about are generalized, that they are reduced to a certain aspect of their general meaning in order that they should be taken up into intelligible talk. But when we have quite a different purpose, that of presenting a world, we experience dissatisfaction. Our descriptions fall short of things, fail to come near their individuality, refer to their *quidditas* but by-pass their *haecceitas*. Language, insofar as it is intelligible, generalizes; the particular lies outside generality. Only proper names elude the curse of generality but they have to be defined ostensively; without such a definition, they are either general ('Claudia – a cat') or meaningless. So we cannot present individuals through language. Now when we want to describe how things *really* are, we are drawn towards the description of individuals, because it is of individuals that the reality that most intimately impacts on us is composed. The generalities, the universals, seem more distant. And it suddenly seems to us that we cannot describe anything at all. There is no language able to capture to the unique features of an individual. We cannot find terms that will uniquely designate the face of the woman we love, the shape of a particular cloud or the tone of the light filtering through it on to the landscape below. Even less do we feel able to create a uniquely identifying description of, say, a city. We pick and choose at random and throw together a few fragments to signify a town that has 50,000 inhabitants, 400 streets, a dozen indescribable smells, and hope that the reader will furnish the rest from his imagination.

We focus on a single object. We multiply the general terms in the hope that each one will modify the other and we shall gradually cone down on our descriptive target. As a result, we learn that there is no intrinsic terminus to any description. Fatigue or some external purpose determines when our description shall seem to have been completed. We are dissatisfied with describing the house as 'cosy'; it is vague, imprecise, insufficiently ambitious. But most forms of available precision fail to help us:

> The floors to the house are of normal traditional suspended timber
> design comprising tongue and groove softwood floorboards on joists
> with ground floor intermediate supports of sleeper walls.

Poor Robbe-Grillet. His descriptions lack fidelity to visual impression, to experience, to impact, to the viewpoint being developed, to the consciousness being displayed. They know more than any eye can see. The realistic novelist wants to describe a world and finds he cannot capture even the specific appearance of a pebble.

Consider the dispiriting advance from 'She had a beautiful face' to an item by item listing and description of all its features: the hair, the eyes, the mouth, the nose, the chin and, lo! there develops on the page an identikit portrait of an anyone. Or the elements simply refuse to add up to any kind of portrait, to fuse in the reader's mind into an impression of beauty or of *that* beauty. The novelist becomes a *chosiste* and finds himself competing with the cinema on its home ground and failing. It's worse, of course, if he tries to describe a scene. How can he make sentences – or sentence-length noticings – add up to the phenomenal appearance of, say, a crowd?

So a commitment to realism means being prepared to face the anguish of the inexpressibility of ordinary things, of the elusiveness of the particular. That tree, that light, that look in the girl's face.

There is a way out. Mallarmé's dictum points to it: *Peindre, non la chose, mais l'effet qu'elle produit* [7] – Don't try to describe the girl. It is sufficient to say that she is beautiful then all that follows – the hero's obsession with her, etc. – will make sense. This beauty, once referred to, will act as a dynamo for the story. But the true artist will resist as long as possible yielding to the temptation to refer to the effect of the thing rather than trying to capture its presence.

4.2 Fact Versus Form

Nabokov once described the novel as the result of a long quarrel between an author and his world. This is well put but perhaps 'quarrel' is too explicit.

---

[7] Stephane Mallarmé Letter to Henri Cazalis October or November 1864. Quoted by Anthony Hartley in his Introduction to *Mallarmé* (London: Penguin 1965), p. ix.

The relationship between the novelist and reality is more one of constant tension that only occasionaliy breaks out into formal bickering. The basis of this tension, which of course lies within the novelist, is a conflict between his desire to be true to a piece of reality and his equally strong desire to advance the business of his novel.

Let us suppose the business of the novel is, as it is most commonly is, to tell a story. The story, reduced to a plot, could be despatched in ten lines. Or less. A falls in love with B's wife and plots with her to murder B. After B's death, the love between A and B's wife is soured by guilt. They quarrel and B's wife betrays A to the police. A hangs. Now the author lighted on the story because he felt there was more to it than could be summarized in the plot. He could imagine A and B's wife – their lust, their hatred for B, their guilt – and he could imagine the kind of lives they lived, the places they lived and loved in. He wants to tell his tale but, also, he wants to imagine and re-create the characters and their setting. He wants to say how A felt when, kissing B's wife for the first time, he tasted the toothpaste in her mouth. He wants to portray the small town in which B's wife lived out her boredom and dissatisfaction with her marriage to B. He wants to remember a world he knows; to preserve it; to celebrate it.

One could simplify the novelist's intentions by thinking of the process of composition as taking place in three dimensions: the forward movement of narrative, the spread of setting, and the exploration of character; or distance, width and depth. From time to time the narrative line fattens into a lagoon as a setting is placed before the reader. The forward movement slows. Or a well is sunk and a character is analysed in depth. Again the forward movement slows. A tension begins to emerge between getting the novel's ultimate business done – telling a story – and satisfying the author's demand to realize the setting and explore the depths of the characters.

This is to put it all very simply. But let us imagine the author writing the scene in which A first sets eyes on B's wife. She is in a cafe, by herself, drinking coffee, smoking a cigarette, looking bored. The cafe must be described, and the way B's wife looks, and her clothes. . . . As he works on the scene, giving it that 'solidity of specification' he requires, the novelist finds the necessary details proliferating; for he is thinking of a particular cafe. Indeed, it is one of his own favourite haunts; it was the place where he had felt the first twinge of the story. How is he to describe the cafe; which comings and goings, what lights, what traffic sounds from without? How, moreover, is he to limit his description? How is he to do justice to what is there while, at the same time, allowing the plot to move at a respectable speed? How shall he reconcile the warring demands of time and space, of speed and mass; and retain fidelity to the exact contours of reality while not allowing the plot to become so viscous with detail that all sense of movement is lost? How is he to mediate between his wish to use reality and his equally strong wish to present (or to preserve) it?

We could look at this tension another way, as a conflict between two desires: to create a form; and to be true to the formlessness of reality. To complete a story with clear lines, and to terminate descriptions and explorations while they are still soluble in the story; and, at the same time, to be true to a real world which is formless. For one of the most potent sources of inspiration behind realism is the intuition that *this* (or, perhaps, any) reality has not yet been expressed, that its true order is quite other than the order of the fictional forms in which it has hitherto been rendered. Once reality is let into the novel, it becomes seemingly impossible to retain formal control over the finished work. Beady-eyed attention to reality is at odds with the shaping of a work that has a satisfying form.

It is to put it too dramatically, even romantically, to describe the real world as formless. Far from being formless, the world is over-provided with forms; far from being storyless, it is seething with stories. The trouble is, the forms are co-present, the stories overlap. A's affair with B's wife is embedded in innumerable other stories and storylets: his many different relationships with his own wife (the story of his marriage which is composed of a thousand smaller stories starting and finishing at different times); his worry about his back pain; the development of his business; the on-going saga of the row with the garage that is servicing his car; his running battle with his mother-in-law; the fluctuation of his feelings about his son; etc., etc. The comings and goings in the cafe are themselves parts of stories that the author has decided, arbitrarily he feels, in the light of his wish to present reality, do not belong to the novel he is writing. Every setting, every view is part of a larger setting, a larger view, indescribable because boundless and inexhaustible. The signal is lost in the noise, the noise itself being composed of events that have as much entitlement to be regarded as signals. The distinction between the signals that belong to the novel, the things that the novel foregrounds, and the noise that belongs outside of it, is purely arbitrary.

For the writer who wishes to do justice to reality, rather than merely tell a tale, or who wishes his telling to take on the shape of reality itself, there is a constant quarrel between the factual reality outside of the novel and the formal reality within it. Between uncovering the real and getting somewhere – advancing a narrative or an argument in the manner to which readers are accustomed.

Importing new aspects of reality into any art form – whether it is ordinary speech in Wordsworth's poetry or conversation that gets nowhere in Pinter's plays – often seems like an assault on form. Compensation is demanded and the author, having admitted the formless into his story, must reassert form. In an extreme instance, form may be explicitly imposed – as in *Ulysses*. In a more typical case, the reassertion of form is less explicit and formal characteristics are less obviously worn on the sleeve.

Flaubert, again, provides us with the paradigm instance of a writer caught in the conflict between 'fact' and 'form'. How does one reconcile the wish to give definitive expression to a piece of reality (precise observation for its own sake, the notebook and the *mot juste*) with the desire to impose an aesthetic order upon it? We know how intense was Flaubert's formal sense, his formalizing ache, how he heard the rhythm of the sentences to come for pages, even chapters ahead. The central agony of his years of composition was that of mediating between the rhythms he heard and the reality he observed and wished to give just expression to. Hardly surprising then that he was tempted by anti-realism and dreamt of a novel that would be severed from reality altogether and would hover self-suspended above the world:

> a book about nothing, a book dependent on nothing external, which would be held together by the strength of its style, just as the earth, suspended in the void, depends on nothing external for its support, a book which would have almost no support.[8]

Thus *La Tentation de St Gustave*, a temptation that must have at times seemed irresistable; for what better way to resolve a quarrel than to walk away from it? But it was left to his successors to succumb to the temptation and, with the help of bad philosophical arguments provided by critics, to make a virtue of it.

Flaubert resisted the temptation and found a solution to the conflict between between form and fact. He did not, like Joyce in *Ulysses* half a century later, allow reality to wash over him so thoroughly as to render forms seemingly recoverable only as an arbitrarily imposed, external, mythical framework. Flaubert's solutions – for example the use of recurrent motifs – have been expropriated by innumerable novelists who have written in his wake. Those famous black and white butterflies have fluttered, in one guise or another, over most of the serious fiction of the last one hundred and thirty years. Few modern realistic writers have not learned, directly or indirectly, from his example. Even authors of serials in weekly magazines resort to recurrent 'symbols' to solve their (scarcely felt) problems of imposing formal order on uncombed, inconsequential reality. Flaubert was not, of course, satisfied with the various devices he used to reconcile his desire for formal perfection with an insistence on fidelity to the non-novelistic truth of actual worlds. These devices served only to reduce his dissatisfaction to bearable levels. A retreat into formalism, and the writing of fanciful fictions readily manipulated according to the formal senses of the author, would have earned his utter contempt.

There are no recipes for successful mediation between the factual and the aesthetic demands of realism, between the crystalline structures of art and the hundreds and thousands of the experience it tries to render. There are no handy algorithms for turning a piece of reality into into a plausible and realistic story; for getting the atmospheric instant or the described moment to

---

[8] *Selected Letters of Gustave Flaubert*, trans. Francis Steegmuller (New York: Farrar Straus & Young, 1954), pp. 127–8. Christopher Nash, in his *World-Games. The Tradition of Anti-Realist Revolt* (London: Methuen, 1987) cites this letter in the context of Flaubert's 'utter exhaustion with the ordeal of mimesis'. Nash's brilliant and comprehensive account of anti-realism was published too late for its arguments to be dealt with in the present book.

unite with its fellows in a narrative unfolding as jointlessly or as disjointedly as ordinary life; for turning arrays of objects and events into sequences that provoke expectations while at the same time doing justice to the temporal structures of experience. Solutions lie readily to hand only when the work does not aim at realism or even plausibility and the writer is entirely in command of content and feels no obligations to follow the contours of daily experience or to be constrained by the laws of actual worlds. It is easy to find arbitrary forms to match arbitrary contents; indeed, they are internally related to one another.

That is why even the most daring formal experiments in non-realistic fiction are of limited interest. To unhinge the search for form from the desire to deepen and extend the sense of the realities one lives in is to render the search pointless. Form in an anti-realistic work is mere formality. Without the external constraints, the counter-currents, arising from experience and memory and knowledge transformed by imagination into possible experience, style is empty stylistics. Fancied events in faked up worlds, however carefully they are 'described', must always be shallower than imagined events in the real world because they are only word deep, having meaning but no reference. Consequently, they yield more readily to narrative organization and accept whatever 'artistic' order is imposed on them.

4.3 Getting Consciousness to Disclose Itself

A recent novel about Lenin takes the form of a diary supposedly kept by him. D.A.N. Jones, reviewing it, notes the following passage: 'My 11-year-old foster-nephew, a child-prodigy adopted by Anna and Mark, and known as Gora, was at school'. Why, the reviewer asks, should Lenin tell himself that, in the middle of the October Revolution? A good question. It is obvious why *the author* should tell us that Lenin's foster-nephew is a prodigy, that he is called Gora, that he has been adopted by Anna and Mark and that he is at school. For his readers need to know these facts so that they can understand what is happening, or what they are going to be told next. Lenin, however, does not need to tell himself these things because he knows them already; and if he didn't know them already he wouldn't be able to learn them from himself anyway.

We have touched the heart of the one of the great problems of realistic fiction – that of getting consciousness to disclose itself. Since Henry James (and after him the critic Percy Lubbock) made the question of *the point of view* the central methodological issue in the writing of fiction, thoughtful writers of realistic fiction have been aware of the problem of remaining faithful to a particular viewpoint and yet giving the reader enough, if not to know what it going on, at least to make sufficient sense of what is 'going on to remain interested. This problem does not arise within a novel whose narrator is impartial, omniscient and invisible. Such a narrator does not suffer from the need to account for his knowledge or for the efforts he is making to share that knowledge. But writers, for a variety of reasons, have been attracted by the idea of adopting the viewpoint of one of the participants in the narrated events, of writing from within the space of the fiction that is unfolding.

The attractions of having an explicit point of view, an internal rather than an external narrator, are many. There is much to be gained in dramatic force from having the story told by someone caught up in it. The events are permeated with personality and may be told in a distinctive voice. Our engagement as readers with the action is enhanced by the evident engagement of narrator. The adoption of a certain point of view allows for a dappling of knowledge and ignorance over the narrated world which will make it seem more like our world. The narrator who does not know what someone is up to, but would like to know, is like us and we can share his or her satisfaction at gradually coming to know. Finally, from the author's point of view, it is salutary and helpful to escape from himself into the viewpoint of another, however similar that other is to himself.

So there are many reasons for abandoning the omniscient viewpoint and the unproblematic, because invisible or implicit, narrator. But adoption of a point of view creates a new set of problems, summarized by Lubbock as 'the question of the relation in which the narrator stands to the story'. It is an enormous question and has attracted proportionate attention. The identification of implied and explicit narrators within a fictional text, the discrimination of narrative voices, the logical relations between the narrative personae, and so on, are the subjects of a huge and often very subtle literature.[9] But little progress has been made in relation to the fundamental problem – that of ensuring that the narrator's commitment to telling the story is adequately accounted for; or, if it is not a question of a story being explicitly told, of ensuring that we have not obtained a piece of information from a character under false pretences. That we haven't, for example, learned about Lenin's foster-nephew simply because he has taken the trouble unaccountably to tell himself about that nephew.

The problem becomes even more acute when a novelist tries to move closer to phenomenological reality and the point of view all but dissolves into that of which it is conscious. All the things that we need to know in order to make sense of what is revealed to the consciousness are known already to that consciousness; their being narrated by the consciousness to itself so that they can be overheard by us seems almost embarrassingly inauthentic. And the problem connects with deeper doubts that reach into the questions that lie unresolved at the centre of philosophical psychology: how far is consciousness verbal? is our immediate self-presence a stream of talk? to what extent is consciousness, explicit being-there, sentential? is the sense the world makes

---

[9] The massive narratological literature (usefully outlined in, for example, Shlomith Rimmon Kenan, *Narrative Fiction: Contemporary Poetics*, (London: Methuen, 1983)) has taken the debate a long way forward from James and Lubbock but has done nothing to render more tractable the problem they first identified and which is my concern here.

to us organized in any narrative, even ur-narrative, form? Whatever the answer to these questions, it is obvious that consciousness does not naturally take an expository stance; it is not a continuous expounding of itself; and even if it were, it would not amount to anything anyone else could make sense of without the very knowledge that, in those moments when we talk to ourselves, we assume.

There are all sorts of tricks. Under what conditions does a consciousness tell itself that it is a man of forty two, that is has two children, that is is five foot eleven tall, that it is slightly balding and that it is unhappy about something that happened ten years before? When, that is to say, does consciousness gather into the *curriculum vitae*, the map, the reader needs to help him through the novel? When, perhaps, it is writing a letter or a diary. But, as we have seen, the diary can prove to be a false solution. And few consciousnesses nowadays write long letters. Even fewer are so articulate as to be able to summarize themselves usefully on the telephone. Few of us, anyway, approach our friends with a ten-page oral self-abstract.

So the narrator has to be provided with a reason for furnishing us with a summary of himself. He is 'obsessed' with the past (guilt, unhappy love, lost content) and must purge himself: the white pages of the novel are the analyst's couch on which he lies, the silent ear into which he speaks. Or he is about to die and a life-review is in order. Not too close to death, of course, because few at the point of death have enough puff to announce that they are dying never mind to review their lives or to expatiate upon the nature of death. So we might have a narrator who decides to write himself down between the diagnosis and its final enactment. And so we have more letters, diaries, etc.

Getting consciousness to talk at once plausibly and interestingly, to speak in its own language and yet to the point, requires an infinity of artistic tact and cunning. The problem is probably insoluble; but the thing is to try to make it seem solved. Or at least to ensure that the point of view doesn't look as if it were that of the author, moved to self-disclosure by literary intent, by the desire to write a realistic novel. Or by the wish to help the author of such a novel.

There are many ways in which characters can assist their authors. Let me describe one such type of character. He, like the author, is fascinated by the other characters in the story. He therefore observes them very carefully. In order to do this, he has to be intelligent, perceptive, articulate and, so that he shall be in no way limited in his access to the objects of his study, he is possessed of a large private income. He has a curiously empty personal agenda – his own private life is quiescent and his days are uninterrupted. He is permitted to enjoy, that is, a unity of preoccupation: he can be undividedly preoccupied with the plot. He has a certain prose style that is not too different from the author's and has the habit of thinking in metaphorical terms about himself and the rest of the world and the metaphors he uses dovetail into the hidden intellectual agenda of the plot. He has a formidable memory for what people say and how they look when they say it. He is Henry James's ideal narrator and he is not very clearly differentiated from Henry James himself – except in respect of one enormous fact which makes him, in the end implausible – he is not a novelist. I say this only to support the contention that, in certain respects, Henry James's great novels represent the infancy, rather than the climax or old age, of realistic fiction.

4.4 Imagining the Actual

We walk away from the bed of someone we have been visiting in hospital. From the top deck we watch someone failing to catch the bus we are on. We see the results of a massacre on the Six O'Clock News. A friend's marriage breaks up. So many things invite our imagination to work on them, but we rarely respond to the invitation; we are on to the next thing, on to the next theme, the next agenda item, the next story. And so we come to know much more than we experience, much more than we can pause to imagine. There comes a time when we feel as if we are passing through the world without ever having been fully there.

Realism answers to this need; it takes up the challenge of trying to enable us to imagine what we know, of imagining the actual, of breaking through the crust of fact to the unformed experience, leading us back from the outcome to the process. It was Shelley who reminded us that we lack 'the creative faculty to imagine what we know'. In advanced civilizations, this takes the form of having more abstract and factual knowledge than (to use Goethe's words) we 'can creatively live up to'. But human knowledge always exceeds that which we can experience or fully imagine. The discrepancy is a disease not of civilization alone (though here it becomes more acute and there is sufficient distance from the struggle for survival to permit it to become a source of dissatisfaction) but of consciousness itself. And although Shelley saw it as the function of *poetry* to enable us to imagine what we know, he included Bacon and Plato among the poets, maintaining that 'the popular division into prose and verse' was 'inadmissable in philosophy'. And in our own day, the division between prose and poetry seems even less absolute, and not only because ninety-nine per cent of contemporary poetry that is not doggerel seems like prose cut up into lengths. Helping us to imagine what we know is the essential function of realistic fiction.

Imagining the actual may be contrasted in Coleridgean terms with merely 'fancying' the possible. Fancy, or fantasy, does not enter creatively into that which is outside of itself into some object or idea, but plays with things as 'counters'. It deals, as Coleridge says, with the world as a group or collection of 'fixities and definites'. It is essentially uncritical, unanalytical, unastonished by things, at best using them to fabricate something that will astonish or at least divert or surprise. The resort to fantasy is not a sign of an active imagination but of an inert one. It is not through an excess of talents that a writer is obliged to turn away from the real world to an invented one. For it is considerably easier to make something up than to follow out the contours of the given. Fantastical beings and events in fancied worlds are easy to describe because, as has already been suggested, their very existence is intra-linguistic. If goblins do not exist, their being is the sum total of the things that have been said about them. Even for those who do believe in them, there is relatively little in the way of extra-linguistic experience of goblins to a challenge the descriptive powers of the writer. On the other hand, it is possible to find words, new, arresting words, to describe the commonplace that surrounds and dominates even the most extraordinary of lives, only in the heat of inspiration. It takes an infinitely greater talent to imagine and express the consciousness of the person sitting opposite you in a train – what she is thinking now, how it connects with what she is feeling and what she may be feeling or thinking next – than to summon up ten thousand demons from some imaginary Hell or send a million rockets to an unknown planet.

At the heart of the realistic novelist's proceedings is an *imaginative extension of experience along lines laid down by knowledge*. Observation and information create the field within which the creative imagination shall set itself to work. Behind the novelist's imaginative effort is a desire to become larger than one's customary self, to enter into the interiority of the others around one, to inhabit them for more than a few moments at a time, to unpeel what one is used to seeing so that one notices, and is astonished by, it. Now it is one of the arguments used to defend fantasy that it enables us to come upon our own world as it were from the outside, so that we can see it from the outside, as if for the first time and thus start to question it. Fantasy, so the claim goes, opens up a space outside the actual world from which it can be seen as but one of many possible worlds, even as *constructed*. In practice, as we have already indicated, fantastical worlds are usually composed of off-cuts from the real world, shallow world-peelings.

Moreover, the actual world is not a unity and there are many worlds within 'the world' to provide the necessary outsides, as many mutually estranged viewpoints within reality as it is useful to conceive. Indeed the most arresting way to come upon one's own life, oneself, from the outside is to view it from within another's life: a man imagining his world, his behaviour, even his smell, as perceived by a woman. Or a Western European imagining his world seen through the eyes of Saharan tribesmen. Or imagining how he looks to his five-year-old son. This is more likely to generate the desired degree of *ostrananie* than a novel dealing with a Western European going on a journey to K9P and conversing with little yellow men, however 'wonderfully realized'. There are greater unspoken, implicit or suppressed distances within the real world than there is between any real and any fantastical one. The most fundamentally de-centring and estranging intuition is that we do not see ourselves as others see us or see or experience the world as others experience it. Writing realistic fiction, imagining the actual, is a way of honouring that redeeming intuition.[10]

5. The Truth of Realism

Truth and fiction are opposing categories. Fiction is mainly about things that did not happen to people who do not exist and assertions in a novel must therefore be untrue. And yet we talk of the truth of fiction. The paradox is apparently readily resolved: fictions are about real events, and real people, but the names and dates and places have been changed to protect the innocent. This is rather naive and would narrow realism down to the category of a non-fiction novel with a few factual alterations to spare blushes. Moreover, the truth of fiction seems to be deeper, as well as wider, than this. The great novel tells the truth not only about the events it describes; it also tells a large truth about the world. 'Realism to my mind implies, besides truth of detail, the truthful reproduction of typical characters under typical circumstances ... true character must combine typicality with individuality'.[11] *War and Peace* is interesting not only as an account of a particular campaign and of the manners and morals of a certain group of people in a certain place and time. It is great because it has much to say about war and peace at other places and other times. The reality described in a great fiction stands metonymically for a larger reality, or for a whole, infinite, class of realities.

5.1 The True and the Plausible

At the very least, a successful realistic novel should seem plausible. But this raises a difficulty; for what is plausible will be different in different epochs. It raises the possibility that realism is merely that which 'conforms to public opinion' – as Barthes, in *L'Effet de réel* claimed.[12] Does this not then mean

---

[10] Nash *op. cit.* cites C.S. Lewis's eloquent defence of fantasy. For example, 'Far from dulling or emptying the actual world', [other-world] fiction 'gives it a new dimension of depth. [The reader] does not despise real woods because he has read of enchanted woods: the reading makes all real woods a little enchanted'. (Nash p. 104). I suppose this is sometimes true; but the overwhelming evidence, both within and about fiction, is that those who are able to inhabit fantasy worlds find the actual one insipid by comparison. And although 'the impossible may be a postulate that will usually point a moral', the best practice for imagining the actual, seeing the world aright, is imagining the actual. The next best is imagining the probable.

[11] Engels, quoted by Terry Eagleton in *Marxist Literary Criticism* (London: Methuen, 1976), pp. 46 and 29.

[12] This suspicion about realism has been given radical and persuasive expression by Catherine Belsey:

> If by 'the world' we understand the world we experience, the world differentiated by language, then the claim that realism reflects the world means that realism reflects the world constructed in language. ... It is intelligible as 'realistic' precisely because it reproduces what we already seem to know.

that the realistic writer will merely lag behind, rather than being instrumental in changing, our conceptions of reality? No; for by organizing our conception of what is real to a higher degree than it is organized in ordinary consciousness – chatter, pub yarns, journalism – it opens that reality to inspection – and hence to criticism and transformation. To render reality visible – even where the nature of reality is determined by public opinion – is to step beyond it. A single quotation from Pierre Macherey will suffice: 'no ideology is sufficiently consistent to survive the test of figuration' (see Chapter 6). If a realistic writer does not swallow received reality whole, it is because he sees more clearly what others, and himself on other occasions, swallow whole. That is why a commitment to realism is compatible with a sophisticated, or guarded, awareness of what is real, or counts as 'real'.

Realism is not a task that can be completed once and for all – for reality itself changes as do our conceptions of it. And our ideas of what is plausible will also change. In ancient times, the interventions of the Gods may have seemed probable, now they do not. But, again, realism is one of the great motors of that change. Fantasy, romance, etc. do not expose reality to scrutiny in the way Macherey pointed out that realism does. This is at least in part because the reader of fantasy, required to 'give himself over' to the story, has to bracket off a good deal of his critical intelligence. It is difficult to suspend one's disbelief without suspending many other things besides.

The sense of reality in fiction is, for Barthes, merely an 'effect' – another *signification*, and conveying it another fictional game for the author to play. When, in his story *Un Coeur Simple*, Flaubert refers to the barometer in Mme Aubain's room, he does not do so, Barthes argues, in order to convey anything about Mme Aubain or to lay the ground for some future development of the story. For the barometer has no place in the story, contributes nothing to the interwoven fabric of character, setting and plot. It is a 'narratological dangler'; and its purpose is to signify a reality outside of, transcending, the tale, to signify matter outside of the narrated events, in short to signify *reality* itself. Reality emerges as that which is not assimilable to human, including authorial, purposes; and the terms that signify it, creating the 'reality effect', belong not to reality itself but to another kind of fictional rhetoric.

We could extend this argument to include anything that makes a story plausible. Since the events described in a novel have not actually taken place – or not, at least to those named persons at those particular places and times – whatever contributes to its plausibility could be counted as 'plausibility effects'. Indeed, anything that helps to create the sense for the

---

Critical Practice (London: Methuen, 1980), p. 46.

If this were true, then there could not be degrees of plausibility; and plausibility could never rank as an *achievement*, as a necessary (though not a sufficient) condition of greatness in a novel. But in practice, some novels are more plausible, more convincing, more vivid than others.

reader that something is happening must, since the events in question did not happen, be 'actuality effects'. With Barthes's dismissal of authors' endeavours to imagine the actual in the course of their fictions as the creation of a mere 'reality effect' ('a mask', according to Todorov, 'in which the laws of text are dressed up, a mask which we are supposed to take for a relation to reality'), we begin the long slide towards the position that the only truthful fictions are those whose constant theme is their own fictive status.

We can look at Mme Aubain's barometer in another way: as part of an attempt to imagine the story beyond the limits laid down by the usual narrative outline, to lead the reader's consciousness away from the smooth running machinery of the plot into the world of those who live the plot. An attempt to *realize* reality by signifying it, not merely to signify the realization of it. And this would connect with the fundamental insight of realism that there is reality beyond the confines of the realistic story, that there is much else, including other stories, beckoning beyond the tale in hand. It is an essentially adult insight.

Stravinsky said: 'Sincerity is the *sine qua non* that guarantees nothing'. The same could be said of plausibility. It is a necessary, but not a sufficient, condition of realism. And it is the most interesting of all the constraints that fancy might place on itself. Without this constraint, fiction is not truly intelligible and the reader is not able to exercise his intelligence, or his imagination, to the full.

5.2 Anticipatory Anaphoric Reference, False Deixis

A story begins as follows: 'He walked into the room'. Who is 'he'? We don't know; the story's universe of discourse has just been opened and the introductions have not yet been made. Normally, pronominal reference is dependent on prior identification – either through prior reference (using a proper name or a uniquely referring expression); or through ostensive definition or some less explicit mobilization of the spatio-temporal coordinates of the discourse. The first case is designated by the term 'anaphora' and the latter by 'deixis'. The former can manage with story-or text-relative identification; the latter requires an absolute or body-relative identification. Anaphora presupposes that the referent should already have its place in the universe-of-discourse. The pronominal reference is therefore false. Or, at least, its reference is given on credit. But in our example, however, there has been no previous reference to the 'he' of the opening sentence of the story.

Fiction is riddled with false (or anticipatory) anaphora and false deixis. Consider another opening sentence: 'The man walked across the road'. We have no idea who the man is, or which road is being referred to. And yet the use of the definite article implies previous reference, as if 'the man' and 'the road' were co-referential with a man and a road to which earlier reference had been secured. We are made to feel as though an earlier portion of the text has been deleted. The purpose of this is clear: it is to imply that we are beginning in the middle of things. And the effect is to suggest that the world of the story pre-exists the story, that the story is merely reporting on, not creating and then reporting on, a set of events.

This is more explicit in the following opening sentence: 'The man walked across the road again'. Or: 'The man was still there when I looked out of the window'. But the fundamental principle is the same: it is that we are allowed in fiction to have *reference on credit*. Anticipatory anaphora, quasi-co-reference to entities to which reference has not yet been secured, is the *sine qua non* of fiction. The reader knows that 'the man' means in practice 'the man [I am going to tell you about]' or 'the man [you are going to hear more of]', though it implies 'the man' [we have just been talking about] or 'the man' [I have just seen]. But the author's play with anaphora, requires the reader's willingness to take reference on credit, so that it is permissible to enter a universe-of-discourse by means of a term that is apparently co-referential with another, preceding term.

As the story unfolds, the initial referential credit is apparently justified. The targets of the reference are identified and the anticipatory reference of the opening sentence is retrospectively vindicated. We get to know who 'the man' is, where 'the road' is, and so on. Or do we? The answer is, of course, that we do not. For 'the man' is a fictional character and 'the road' a figment of the author's imagination. They may be possible instances of general types but they do not actually exist. Now most linguists believe that anaphora is ultimately rooted in deixis; that text-relative identification is absolute only it if is based in body-relative identification. It is body-relative identification that, outside of fiction, provides the ultimate frame of reference for absolute identi-fication. (Unless, that is, we standardize spatial and temporal references in relation to a public frame of reference such as Greenwich Mean Time.) Now it is clear that the non-existent cannot be located in relation to the body of the speaker or writer. Anaphora in fiction, therefore, remains free-floating, even when all the referential debts have been apparently paid off.

In practice, however, the difference between true stories and realistic fictions is not so great. We are able to refer very little of what we are told or read to our own bodies (see Chapter 4). The anaphora of true stories is as rootless as that in fictions. Reference is virtual in both factual and fictional discourses. In this absolutely fundamental respect, the truth of fiction is not qualitatively different from the truth of 'true' stories which we hear or read.

6. Concluding Theses

6.1 Reality is the *asymptote* of narration; and a just expression of reality – one that is equal to its greatness and its misery, to its distances and its depths – is one of the central 'regulative ideas' (in the Kantian sense of this phrase) of literature and the supreme regulative idea of fiction. Realistic fiction is capable of being the highest expression of the fundamental task of conscious-ness – that of imagining what is actually *there*.

6.2 Fiction is less important as a source of new knowledge than as a means of reminding us of what we already, tacitly, know; or as a means of transforming that knowledge into experience.

'How can thinking about something help us to learn more about it?' – 'Just as you see something more clearly if you draw it'. A careful reading of a novel is a response to an invitation to draw part of what we know; or to use what we know to imagine into what we don't.

6.3 The novelist doesn't merely tell the truth but uses the truth to illuminate itself. A world made explicit as truth is, however horrible, a world celebrated: the actual is miraculous. It *exists*; this is what makes it more interesting than the possible, though we sometimes need the counterfactual possible to show it to us, as shadows will reveal the light.

6.4 Man is the only form of matter that is astonished at its own existence and capable of conceptualizing its own mutability in the terrifying idea of death. Realistic fiction, linking the small facts that engage us with the great facts that enclose us, mediating between the truths that are uncovered by abstract thought with the small-scale truths of daily life, is the most compendious expression of that astonishment and that error. It is, potentially, the highest achievement of man, *the explicit animal*. But with this definition of man, we have arrived at the subject of another book.

Closure: Realism and Anti-Realism

God was not too bad a novelist except he was a realist.

John Barth

I am conscious that in my defence of realism I have run the risk of overstating my case. It is a natural, though rarely desirable, reaction to respond to hysterical and unfair attacks on something that one cherishes and considers to be of immense value with counter-attacks that are equally hysterical and unfair. Consequently, I may have underestimated the *value* of the hostility directed towards realistic fiction – explicitly by certain critics and theoreticians of the novel and implicitly by the practitioners of anti-realistic fiction. For this reason, I should like to end on a note of conciliation.

It would be absurd to deny the delight that some readers derive from fantasy, from whimsy, from fictions that play with the idea of fiction, from self-referential discourses that behave like staircases in Escher drawings. I, too, have derived enormous pleasure from A.A. Milne and the Rev. W. Awdrey. But the claims of anti-realism go further than fun. And I will happily concede one such claim: anti-realism is an invaluable critique of realism.

Anti-realistic fiction and the debate it has occasioned have forced all who write fiction or who think about it, either as critics or ordinary intelligent readers, to look critically at the habits and rituals and rules and assumptions of realism. Those once-innovatory techniques that have become embalmed as routines are made visible by the anti-realist challenge, as also are the metaphysical, ideological and social assumptions that have hitherto been passed 'on the nod'. Certain anti-realistic texts have been successful in their intention of making us aware of the artifice concealed in the most 'natural' of styles. Behind much anti-realism is a protest on behalf of a reality that is being traduced by fictions in the grip of stylistic tricks the author has borrowed without being fully aware of having done so, of mannerisms that imply a certain metaphysic of the self or a certain world picture when neither of those has been thought through or even consciously considered.

If the aim of realistic fiction is to express an uncircumscribed attempt to *notice* reality, to reveal it as it appears to the widest of wide-angled consciousnesses, then it needs to be prevented from lapsing into a stupor composed of its own habits. The anti-realist critique, keeping realism on its toes by continually questioning the received version of the nature of reality and mocking the fictional conventions by which reality is captured for the printed page, is an essential goad, an irritant driving the realistic novelist towards a more self-critical and conscious confrontation with reality, a greater willingness continually to compare what he writes with the world he is experiencing outside of his moments of writing. It forces realism to notice itself, causes it to be more conscious of its own practices and so makes it less likely to confuse those practices with the laws of the universe, its forms with the structure of the world.

It would, therefore, be a serious mistake to dismiss anti-realism and to imagine that the house of fiction, or even the house of realistic fiction, would be better off without it. Yes, there are many anti-realistic writers whose work is worthless – little more than whimsy grotesquely over-rated by deeply muddled critics who have overheard many more ideas than they can understand or think through. But there are others who have contributed importantly to, say, the transformation of our ideas about the representation of the self in fiction and the idea of a fictional character. Few serious writers of realistic fiction could be unaffected by the example of Robbe-Grillet (*minus* his inconsistencies and absurd pomposities) in their thinking about the role of material objects in the construction of human reality. He makes it more difficult to psychologize objects or to dissolve them into the psychological interplay of characters. The impact of Beckett's characters, talking with manic pedantry about recherché topics from the bottom of the 'messed sockets of existence' into which they are fastened, is not nullified by their unrealistic implausibility. For the writer of realistic fiction, this is a dramatic, indeed dramatized, exposition of the problem of getting consciousness to disclose itself. It is a reduction to absurdity of those fictions in which the least articulate somehow manage to articulate themselves for the benefit of the reader: where the dying man takes the trouble to inform the absent millions that he is dying; where the philosophically inclined author ventriloquizes through characters that are unlikely to philosophize – or not at that moment or in that way. Anti-realistic mockery makes realistic fiction more difficult to write; or makes writers more aware of the difficulties that have to be overcome if realism is to re-possess the territory lost to the cinema, to the documentary and to verse and to expropriate the high ground that seems to have been seceded to philosophy. The great realistic novelist is unsleepingly aware of the complexity of ideas and the uncombed nature of reality, of the provisionality and incompleteness of the sense we make of the world. Anti-realism at its best helps him to maintain that wakefulness.

It would be a mistake, then, to dismiss anti-realism as a series of aberrations. But it would be equally a mistake to see anti-realism as somehow superseding realism, as once and for all showing the realistic enterprise to be a phase of naivety from which fiction has now grown up. This mistake is one, as we have discussed, that is more easily made if 'realism' is taken to refer to a particular manner of fictionalizing reality – as a set of techniques, tricks, beliefs – instead of as referring to a *project* – that of doing some kind of fictional justice to the world in which a group of people pass their lives. Anti-realism correctly regarded is not the successor to realistic fiction but its servant, a means of deepening it, sharpening it, and so assisting it in its task of approximating reality. It does not spell the end of realism (or even of fiction); rather it is the precursor to another phrase of realism, a realism made more sophisticated by the anti-realistic critique. Under this interpretation, anti-realism is secondary, even marginal, but certainly not worthless.

Realism, however, remains central. Motivated by an unflashy radicalism that does not depend on labels, it takes up the challenge of all literary art most directly and most compendiously: to discover a significant order (or disorder) in common experience; to deepen and sharpen our sense of reality; and, ultimately, to mediate between the small facts that engage us and the great facts – that we are unoccasioned, that we are transient, that we nonetheless make sense of the world – that enclose us. The writer who faces that challenge does so, as Flaubert did, in solitude, alone with his sense of astonishment, his terror, and his joy.

Index